The
Spirit
of
Anglicanism

HOOKER, MAURICE, TEMPLE

William J. Wolf, Editor
John E. Booty
Owen C. Thomas

MOREHOUSE–BARLOW CO., INC.   WILTON, CONNECTICUT

Published 1979 by Morehouse-Barlow Co., Inc.
78 Danbury Road, Wilton, Connecticut 06897

ISBN 0-8192-1263-6

Published in the United States of America

ACKNOWLEDGEMENTS

Thomas Hooker: from an engraving in the 1672 edition of Sparrow's *Rationale*. The copy used was loaned to John Booty by Professor W. Speed Hill, editor of the new edition of Hooker's *Works*.

Frederick Denison Maurice: from *Theological Essays* by Maurice; published by Harper & Brothers printed in Great Britain, copyright © 1957 by James Clarke & Co., Ltd.

William Temple: from *William Temple: His Life and Letters* by F. A. Iremonger; published by Geoffrey Cumberlege, Oxford University Press, London, New York, Toronto; Third Impression 1949.

CONTENTS

Preface

The Episcopal Church and the worldwide Anglican Communion of which it is a part are, to use a phrase of Arnold Toynbee's, in a "time of troubles." Revision of the Book of Common Prayer, radical questioning of the Incarnation, liberation theology and the empowerment of the oppressed, the ordination of women, the position of homosexuals, the breakaway of dissident groups, the fear of or the desire for being "trendy," the very credibility of the church's leadership — all these issues are seething in the Anglican cauldron. This book is not directed to these problems, but to something more basic. We will be trying to assess the strengths and weaknesses of the Anglican Communion by taking inventory of its resources and direction — in short, of its fundamental spirit.

There have been other books which describe the spirit of the varying denominational ways of being Christian. Karl Adam's *Spirit of Catholicism* and Robert McAfee Brown's *Spirit of Protestantism* have become classics.[1] Professor Brown, an American Presbyterian, appreciates the difficulty of writing on Anglicanism. "This diversity of theological belief within Episcopalianism, while the despair of those who try to describe it simply, is one of the sources of its greatness, for the church has managed to conserve within its diversity many of the best features of historical Catholicism and Protestantism."[2] In writing this book, we have had in mind both Anglican and non-Anglican readers who might appreciate some explanation for this "diversity of belief."

There have been many books about Anglicanism, but few about "the spirit of Anglicanism." Bishop McAdoo's book of that title has a subtitle which states his real subject matter: "A Survey of Anglican Theological Method in the Seventeenth Century."[3] Bishop Neill's *Anglicanism* is still a useful historical study that, despite additions at the end of the book in 1977 and the strange omission of the last and

finest chapter in the previous edition, has never been fundamentally revised since its publication in 1958.[4] We still need
a book on Anglicanism comparable to the excellence of Tim-
othy Ware's *The Orthodox Church*, a study which brings together history, theology and spirituality, communicating at
the same time the spirit of Eastern Orthodoxy.

This book makes no modest or even immodest claim to
have filled that gap. Its focus is both narrower and yet more
comprehensive. It necessarily paints Anglicanism with
quick strokes of the brush in order to sketch its overall
spirit. The book uses a special method to get at the spirit of
Anglicanism, namely the study of three of its giants: Richard Hooker, Frederick Denison Maurice and William Temple. It is a method that, while chiefly theological in analysis,
incorporates some history, biography, liturgical and pastoral concerns and spirituality into its interpretations.

Some may be skeptical of the word *spirit*. The word is
often used to cloak vagueness and sloppy thought. As used
here, *spirit* refers to the wholeness of life within the Anglican Communion. It points to a sense of direction and identity, to a *Gestalt*, and to a *milieu* in the sense in which the
French word signifies both a field of attraction and the at-
tracting pole at its center. It also suggests continuity within
a historical development. *Spirit* is elusive (witness our re-
course to two foreign words for help), but not in itself vague
or indefinable. Norman Pittenger once captured its essence
in a partial sentence that will take us a book to explain.
"The Anglican spirit," he wrote, "in which conservatism
and liberalism are held in balance by the constant appeal to
Scripture, history, reason and experience."[5] With this understanding of *spirit* it becomes clearer why the study of the
life, work and thought of three representative Anglicans offers a fresh and fruitful way into that sense of ecclesial
wholeness which, in many respects, is akin to the meanings
of *catholicity* in the patristic period.

Each of us has published before on the subject of our respective chapters in this volume. Because we are colleagues
on the faculty of the Episcopal Divinity School, our discussions over the years have sometimes centered around
Hooker, Maurice and Temple as we have participated in and
discussed the challenges to contemporary Anglicanism. The

book will show strong convergence between the three of us. Our agreement may reflect the fairly substantial agreement in position and orientation of our three Anglican proto-types. The astute reader, however, will perceive some differences in our analysis and evaluation which we hope should make for enrichment rather than confusion.

Each of us has read and discussed the contributions of his colleagues before they were put in final form. Then our conscientious editor, Robert Gilday, submitted the manuscript to two anonymous scholars, one an Anglo-Catholic and the other an Evangelical. We are grateful for their vigorous criticism and thorough evaluation even when, at times, we disagreed with them. We have taken their comments very much to heart in our final revision. Each of them wanted the book to contain one more chapter. In the first case the recommendation was for a "more catholic" theologian and in the second case for a more decisively evangelical one than Hooker, Maurice or Temple. Although we dislike being labeled, our own position and slant, perhaps not surprisingly, is "broad church"; yet we should want to define that elusive term ourselves. A special chapter for a representative of each of the four basic Anglican positions and a fifth chapter on the "broad church" way of being an Anglican would have enriched our book and made it more representative, but it would also have made it much too long. We feel there may be something valuable and typical in the dialogic way we have approached a definition of the spirit of Anglicanism.

At this point the reader may be asking: "But why these three and not some others?" Any selection is debatable. Yet it is highly probable that if teachers of Anglican studies were asked to list, say, twelve leading Anglican thinkers and then were asked to rate their choices in terms of importance, the names of these three would head a substantial majority of the lists. There would, however, be wide diversity as to which of these men would be first, second or third. We have not yet settled that issue between ourselves. Recently, more testimony to the centrality of the three has been provided by a generally hostile witness. Stephen Sykes, in his *Integrity of Anglicanism*, notes the importance of Hooker and then attacks Maurice and Temple as dangerous and confusing influences in the Anglican Communion responsible, he believes, for a lack of systematic theology and clear thinking, especially on the nature of the comprehensiveness of Anglicanism.[6]

As a further step in the analysis of the contributions of Hooker, Maurice and Temple to the spirit of Anglicanism, we shall examine in a final chapter the emergence of a corporate and contemporary consciousness of Anglicanism. Our conclusions on the spirit of Anglicanism can best be illustrated by the decennial Lambeth Conferences, for nearly every meeting has wrestled with the problems of identity, image and the basic interrelationship of the churches making up the Anglican Communion. The direct contributions of Temple as drafter of Lambeth 1930 were immense. He was also preparing for Lambeth 1948 when he died. We are aware that our choice of these three representatives — men, English and clerics — give us a skewed picture of the Anglican Communion which is now a far richer reality than the Church of England which gave birth to it. At the urging of Lambeth 1968, in order to secure a more representative and more frequent expression of the mind of Anglicans, the constitutive churches authorized and then set up the Anglican Consultative Council. It meets every two years and includes laity and priests as well as bishops. At its third meeting in 1976 in Trinidad, the delegates discussed the role of the church in contemporary society and the functioning of multinational corporations. The very place of meeting was a symbol that Anglicanism is now a body composed more of Third World people than of Anglo-Saxons. It is said that there are now more Anglicans in Uganda than in the United States. What is of particular interest to us, however, is the naming of two of our theologians in their report. The spirit of Anglicanism typified by Hooker, Maurice and Temple within the Church of England still lives as a prophetic witness within the far wider Anglican Communion.

"In seeking to determine its attitude to society and social problems, the Anglican Communion must be conscious both of strength and of weakness. Its strength derives from some notable examples of social awareness and action in the eighteenth and nineteenth centuries, and from an all-too-short theological tradition examplified by such persons as F. D. Maurice and William Temple — a tradition which still does not receive the attention it deserves. Its weakness lies in its long history of uncritical acquiescence in the prevailing social order."[7]

Chapter I has been written by John Booty. After a brief description of Richard Hooker's life and works, he presents an exposition of Hooker's theological views — from natural law to social ethics — and ends with a critique. Booty's special insight is to see Hooker's importance in Anglican tradition in relation to his theology of participation. Chapter II is by William Wolf who, following an account of Maurice's life and works, emphasizes his pioneering work in social action and in the principles of an ecumenism that have yet to be accepted in the churches. Wolf shows how Maurice's understanding of Christ as "the transformer of culture" saves Maurice from having to construct a system, but still allows him to "dig down" to the Christological foundation of reality. Chapter III on William Temple is by Owen Thomas. Thomas explores the life, work and thought of Temple as an example of the spirit of Anglicanism. Special attention is devoted to Temple's view of the Incarnation, the church, Christian social witness, Christian reunion, the ministry and Anglicanism. Chapter IV by Wolf moves toward a description of Anglican identity as "a way of being Christian that involves a pastorally and liturgically oriented dialogue between four partners: catholics, evangelicals and advocates of reason and of experience." There is special emphasis upon the Lambeth Conferences and their emerging criterion of "comprehensiveness" and upon Anglican spirituality as clues to the spirit of Anglicanism. At the end of the book, there is a selective bibliography for each of the chapters with some suggestions for a beginner on how to start reading in these three fascinating Anglicans who, in their life, work and thought, incarnate much of the best in the spirit of Anglicanism.

We want to thank Frances Ricker for typing most of the manuscript.

John E. Booty
Owen C. Thomas
William J. Wolf

By the Authors:

William J. Wolf

Man's Knowledge of God
No Cross, No Crown: A Study of the Atonement
The Almost Chosen People
A Plan of Church Union
Thoreau: Mystic, Prophet, Ecologist
Freedom's Holy Light: American Identity and the Future of Theology

John E. Booty

John Jewel As Apologist of the Church of England
John Jewel, Apology, editor
Book of Common Prayer, editor
The Church in History (The New Church's Teaching Series)

Owen C. Thomas

William Temple's Philosophy of Religion
Science Challenges Faith
Attitude Towards Other Religions
Introduction to Theology

CHAPTER I

Richard Hooker

Ætat: suæ. 50

M: Richard Hooker,
Author of the Bookes of Eccle
siasticall Politye.

—I—
Richard Hooker

The Importance of Richard Hooker

Richard Hooker's importance for our day is suggested not
so much by the work of modern Anglican theologians as by
that of others who have contributed to a growing number of
Hooker studies. Scholars of various nationalities, including
a French Roman Catholic and a Swedish Lutheran, and various disciplines, including philosophers, historians and professors of English literature, have given years of their lives
to study and write about Hooker and his thought.[1] Furthermore, a new, critical edition of his *Works* — sponsored by
the prestigious Folger Shakespeare Library and financed by
the American government's National Endowment for the
Humanities — is in the process of being published.[2]

Why is there such interest in this sixteenth-century theologian now? H. R. Trevor-Roper, Regius Professor of Modern History at Oxford, suggests that Hooker's importance
is based on his provision of a philosophical foundation for
the sixteenth-century Church of England, a foundation dealing with profound issues in a large and ecumenical spirit. It
is his profundity, breadth and depth which draw people to
Hooker today, whether they are Anglicans or not. "Like
Hooker," says Professor Trevor-Roper, "we wish to look
past doctrinal controversies to the profounder issues which
they so often concealed; and we may find ourselves in agreement with that uncomfortably isolated Roman Catholic
scholar of the nineteenth century, Lord Acton. 'In the six-

1

teenth century,' wrote Acton, 'as a serious quest for a set of principles which should hold good alike under all changes of religion, Hooker's *Ecclesiastical Polity* stands almost alone.' "[3]

Hooker's profundity is related to a habit of mind or theological method to which Samuel Taylor Coleridge referred when he said that Hooker's mind was forever flying from the particular "to the *General*."[4] That is to say that, when Hooker was confronted by particular controversial issues involved in the struggle between Puritans and Anglicans, he dug beneath them to their philosophical and theological roots.[5] He did this over and over again, searching for roots and ends, questing to understand the purposes involved in the particular issues. Although this habit was frustrating to the Puritans, and even to some of his friends, it was not one which he could break for it was an intimate part of that personality which identified Richard Hooker.

For instance, Hooker confronted the major issues underlying all of the theological controversies of the sixteenth century: On what authority is anything positive and pleasing to God done? Suspicious of human nature, Puritans relied on Scripture as interpreted by the Holy Spirit in the individual. Scripture provided the only adequate authority for doing that which is meritorious in God's sight. For Hooker this position was too narrow and too dependent upon individuals who are inclined to confuse "private fancies" with the promptings of the Holy Spirit (Pref.3.10).[6] God's ways are many and various (III.11.8), working through a universal hierarchy of laws, a complex structure of relationships fundamentally harmonious but often marred by human sin. An important element in the complex structure is reason[7] which possesses authority not only in the sciences, as the Puritans allowed, but in things divine (II.7.3–4). Scripture presupposes that God works through reason in determining its authority and interpreting its meaning. Therefore, although under the conditions of human existence they are in tension, yet Scripture and reason (or nature) require one another. "Nature and Scripture do serve in such full sort, that they both jointly and not severally either of them, be so complete, that unto everlasting felicity we need not the knowledge of any thing more than these two, may easily furnish our mindes with on all sides" (I.14.5).

The breadth of Hooker's thought is impressive, as was that of Augustine and Thomas Aquinas, both of whom influenced him. Moreover, for several reasons this breadth is partially responsible for the interest now shown in him. First, his teaching is broad enough to take account of non-Christians with whom God communicates through nature. Second, Hooker's teaching emphasizes the dignity of human nature. Finally, there is humility expressed in his prose indicative of the spirit of one who not only writes about but worships God. Time and again this finds expression in writings which are not intentionally devotional.[8]

In a time when there is growing interest in spirituality, Hooker appeals not only because he wrote on prayer (V.20f.), but because there is spiritual depth in all of his writings. His spirituality is not, however, introverted or individualistic. His writings are rooted in tradition and grow out of his social views. In a time when there is concern for the fate of tradition and its values, Hooker provides an example of one steeped in tradition who nevertheless seeks to evaluate that tradition, discerning between that which is essential to salvation and must be retained and that which is of indifference and need not (indeed at times should not) be retained. In discerning this difference, Hooker assesses that which is received from the past in terms of purposes and ends, but also in relation to changing times and circumstances. On the one hand we find in Hooker devotion and humility, on the other evaluation and advice concerning things to be defended and things to be changed. In an era of rapid social and religious change, Hooker can be of help, as those who read him well know.

Hooker's Life: A Brief Sketch

Richard Hooker was born in 1554 at Heavitree in Exeter of prominent but not wealthy parents. Educated at the Exeter Latin School, where he demonstrated scholarly aptitudes, Hooker was early destined for a university education. John Hooker, his uncle and Chamberlain of Exeter, pre-

sented the boy to John Jewel, Bishop of Salisbury, who became his patron at Oxford. In 1568 Hooker became a clerk
in the company of Corpus Christi College, where he fared
well under the guidance of the Puritan John Rainoldes. A
fellow of Corpus in 1577, Hooker lectured on logic and, two
years later, began giving the Hebrew lecture in the university.

In 1580 Hooker was involved in a dispute as to who
should be president of the college — his former tutor Rainoldes or one Barfoot, vice president and chaplain to the
powerful Earl of Warwick. Hooker campaigned for Rainoldes, was expelled for contentiousness, but was restored
when Rainoldes assumed the presidency. In this campaign
Hooker was supporting a man who would be a leader of the
Puritans at Hampton Court in 1604 and a lifelong friend.

In 1581 Hooker was a priest of the Church of England and
preached at Paul's Cross, the preaching station outside of
St. Paul's Cathedral, London. There, where great throngs
gathered, including the Lord Mayor and Aldermen of London, as well as members of the Queen's Court, Hooker began
that controversial work which was to occupy him for the
rest of his life. Izaak Walton, his first biographer, reported
Hooker as saying that "In God there were two wills; an an-
tecedent, and a consequent will: his first will, that all mankind should be saved; but his second will was, that those
only should be saved, that did live answerable to that degree
of grace which he had offered, or afforded him."[9] Hooker
was not allowed to forget this early sermon. Its teaching
was like that of Peter Baro who said that " 'God, who is in
his nature good, created man for what is good, that is, for a
life of blessedness.' God 'every day truly calls and invites all
men, without any limit, to repentance, faith, and salvation.' "[10] The Calvinist Puritans, who believed that "God
eternallie predestinateth by a constant decree,"[11] and that
therefore since some are damned God does not will that all
be saved, regarded such teaching as Baro's and Hooker's as
dangerous, not only because it was false, but because it was
popish. The fact that Hooker laboriously explained and
qualified his early teaching and that he was defending the
doctrine of predestination as he understood it was to no
avail.

While in London in 1581, Hooker was introduced to the Churchman family and was befriended by its head, John Churchman, a distinguished London merchant. In 1584 Hooker left Oxford to make his residence in London. He had been presented to the living of Drayton-Beauchamp in Buckinghamshire but probably never lived there. In fact he seems to have joined the Churchman family, with which he lived off and on until 1595, marrying Joan Churchman in 1588, and being assisted in his literary activities by Benjamin Pullen, a Churchman family servant. Contrary to Walton's testimony, Hooker seems to have been well treated and considerably assisted by John Churchman and his wife.[12]

In 1585 Hooker was appointed Master of the Temple by the Queen. He thus became "vicar" to the legal profession centered in the Inns of Court. He was not the first choice for the Temple. The favored candidate was Walter Travers, the Puritan, who was then Reader of the Temple, a position subservient to the Master. Travers had the support of lawyers and of the Lord Treasurer of England, William Cecil, Lord Burleigh. John Whitgift, the Archbishop of Canterbury and scourge of the Puritans, preferred Nicholas Bond, a chaplain to the Queen but otherwise not remarkable. The great men struggled and Hooker emerged as the victorious alternative.[13]

At once another struggle began, now between Travers and Hooker. The former tried to win the latter over to his presbyterian views. They discussed matters but firmly disagreed. Eventually their disagreement was made public in sermons preached at the Temple, Hooker on Sunday mornings, Travers in the afternoons. The Puritan reminded Hooker of his sermon at Paul's Cross in 1581, attacked his teachings on the assurance of God's Word (Hooker believed that the assurance "is not so certain, as that we perceive by sense") and expressed his alarm at the way Hooker argued that some Roman Catholics had been saved.[14] It was Hooker's attitude toward Rome which aroused the greatest opposition.[15] The controversy progressed until, suddenly, in March 1586, the Archbishop silenced Travers. The Puritan appealed to the Privy Council for support but to no avail. He was at fault, it was said, for engaging in debate on religious matters, contrary to the statutes. Furthermore, his orders were defective, Travers having been ordained in a presbyterian ceremony in Antwerp.[16]

It was then, seemingly, that Hooker began to conceive his major work, *Of the Laws of Ecclesiastical Polity*, in which his intent was to lay bare the falsity and danger of the Puritan cause in relation to the Church of England as reformed, with its Book of Common Prayer, its episcopal government and its intimate connection to the Tudor state, but also to the most fundamental philosophical and theological principles essential to Christianity everywhere and recognized as such by all reasonable people. He wrote a draft of the *Laws* while resident in London living at the Churchman house on Watling Street.

In 1591 Hooker left the Temple and, in order that he might devote his time to his writing, Whitgift presented him to the living of Boscombe in Wiltshire. There is no conclusive evidence that he was ever resident there, but there is some evidence that he spent a prescribed amount of time each year at Salisbury where he was subdean and canon of Netheravon.[17] In all likelihood his principal residence was then in London, while he resided at the house provided for him in the Salisbury Close for a few weeks each year, working at the Cathedral Library and conferring with the dean, John Bridges, a noted enemy of the Puritans and author of a defense of the Church of England.[18]

It is also evident that Hooker had the advice of Edwin Sandys and George Cranmer, his tutees at Oxford. The former was the son of the Archbishop of York, Hooker's patron after Jewel's death in 1571. The latter's father was a nephew of the famed Archbishop of Canterbury. Sandys was a lawyer, member of the Inns of Court and, in time, a member of the House of Commons. Cranmer was first secretary to William Davidson, secretary of state, and then to Sir Henry Killigrew on embassy to France. Both Sandys and Cranmer were anti-Puritan at a time when the government's pursuit of Puritans and Separatists was most intense. We believe that they read Hooker's drafts of the books of the *Laws*, criticizing them and urging Hooker to deal less with the high principles of philosophy and theology and more with the specifics of the Puritan bill of complaint, refuting their arguments point by point.[19]

In 1572 the Puritans produced an "Admonition to Parliament," together with "A View of Popish Abuses," attacking the three articles contained in the oath they were forced to take.[20] The "Admonition" was answered by Whitgift, who was in turn answered by the Puritan Thomas Cartwright. The literature of the Admonitions controversy contains the specifics which were to be debated for the rest of the century and beyond. The debate intensified during the 1580s as some Puritans sought to institute presbyterian government in England, as radical separatists such as Penry, Harrison, Browne and Greenwood openly defied the law, and as the church under Whitgift became increasingly concerned to put a stop to the subversion. With Sandys and Cranmer bringing pressure to bear, Hooker revised his early drafts to address the Puritans more directly. And yet he did not yield to such pressure to the extent that his main purposes were obscured.[21]

The first four books of the *Laws*, originally intended to be one half of the entire work, were published in 1593 with the printing subsidized by Sandys. A copy of the work was in the Lord Treasurer's hands by March, at a time when Parliament was enacting a statute that greatly damaged the Puritan movement.[22] Some regarded Hooker's book as a strong weapon in the arsenal of weapons which the government was using to defeat the Puritans. Men such as Sandys and Cranmer were eager for the second volume to be published. Indeed, there is reason to believe that all of the eight books of the *Laws* were ready in the winter of 1592–93. Only the first four were published. Hooker seemingly delayed publication of the last four in order to revise them further.

In 1595 Hooker was presented to the living of Bishopsbourne in Kent and with his family retired into the country, near Canterbury, to continue his writing. The fifth book of the *Laws* was published in 1597 and was as long as the first four books together. In 1599 *A Christian Letter of Certain English Protestants* was issued attacking Hooker and all five books of the *Laws* then in print. A slender volume, published anonymously, it concentrated on Hooker's treatment of basic Christian doctrines, seeking to prove that he disagreed with the Thirty-Nine Articles of Religion, the English Reformers and the Fathers of the Early Church.[23] When Hooker died in 1600 he was preparing an answer to the *Letter*, of which we possess but fragments and his own copy of the tract heavily annotated.[24]

After Hooker's death there was a legal contest over his literary estate, in the course of which his wife and his in-laws were badly maligned.[25] The manuscripts on which he had been working were dispersed and appeared in print piecemeal, books six and eight in 1648, and book seven in 1662. There has been suspicion that these posthumously published books were tampered with and there have been those who have argued that book six is not properly a part of the *Laws*.[26] We may never be altogether certain of their authenticity, although there is no question that in them we possess material from Hooker's pen.

Hooker himself would have been amazed at his posthumous fame. His reputation was not great during his lifetime. No publisher would venture to print his work without a subsidy. Nor was he an exciting person. The historian Fuller, writing in the seventeenth century, said that "his voice was low, stature little, gesture none at all, standing stonestill in the pulpit, as if the posture of his body were the emblem of his mind, unmoveable in his opinions." Furthermore, his "sermons followed the inclinations of his studies, and were for the most part on controversies and deep points of school divinity."[27] Fuller is not altogether accurate. In his writings, published and unpublished, Hooker is at times vigorous, even passionate, capable of anger and of wit edged with sarcasm.

We turn now to his writings, not using them as a means of summarizing his thought, but taking note of them as the basis of that summary of his theology which constitutes the most substantial part of this chapter, a reconstruction of his theology in relation to his understanding of participation in Christ.

Of the Laws of Ecclesiastical Polity: A Description

Hooker's *magnum opus* was addressed to Puritans who attacked the Church of England in the name of a purer, more scriptural ecclesiastical settlement. In the process, so Hooker asserted in his preface of the *Laws*, they engaged in illegal and unreasonable activities. Granted that there were abuses which should be corrected, yet,

> sith equitie and reason, the law of nature, God and man, do all favour that which is in being, till orderlie judgement of decision be given against it; it is but justice to exact of you [Puritans], and perversnes in you it should be to denie thereunto your willing obedience (Pref. 6.5).

Hooker was not concerned to argue about any specific law or laws objected to by the Puritans. His intent was to show that those laws which they disobey are part of a universal pattern of laws established by God and possessing ultimate authority.

It was in the light of this assertion that Hooker discussed the overall plan of the eight books. Since he was intent on convincing the Puritans that "equitie and reason, the law of nature, God and man do all favour that which is in being," and that they commit grievous error who impugn the present order of things, he began with a discussion of law in general. He drew upon Aristotle, Thomas Aquinas and others out of the past, along with those of his own age, in depicting the universe as composed of a hierarchy of laws designed to serve "fore-conceived" ends. Laws[28] are thus reasonable and of great variety, composed by God for the sake of creation. Hooker began with "*the first eternall law*" (I.3.1.). This is God's law by which he governs himself through his own voluntary act. All else is governed by the "*second law eternall.*" This law is divided into physical laws governing "naturall agents," the "*law* Celestial" governing angels, "the law of *Reason*" governing rational creatures, the "Divine law" which is God's revelation through Scripture and "Human law," or positive law, which humans devise on the basis of Reason and divine law. Basic to Hooker's understanding is the principle of "correspondence" (I.16.4), which teaches that inferior laws are derived from the supreme or highest law; positive human laws are good in that the eternal law "worketh in them."

Hooker then turned from a general consideration of law to discuss specifics. First he dealt with the Puritan contention that "Scripture is the onely rule of all things which in this life may be done by men" (title, Book II). Against this, Hooker held that "God hath left sundry kindes of lawes unto men, and by all those lawes the actions of men are in some sort directed" (II.1.2.). He wrote:

> Whatsoever either men on earth, or the Angels of heaven do know, it is as a drop of that unemptiable fountaine of wisdom, which wisdom hath diversly imparted her treasures unto the world. As her waies are of sundry kinds, so her maner of teaching is not meerely one and the same. Some things she openeth by the sacred bookes of Scripture; some things by the glorious works of nature; with some things she inspireth them from above by spirituall influence, in some things she leadeth and trayneth them only by worldly experience and practice. We may not so in any one speciall kind admire her that we disgrace her in any other, but let all her wayes be according unto their place and degree adored (II.1.4).

It was in this context that Hooker asserted the rightful authority of human judgment, even in things divine (II.7.4–5).

In the third book Hooker sought to refute the Puritan contention that "in Scripture there must be of necessitie contained a forme of Church-politie the lawes whereof may in no wise be altered" (title, Book III). He began with a discussion of the church, the church mystical which is known to God alone and the church visible composed of those who confess Christ as Lord, profess the faith he delivered and are baptized. This visible society contains the faithful growing in holiness, but also those who are unfaithful and corrupt. Furthermore, the visible church is divided by local distinctions so that we speak of the Church of Corinth, of Rome and of England, each church having its own characteristics, functions and way of life. Each such church possesses a polity or form of government with orders of ministry and with rites and ceremonies. It is Hooker's contention that while each church is bound by certain general principles governed by Scripture, there are areas dependent on human judgment, such as Scripture presupposes (III.11.20). The authority of Scripture is thus limited, presupposing knowledge derived from reason, the operation of positive human laws made by human assemblies, and by human authority establishing the authority of God's Word in Scripture, and the activity of reason for the interpretation of Scripture. Hooker emphasizes the necessity of grace (III.8.10,17) and the necessity of reason's operation. And so he concluded:

> We have endeavoured to make it appeare how in the nature of reason it selfe there is no impediment, but that the selfe same spirit, which revealed the things that god hath set down in his law, may also be thought to aid and direct me in finding out by the light of reason what lawes are expedient to be made for the building of his Church, over and besides them that are in scripture" (III.8.17).

The fourth book addressed the Puritan "assertion, that our forme of Church-politie is corrupted with popish orders rites and ceremonies banished out of certaine reformed Churches whose example therein we ought to have followed" (title, Book IV). Hooker began considering the purpose of ceremonies: "We are to note that in every graund or maine publique duty, which God requireth at the hand of his Church, there is, besides that matter and forme wherein the essence thereof consisteth, a certaine outward fashion whereby the same is in decent sort administered" (IV.1.2). Such outward fashions, both words and sensible actions, must edify, communicating that for which they are intended. Turning to the Puritan assertion, Hooker refuted the argument that the church in the sixteenth century must imitate the apostolic church. "The glorie of God and the good of His Church was the thing which the Apostles aymed at, and therefore ought to bee the marke whereat we also levell" (IV.2.3); therefore, given the changes of times and circumstances, the "outward fashions" will not always be the same. Hooker also denied that the Church of England must imitate continental reformed churches. Willful singularity must be avoided, but so must rigid uniformity amongst churches (IV.13.2–10). As to the charge that the ceremonies of the English church are popish, Hooker wrote:

> We hold it better, that the friends and favourers of the
> Church of Rome should be in some kind of hope to have a
> corrupt religion restored, then both we and they conceive
> just feare, least under colour of rooting out Poperie, the
> most effectuall means to beare up the state of religion be re-
> mooved, and so a way made eyther for Paganisme, or for ex-
> treme barbaritie to enter" (IV.9.3).

The fifth book marks a transition from the general discussion of the law as applied to Puritan objections, to a detailed
defense of the particular ceremonies under attack in the
Book of Common Prayer, then to the issue of lay elders in
Book VI (although this is not the subject of Book VI in the
printed works),[29] then to a defense of the episcopal government of the Church of England in Book VII and, in Book
VIII, to a defense of the English Crown and the exercise of
"Ecclesiastical Dominion" by persons other than those ordained.

The outline of Book V coincides with the outline of the
Prayer Book, but focuses attention on the sacraments. The
sacraments are treated as means toward participation in
Christ, which is salvation (V.50.1, 57.5). It is this end which
Hooker has in mind throughout the book and shall provide
the focus for our discussion of his theology.[30] Book VII addresses the Puritan assertion "that there ought not to be in
the Church, bishops endued with such authority and honour
as ours are" (title, Book VII). Hooker argued that episcopacy was instituted by Christ (VII.4.2–4), but he was otherwise of the opinion that the churches as politic societies had
the right to establish their own forms of government. Episcopacy concerned positive human law. It followed that it
could be abolished "by universal consent upon urgent
cause" (VII.5.8). That the church retained episcopacy was a
matter of its lawful authority to do so or not, and did not
concern any immutable divine command.[31] His argument
satisfied neither Puritans nor those Anglicans in later times
who believed episcopacy to be of the essence of the church
without which the church ceased to be.

Book VIII is a defense of Royal Supremacy or the right of
the civil magistrate to exercise power in the church. The Pu-

ritans could not directly attack the Queen, but they believed that church and state were two separate, although related, kinds of society, exercising power independently. Hooker, on the basis of his earlier books, argued that church and commonwealth (as the state was called) were distinct when, as in the early church, the state was non-Christian. The situation is different in England: "The Church and commonwealth . . . are in this case personally one society, which society being termed a commonwealth as it liveth under whatsoever form of secular law and regiment, a church as it hath the spiritual law of Jesus Christ" (VIII.1.4). Hooker was careful to limit the authority of any earthly governor, resisting the idea that the Queen was supreme over the church by an immutable divine command. "As for the supreme power in ecclesiastical affairs, the word of God doth no where appoint that all kings should have it; for which cause it seemeth to stand altogether by human right, that unto Christian kings there is no such dominion given" (VIII.2.5). Once more, Hooker pleased neither Puritans nor their enemies, the staunchest supporters of Royal Supremacy.[32]

Hooker's Other Writings

The lesser writings of Hooker are few in number but, nevertheless, important. They can be considered in three groups: works concerned with the controversy between Hooker and Travers at the Temple; works concerned with the preparation of the last books of the *Laws* and with Hooker's proposed reply to the Puritan *Letter*; and miscellaneous sermons.

Travers' *Supplication,* or appeal to the Privy Council, has already been mentioned.[33] In the course of his account of the dispute with Hooker, Travers refers to four sermons, one being that preached at Paul's Cross in 1581, of which we have an account in Walton's *Life* but no copy. In that sermon, says Travers, Hooker "taught certain things concerning predestination otherwise than the word of God doth."[34] The other sermons were all on texts from Habakkuk and we do have copies of them. "A Learned and Comfortable Sermon of Certainty and Perpetuity of Faith in the Elect," concerns assurance. It aroused the ire of the Puritan who taught that "the assurance of faith [is] greater, which assured both of things above, and contrary to all sense and human understanding."[35] Hooker's view contains an important epistemological principle:

> The angels and spirits of the righteous in heaven have certainty most evident of things spiritual: but this they have by the light of glory. That which we see by the light of grace, though it be indeed more certain; yet is it not to us so evidently certain, as that which sense or the light of nature will not suffer a man to doubt of.[36]

Hooker was concerned to define and defend the nature of faith by which the Christian understands the things of God "not only as true, but also as good."[37]

The second sermon on a text from Habakkuk is "A Learned Discourse of Justification, Works, and How the Foundation of Faith is Overthrown." Travers accused Hooker of preaching doctrine favorable to the Church of Rome. In fact, Hooker sought to describe both the agreement and the disagreement of the churches of Rome and England on the doctrine of justification. His approach to the Roman Church was irenical, but it was also critical: "What is the fault of the church of Rome? Not that she requiereth works at their hands that will be saved: but that she attributeth unto works a power of satisfying God for sin; and a vertue to merit both grace here and in heaven glory."[38] Hooker explained his understanding thusly:

> Christ is the matter whereof the doctrine of the gospel treateth; and it treateth of Christ as of a Saviour. Salvation therefore by Christ is the foundation of Christianity: as for works, they are a thing subordinate, no otherwise necessary then because our sanctification cannot be accomplished without them.[39]

Works, according to Hooker and sixteenth-century Anglican theology, do not cause justification. They are the necessary expression of thanksgiving on the part of a Christian for unmerited justification by a merciful God.[40]

The third sermon on a text from Habakkuk is "The Nature of Pride." It deals with pride, but also with a wide range of subjects including law, divine justice, salvation and the spiritual life. Domestic and public strife, heresy, schisms — pride is "the mother which brought them forth, and the only nurse that feedeth them. Give me the hearts of all men humbled; and what is there that can overthrow or disturb the peace of the world?"[41]

Travers aimed his attack at such sermons, seeking in his *Supplication* to prove that Hooker erred and was dangerous. Hooker's defense is called an "Answer to the Supplication." In it, by the way, we find the beginnings of certain threads of thought leading to the *Laws*. For instance, Hooker defends the use of Reason:

> Not meaning thereby mine own reason as now it is reported, but true, sound, divine reason; reason whereby those conclusions might be out of St. Paul demonstrated, and not probably discoursed only, reason proper to that science whereby the things of God are known; theological reason, which out of the principles in Scripture that are plain, soundly deduceth more doubtful inferences, in such sort that being heard they neither can be denied, nor any thing repugnant unto them received, but whatsoever was before otherwise by miscollecting gathered out of darker places, is thereby forced to yield itself, and the true consonant meaning of sentences not understood is brought to light.[42]

The second grouping of lesser writings pertains to the *Christian Letter* and Hooker's response in notes on his copy of the tract,[43] in one leaf of a manuscript of rough notes recently discovered which deals with predestination,[44] and in certain "fragments" of an answer to the *Letter,* constituting a major theological treatise, its three sections giving us Hooker's most substantial treatment of grace and predestination.[45] Through his treatment of grace and free will, sacraments as a means of grace and predestination to grace, grace is at the center of Hooker's attention: "The grace of God hath aboundantlie sufficient for all. We are by it that wee are, and att the length by it wee shall bee that wee would."[46]

The third group of lesser writings — miscellaneous sermons — includes a funeral sermon called "A Remedy Against Sorrow and Fear." It is the work of a pastor, counseling against excessive sorrow and fear, ending with a memorable statement: "For our direction, to avoid as much as may be both extremities, that we may know as a ship master by his card, how far we are wide, either on the one side or on the other, we must note that in a Christian man there is, first, Nature; secondly, Corruption, perverting Nature; thirdly, Grace correcting and amending Corruption."[47] There are two sermons on the Epistle of Jude, the first noteworthy for its definition of the body of Christ and what constitutes separation from it.[48] The second sermon concerns edification, the church and the ministry. Hooker's argument for an ordained ministry distinct from the ministry of the laity is here based on the analogy of building, the distinction between laborers and the building: "They which are ministered unto, and they to whom the work of the ministry is committed; pastors, and the flock over whom the Holy Ghost hath made them overseers."[49] A sermon on Matthew 7:7–8 is concerned with petitionary prayer, describing those conditions necessary to acceptable prayer and emphasizing God's love and mercy.[50]

Finally, there are newly discovered fragments of three sermons attributed to Hooker.[51] One is on Matthew 27:46 and is a fragment concerning the "dereliction of probation and reprobation." Another is on Proverbs 3:9–10 and is concerned with the nature of divine providence. The third, seemingly more than a fragment, is on Hebrews 2:14–15 and was probably preached at Eastertide. It is a strong affirmation of the death of death by means of Christ's death and of the salvation which ensued. In it there is a characteristically Anglican warning against trying to discover why some are saved and some not: "Let not men . . . dig the clouds to find out secret impediments; let them not, according to the maner of infidels and heathens, stormingly impute their wretched estate unto destinie."[52]

Participation: The Key to Hooker's Theology

Hooker wrote in the midst of controversy. There is no doubt that Hooker's *Laws* is "thoroughly grounded in polemic and controversial advocacy."[53] But it is also true that, in the *Laws,* Hooker presented his deepest thoughts and on occasion rose "above ecclesiastical bickering." When this happens he may be using essays written earlier without reference to the Puritan attacks. An example is found in Book I with its majestic description of the hierarchy of laws. The central portion of Book V is another example. Here in chapters 51 through 56 he lays the foundation for a discussion of the sacraments without any mention of Cartwright or any other Puritan. This section, and especially chapter 56 which summarizes the whole, is at the heart of the *Laws*, revealing the true nature of Hooker's theological point of view and providing the key to its interpretation.

It is significant that this most theological section of the *Laws* occurs on the threshold of Hooker's discussion of the sacraments and in the midst of his defense of the Book of Common Prayer. The seriousness of Hooker's concern for liturgy and sacraments reflects a major Anglican concern. The Prayer Book provided for many, as it did for Hooker, the liturgical experience which often — quite unconsciously — formed the basis of their theological understanding in general.

Chapter 56 of Book V begins with the definition of a key word. The word *participation* was seemingly first brought to prominence for Hooker in connection with St. Paul's discussion of the Lord's Supper in 1 Corinthians 10 and in that which he understood to be a liturgical statement in John 6. Hooker defines participation as being "that mutuall inward hold which Christ hath of us and wee of him, in such sort that ech possesseth other by waie of speciall interest propertie and inherent copulation" (V.56.1). In his use of the word, Hooker rejected two extremes represented by two of the six Greek words translated into English as *participation*. This is to say, he steered a course between participation as complete union or deification (*theosis*) and as mere kinship (*sungeneia*). In so doing, he probably had in mind, at one time or another, four other Greek words, all used in the New Testament. Of lesser importance are *metousia* (*metechō*), meaning to share or partake in (1 Cor. 9:10,12; 10:17, 21, etc.), and *metalambanō*, meaning to partake of or share in (Acts 2:4, etc.). Those Greek words of greater importance to Hooker are *koinonia* and *menō* (*menein*). The former means fellowship, a two-sided relationship with emphasis on giving and receiving. As used in the New Testament, *koinonia* draws on the concern of primitive religion for the inward reception of divine power (*mana*) in eating and drinking. In this way the word was a logical one to use in connection with the Lord's Supper (1 Cor. 10:16, 1 John 1:3, etc.). The latter word (*menō*) means to abide in or be in union with, as in John 6:54. In this sense it describes the "community of life between Father and Son" and also the disciples' sharing in Christ's life as they do his works. "This is what is meant by the expression, 'I in you and you in me.' "[54] It is seemingly what Hooker had in mind when thinking of the verse as used by Cranmer in the Prayer Book Eucharist.[55]

From the New Testament on, the various meanings of *participation* and the confluence of a variety of meanings loomed large in Christian thought. Hooker was aware of erroneous and dangerous definitions which tended toward the obliteration of personal identity in a mystical union or, quite the opposite, a casual, passing relationship. Thus in his Sermon on Pride, while discussing the manner in which Christ is in the Christian and the Christian in Christ, Hooker writes that some view this as a mystery while others have

> expounded our conjunction with Christ to be a mutual participation whereby each is blended with the other, his flesh and blood with ours, and ours in like sort with his, even as really materially and naturally as wax melted and blended with wax into one lump; no other difference but that this mixture may be sensibly perceived, the other not.

Hooker contends that this way of thinking is irrational, for Christ and the Christian continue to be personally distinguishable. The way in which participation must be understood is in terms of "that intellectual comprehension which the mind is capable of. So that the difference between Christ on earth and Christ in us is no less than between a ship on the sea and in the mind of him that builded it; the one a sensible thing, the other a mere shape of a thing sensible."[56] And yet Hooker does not wish to overemphasize the distinction. The union between Christ and the Christian is the vital fact. Thus, when discussing Christology, Hooker set forth this clarifying statement: "Sith God hath deified our nature, though not by turninge it into him selfe, yeat by makinge it his own inseparable habitation, wee cannot now conceive how God should without man either exercise divine power or receive the glorie of divine praise" (V.54.5).

Hooker has in mind the Trinity, involving a strong affirmation of the conciliar conclusions concerning both the Trinity and the relation of the divine and human in Christ. The four councils (Nicea, Constantinople, Ephesus, Chalcedon) and the four heresies they condemned (Arianism, Apollinarianism, Nestorianism, Eutychianism) encompass all that need be said on the Trinity and Christology. The fact that these conciliar conclusions and the thinking behind them are rooted in the Greek understanding of substance has been a stumbling block for moderns. In 1938 the Anglican Commission on Doctrine wished to affirm "that which was affirmed in the language of its own time by the Council of Chalcedon. But we wish to assert that the Church is in no way bound to the metaphysic or psychology which lie behind the terms employed by the Council."[57] A similar attitude can be taken toward Hooker's statements, emphasizing the aim and not the language or other details. Thus, in defining "participation" he explained:

> The persons of the Godhead, by reason of the unitie of theire substance, doe as necessarilie remaine one within an other as they are of necessitie to be distinguished one from an other ... the persons of the Trinitie are not three particular substances of whome one *generall* nature is common, but three that subsist by one substance *which it selfe is particular*, yeat they all three have it, and theire severall waies of havinge it are that which maketh their personall distinction (V.56.2).

Participation thus means both union and distinction in the Godhead and between Christ and the Christian. This becomes more apparent and convincing as Hooker moves from the level of substance to that of personal relationship, as he does in discussing Christ. The Son "which is in the father by eternall derivation of beinge and life from him must needes be in him through an eternal affection of love" (V.56.3). It is on the level of personal relationship that Hooker's definition of participation can be most useful to us now. In this regard Hooker's definition is not opposed to Paul Tillich's understanding of the ontological elements of individualization and participation: "When individualization reaches the perfect form which we call a 'person,' participation reaches the perfect form which we call 'communion.' "[58] To be a person involves encounter and communion with other persons. Our being and our salvation depend upon participation in the Ultimate known in and through the Trinity and through participation in Christ.

Participation and the Laws of Nature

Having presented his definition of *participation*, Hooker set down two basic principles:

(1) *"That everie originall cause imparteth it selfe unto those thinges which come of it,* and

(2) *"Whatsoever taketh beinge from anie other the same is after a sorte in that which giveth it beinge"* (V.56.1).

These principles point to the all important Book I of the *Laws* where Hooker affirms that God is in whatsoever may be and "in all things an appetite or desire exists whereby they incline to something they may be" (I.5.1).

God, working in humanity, directs our actions toward the imitation of God, that is, toward those perfections "conteyned under the generall name of *Goodnesse.*" Hooker wrote:

Sith there can bee no goodnesse desired which proceedeth not from God himself, as from the supreme cause of all things; and every effect doth after a sort conteine, at least wise resemble the cause from which it proceedeth: all things in the worlde are saide in some sort to seeke the highest, and to covet more or lesse the participation of God himselfe (I.5.2).

This statement, found in a description of the universe of laws, is reminiscent of Gregory of Nyssa who presupposed a hierarchy of being, ranging from the Uncreated intelligible being to the created sensible beings devoid of life. Humanity is in the middle where the celestial and the terrestrial participate in one another's attributes. This participation, involving the mediation of the Incarnate Logos, is participation in the divine goodness and, thus, "the source and origin and supply of every good is found in the Uncreated Nature, and the whole creation inclined toward It, attaining to and partaking of (*metechousa*) the lofty nature through the communion (*koinonias*) of the First Good" (*Contra Eunomium*, I, 274).[59]

Hooker does not, however, cite Gregory in this place, but rather Aristotle, a source common to both Gregory and Hooker. Aristotle affirmed that the human soul, by means of reproduction, is able to "partake in the eternal and divine. That is the goal towards which all things strive" (*de Anima*, II,iv; 415b). And it is possible that Hooker had Thomas Aquinas in mind, particularly in this passage:

> All things, by desiring their own perfection, desire God Himself, inasmuch as the perfections of all things are so many similitudes of the divine being ... And so of those beings which desire God, some know Him as He is in Himself, and this is proper to a rational creature; others know some participation (*participationes*) of His goodness, and this belongs also to sensible knowledge, as being directed to their end by a higher Knower (*S.T.*, 1a 6.1,2).

Hooker's understanding of God working through the Second Law Eternal to arouse a desire for that Goodness which is divine, aiming at participation in the divine, shares much with and perhaps owes something to Thomas' argument.

In his Sermon on Pride, discussing divine justice, Hooker says:

> God himself being the supreme cause which giveth being unto all things that are, and every effect so resembling the cause whereof it cometh, that such as the one is the other cannot choose but be also; it followeth that either men are not made righteous by him, or if they be, then surely God himself is much more that which he maketh us.[60]

For Hooker the cause-effect nexus is self-evident. But this is so largely because of his conviction, derived from experience, that God is, that God created all that is and that God continues to work through that creation.

In chapter 56 Hooker explains that God is in all that is since all proceeds from him and yet, since his substance and created substance differ, communion with God and with one another are not the same as that communion which characterizes the Trinity or the relation of the divine and human in Christ. He then makes a statement which proceeds from faith informed by reason:

> God hath his influence into the verie essence of all thinges, without which influence of deitie supportinge them theire utter annihilation could not choose but followe. Of him all thinges have both receaved theire first beinge and their continuance to be that which they are. All thinges are therefore pertakers of God, they are his offspringe, his influence is in them, and the personall wisdome of God is for that verie cause said to excell in nimbleness or agilitie, to pearce into all intellectual pure and subtile spirites, to go through all, and to reach unto everie thinge which is (V.56.5).

Furthermore, God's influence works by means of his goodness (the Father), which moves him to work by means of his wisdom (the Son), which orders his work, and which perfects his work by means of his power (the Holy Spirit). It is thus that "all thinges which God hath made are in that respect the offspringe of God, they are *in him* as effectes in their highest cause, he likewise actually is *in them*, the assistance and influence of his deitie is their *life*" (V.56.5).

Hooker constantly and emphatically asserted the importance of creation and its worth: "All things that are, are good" (I.5.1). All things are good because God is in all as all is in him. Hooker provides a positive view of all nature, as well as human nature, and thus provides the basis for a theology which is ecologically attuned. There is also a personal, interrelational dimension to his thought here, as indicated by the use of personal terms such as love, assistance and influence, all concerned with personal mutuality. The way is open for the use of personal analogies concerning God's relationship to creation such as C. W. Emmet uses in writing of the influence of the gifted orchestral conductor or of the effective teacher.[61] Affirmation of the goodness of creation and of the personal character of the Creator's relationship to the created order are important facets of the Anglican theological ethos.

Another facet of the Anglican ethos concerns morality and the moral character of God, the universe and humanity. The aim of all is that Goodness which is God. There are two degrees to that Goodness to which humans aspire. The first "is that generall perfection which all thinges doe seeke, in desiring the continuance of their being." That is to say, all things seek to imitate God in his everlastingness and do so through propagation. On this foundation sex, marriage and the family as an institution of personal continuance are to be understood. The second "degree of goodness is that which each thing coveteth by affecting resemblaunce with God, in the constancie and excellencie of those operations which belong unto their kinde." Constancy is defined as "working eyther alwaies or for the most part after one and the same manner." Excellency of operations appropriate to any given kind or order of nature concerns the imitation of God's exactness "by tending unto that which is most requisite in every particular" (I.5.1). Out of such a foundation the Christian doctrine of work proceeds

These two degrees of Goodness pertain to people as they are in themselves. There are more external perfections, involving desires which reflect the goodness of God. Such are "proceeding in the knowledge of truth" and "growing in the exercise of vertue" (I.5.3). Hooker referred in this way not to detailed ethical issues and moral codes, but to basic principles from which Christian ethics and moral codes develop. Such basic principles as we have observed are implanted in and a part of the created order. "Goodnesse is seene with the eye of the understanding. And the light of that eye, is reason" (I.7.2). We know Goodness through knowledge of the causes whereby it exists or through "observation of those signes and tokens, which being annexed alwaies unto goodnes, argue that where they are found, there also goodnes is, although we know not the cause by force whereof it is there." The chief of such signs is the general consent of all people that such and such are good (I.8.2). "The generall and perpetuall voyce of men is as the sentence of God him selfe" (I.8.3).[62] The presupposition is that humanity, which excels the rest of nature in ability to reach unto spiritual things, can know the good, desires the good — the good as defined by the nature of the Godhead. We are now confronted by the question of whether or not humans can will and do the good.

Participation as Saving Efficacy

The fact is that humanity is fallen and therefore in itself incapable of the perfection for which it yearns. Humans make unreasonable and wrong choices. Hooker wrote:

> There is in the will of man naturally that freedome whereby it is apt to take or refuse any particular object whatsoever being present unto it. Whereupon it followeth, that there is no particular object so good, but it may have the shew of some difficultie or unpleasant qualitie annexed to it; in respect whereof the will may shrinke or decline it: contrariwise (for so things are blended) there is no particular evill which hath not some appearance of goodness whereby to insinuate it selfe (I.7.6).

Hooker attributed the first sinful choice, and all subsequent sin, to sloth: "We suffer the gifts of God to rust, and but use our reason as an instrument of iniquity: our wits we lend not towards that which should do us good."[63] Although the human will retains the "aptness" or potential to choose the good, it has lost its ability and, consequently, Hooker can say that reason has been darkened and covered "with the foggy damp of original corruption."[64] The result is that, although humans yearn for God and Goodness, their reasons are so clouded and their wills so perverted that they cannot achieve their deepest desire.

In that central chapter of Book V which has been our key to Hooker's theology, sin and salvation are dealt with initially in terms of the first and second Adams. We are by nature the sons of the first Adam and are thus fallen. By grace we are the children of God, and thus we are saved. We have the necessary saving efficacy or grace through the second Adam from whom we are descended by "spiritual and heavenly birth." To put it another way: God loves people because he loves the Son eternally. God is now viewed as Savior as well as Creator (V.56.6). Indeed, as was true of John Donne,[65] Hooker recognized God's essential nature as merciful and loving toward his creation and especially toward those spiritually descended from his Son. "It was the purpose of his *savinge* goodnes, his *savinge* wisdome, and his *savinge* power which inclined it selfe towards [us]."

Hooker indicated his basic understanding of the Atonement when he wrote:

[1] Adam is in us as an originall cause of our nature and of that corruption of nature which causeth death,

[2] Christ as the cause of originall restauration to life [Heb. 5:9];

[1] the person of Adam is not in us but his nature and the corruption of his nature derived into all men by propagation,

[2] Christ havinge Adams nature as wee have, but incorrupt, deriveth not nature but incorruption and that immediatlie from his owne person into all that belonge unto him.

[1] As therefore wee are reallie partakers of the bodie of synne and death received from Adam,

[2] so except wee be trulie partakers of Christ, and as reallie possessed of his Spirit, all wee speake of eternall life is but a dreame (V.56.7).[66]

This makes it clear that salvation, which is participation in Christ, is the work of Christ's Spirit who has power to restore clarity to reason and ability to will. Hooker explained: "Seeinge . . . that Christ is in us as a quickeninge Spirit, the first degree of communion with Christ must needes consist in the participation of his spirit which Cyprian in that respect termeth *germanissimam societatem*, the highest and truest society that can be between man and him which is both God and man in one" (V.56.8). Once more the emphasis is on the interpersonal.

Hooker then dealt with two further points: First, that none should be misled to believe that the saving conjunction with Christ is solely spiritual, Hooker writes of the conjunction of Christ's body with our bodies. Christ's body is in our bodies as "a cause by removinge through the death and

merit of his owne flesh that which hindered the life of ours"
(V.56.9). He believes that the saving efficacy extends
through all human nature and is not restricted to that which
is "spiritual." From Christ's flesh "our verie bodies doe receive that life which shall make them glorious . . . and for
which they are allreadie accompted partes of his blessed
body."[67]

Second, our participation in Christ is gradual, by degrees,
because sin and death hinder the work of the Spirit. Hooker
is rather obtuse here, but his understanding is still governed
by his belief in the mercy of God. Thus he writes:

> It pleaseth him in his mercy to account himself incomplete
> and maimed without us. But most assured we are that we all
> receive of his fulness, because he is in us as a moving and
> working cause; from which many blessed effects are really
> found to ensue, and that in sundry kinds and degrees, all
> tending to eternal happiness (V.56.10).

Hooker is realistic in recognizing that sin and death continue in the world, although defeated, that some participate
in Christ as creator and governor of the world but not as
Savior, and that not all Christians achieve the same degree
of holiness.

Human beings are endowed with grace through participation, but the fruits of grace do not follow automatically.
There is work yet to do: "Grace is not given to abandon
labour, but labour required lest our sluggishness should
make the grace of God unprofitable."[68] Then, too, Christ
works in various ways in those whom he indwells, making
such effects as are derived from his human and divine natures the possession of those who participate in him. He
works by imputation and infusion, imputing to us those
things which he did and suffered for us, for the sake of righteousness. He infuses in us his Spirit.

Hooker is at pains to avoid novelty. Speaking in a language which he believes can be understood in his own time,
he strives to preserve the theological tradition of the church.
He was well-read in the Fathers of the early church, as were
all theologians of his time, and in his writing cited them
time and again to support his basic arguments. In this he re-

flected the conviction of the sixteenth-century Church of England that the church of the first five or six centuries was authoritative.[69] But he also read the theologians of his own day. He did not cite them as often as he cited the Fathers; they did not possess the same weight of authority. If he used their insights, he did not always acknowledge the fact; it was not customary to do so. Thus it is that we find many of those ideas which seem most typically Hooker's stated by others. For instance, Hooker's protest against arguing the mode of Christ's presence in the Eucharist is similar to statements made by Martin Bucer and John Calvin, but most strikingly like the teaching of the German Lutheran, Martin Chemnitz.[70]

Concerning participation in Christ, Hooker is in agreement with Calvin, whose teaching Paul van Buren summarizes in this way:

> The whole purpose of the mercy of God as Father and His influence upon us as Holy Spirit is to bring us to a participation in Christ (*Inst.* 4.1.3). The Spirit, therefore "has chosen His residence in Christ, that those heavenly riches which we so greatly need may flow out upon us from Him" (2.15.5). In a word, the Spirit is Christ reaching out to men to give them all that He has won. Calvin's way of saying this is that "the Holy Spirit is the cord by which Christ efficaciously binds us to Himself" (3.1.1). Note that Christ is the author of the union: "Christ, when He enlightens us with faith by the power of His Spirit, at the same time grafts us into His body, that we may be partakers of all His benefits" (3.2.35).[71]

Although he may be in general agreement with Calvin on this vital matter, Hooker is at odds with Calvin's followers in England concerning the way to salvation and specifically the relation of grace and free will. Hooker's opponents misunderstood his view of grace and free will. His concern was to limit free will, which he did by differentiating between the will's aptness and the will's ability to do good. The will may be apt, but it is not able. Grace is all important: "Seing all that wee of ourselves can doe, is not only nothing, butt naught, let him alone have abilitie and power of well doing."[72] And yet this does not mean that humanity is lost, far from it. The reason is clouded, not destroyed. Nor can Hooker endorse any full-blown doctrine of predestination which says that God predestines some to eternal damnation. He relies upon his understanding that there are two wills in God, the one a general will that all may be saved and the other occasioned by human perversity and involving divine prescience ruling to the contrary. In writing of the two wills in God, Hooker is influenced by theologians such as John of Damascus and Thomas Aquinas. But his theological point of view is also influenced by his conviction, born and nurtured by experience, that God wills the salvation of all: "He desireth not the death, no not of the wicked, but rather that they might be converted and live. He longeth for nothing more than that all men might be saved."[73] Some are damned because at times human maliciousness overreaches "the highest measure of divine grace." Some are damned "not because God will not save them but because he cannot, though of course their obstinacy cannot be said to excel or defeat the eternal will of God nor call into question his power and goodness."[74] In the end there is mystery, although Hooker is certain that whatever happens is in accord with God's general will.

In all of this Hooker is seeking to state the case of the Church of England as found in Articles 10 and 17 of the Thirty-Nine Articles of Religion, as well as in the so-called Lambeth Articles.[75] He is also interpreting the nascent Anglican tradition when he speaks of grace by degrees, for one characteristic of Anglicanism has been its emphasis on nurture in faith and works. In defending infant baptism and the interrogations put to infants, Hooker believed that the first foundation of faith is laid in baptism, a foundation to be built upon. "For that which there we professed without anie understandinge, when wee afterwardes come to acknowledg, doe wee any thinge els but onlie bringe unto ripenes the verie seed that was sowne before?" (V.64.2) The satisfying of the desire for Good, the achievement of that Wisdom which is "faith seeking understanding" and the strengthening of that Power needed to do the Good which reason and faith reveal — this is a lifelong task.

Participation and the Church

Salvation comes from God by the Son through the Spirit in the church. "But in God," wrote Hooker, "we actuallie are no longer then onlie from the time of our actuall adoption into the bodie of his true Church, into the fellowship of his children." He further emphasizes this:

> Our beinge in Christ by eternall foreknowledge saveth us not without our actuall and real adoption into the fellowship of his Sainctes in this present world. For in him wee actuallie are by our actuall [2 Cor. 2:10] incorporation into that societie which hath him for theire head and doth make together with him one bodie (he and they in that respect havinge [1 Cor. 12:12] one name) for which cause by vertue of this mystical conjunction wee are of him and in him even [Eph. 5:30] as though our verie flesh and bones should be made continuate with his (V.56.7).[76]

The church is formed by God "out of the verie flesh, the verie wounded and bleedinge side of the Sonne of man. His bodie crucified and his blood shed for the life of the world, are the true elements of that heavenlie beinge, which maketh us [1 Cor. 15:48] such as him selfe is of whom wee com" (V.56.7). The church so understood is indeed One, Holy, Catholic, worthy of respect and reverence.

The church is the place in which the Holy Spirit lives and works. And so, Hooker wrote of the people of God:

> They which belonge to the mysticall bodie of our Savior Christ and be in number as the starres of heaven, devided successivelie by reason of their mortall condition into manie generations, are notwithstandinge coupled everie one to Christ theire head and all unto everie particular person amongst them selves, in as much as the same Spirit, which annointed the blessed soule of our Savior Christ, doth so formalize unite and actuate his whole race, as if both he and they were so many limmes compacted into one bodie, by beinge quickned all with one and the same soule (V.56.11).

This statement provides a basis for discussing Hooker's views of church and society, as shall be done presently, his understanding of the church and of the doctrine of the Holy

Spirit. It is sufficient for our purposes here to note that it is the church, a people united by the Holy Spirit, professing "one head, one Faith, and one Baptism" (III.1.3), a mixed lot of fallible human beings, which provides the context and the means for growing participation in Christ.

Prayer and preaching are among such means. For Hooker, preaching includes the public reading of Scripture or, in a more general sense, any means by which the Word of God is communicated to people. In a passage reflecting the medieval world view, Hooker wrote of the continuous coming and going of angels between God and his church on earth, descending with doctrine, returning with prayer, descending with "heavenly inspirations," returning with "our holie desires" (V.23.1). The image suggests the dynamic movement of the daily offices, the faithful hearing God's Word, inspired thereby to pray. In such a way — which is central to Anglican spirituality — people grow in Christ.

What is that doctrine which inspires? It is the saving Word of God, rightly called "the word of life." "The waie for all men to be saved is by the knowledge of that truth which the word hath taught. And sith eternall life is a thinge of it selfe communicable unto all, it behoveth that the word of God the necessarie meane thereunto be so likewise" (V.21.3). Such conviction accounts for the emphasis given in Anglicanism to the public reading of Scripture and to preaching.[77]

What is prayer? Hooker's explanation is important and deserves close attention, especially at a time when there is so much sloppy, sentimental talk about prayer:

> Mindes religiouslie affected are woont in everie thinge of waight and moment which they doe or see, to examine accordinge unto rules of pietie what dependencie it hath on God, what reference to them selves, what coherence with any of those duties whereunto all thinges in the world should leade, and accordinglie they frame the inwarde disposition of theire mindes sometyme to admire God, some tymes to blesse him and give him thankes, sometime to exult in his love, sometime to implore his mercie. All which different elevations of spirit unto God are conteined in the name of prayer (V.48.2).

Fundamentally, "Everie good and holie desire though it lacke the forme, hath notwithstandinge the force of a prayer" (V.48.2).

Hooker, like John Donne, believed that personal prayer was difficult and could only achieve its desired ends when nourished by common prayer.[78] People, he wrote, are inclined to prefer common to private prayer because of the "vertue, force and efficacie" it possesses "to help that imbecillitie and weaknes in us, by meanes whereof we are otherwise of our selves the lesse apt to performe unto God so heavenlie a service, with such affection of harte, and disposition in the powers of our soules as is requisite" (V.25.1). He might have said that common prayer is necessary because through it the Word which inspires prayer is preached and the people are taught to pray in response to the Word.

Sacraments are means of participation in Christ. Hooker is most forceful here. Asking to what end sacraments are given, he answered that we may participate in Christ. Baptism is the sacrament by which we begin on the way to fuller participation. That is not to say that it is incomplete; it is complete in terms of the end for which it exists. In Baptism we receive Christ "once as the first beginner, in the Eucharist often as beinge by continuall degrees the finisher of our life" (V.57.6).[79]

Much of what Hooker had to say about the Eucharist was written in protest against the quarrels of his day over the mode of Christ's presence in the sacrament. Looking at the end for which the sacrament was given — participation in Christ — it is enough to regard the bread and wine as the body and blood of Christ in a symbolic fashion "because they are causes instrumental upon receipt whereof the *participation* of his body and blood ensueth" (V.67.5). Not transformation of bread and wine, but rather of persons is the aim. "The real presence of Christ's most blessed body and blood is not to be sought for in the sacrament, but in the worthy receiver of the sacrament" (V.67.6).

That Hooker's teaching did not testify to any depreciation of the sacrament's worth is made abundantly clear as he speaks of the way it makes us partakers of eternal life. He becomes most impassioned when he writes:

These mysteries doe as nailes fasten us to his verie crosse, that by them wee draw out, as touchinge efficacie force and vertue, even the blood of his goared side, in the woundes of our redeemer wee there dip our tongues, wee are died redd both within and without, our hunger is satisfied and our thirst for ever quenched . . . this bread hath in it more then the substance which our eyes behold, this cup hallowed with sollemne benediction availeth to the endles life and welfare both of soul and bodie, in that it serveth as well for a medicine to heale our infirmities and purge our sinnes as for a sacrifice of thanksgiving, which touching it sanctifieth, it enlightneth with beliefe, it trulie conformeth us unto the image of Jesus Christ (V.67.12).

Hooker's doctrine avoids the temptation to define Christ's presence in precise philosophical terms. He argues that the sacrament becomes that which it is meant to be in the use of it, as the faithful receive the body and blood of Christ, transforming them to participate ever more fully in Christ's life, death, resurrection and continuing work in the world.

Another means of participation is the ordained ministry. When treating the ministry in Book V Hooker goes to the roots of the matter, beginning with the importance of religion to the achievement of God-given ends in life (V.76.1–9). The ministry is created by God that human needs may be ministered to and the people of God participate more fully in Christ.

The power of the ministrie of God translateth out of darknes into glorie, it rayseth men from the earth and bringeth God himself down from heaven, by blessing visible elementes it maketh them invisible grace, it giveth dailie the holie Ghost, it hath to dispose of that flesh which was given for the life of the world and that blood which was poured out to redeeme soules, when it powreth malediction upon the heades of the wicked they perish, when it revoketh the same they revive (V.77.1).

Hooker thus held a very high view of the ordained ministry, but it must be emphasized that he valued the ministry not in and for itself alone. Its value consisted in its service toward that end for which it was created. It was to be the means of assistance by which the "Order of Laity" (as he called it) achieved fuller participation in Christ. His views did not encourage sacerdotalism; he preferred the title "presbyter" or fatherly guide to "priest." Furthermore, he could be very critical of the ordained ministers of the church, including bishops, when they served their own selfish ends rather than that end for which they were appointed. But he was also concerned for the condition of the ministry, the poverty and ignorance of so many clergy, conditions for which the laity were often responsible to the great detriment of themselves and others. Hooker wished to see the ordained ministry respected and self-respecting, without idolatry or pride, but with strength and humility.[80]

Hooker was not unique in his views; he avoided novelty. His understanding of the Eucharist is similar to that expressed by Calvin when he wrote:

> Christ is by his boundless and wonderous powers united us unto the same life with himself, and not only applies the fruits of his passion to us, but becomes truly ours by communicating his passion to us, and accordingly joins us to himself (ideoque nos sibi coniungere), as head and members unite to form one body.[81]

And yet Hooker differs from others, generally speaking, in that which is typically Anglican. Participation is viewed in relationship to the liturgy of the Book of Common Prayer. His exposition of the Prayer Book influenced generations of Anglicans. The emphasis on participation, the distinction between the essential and the indifferent, the protection of the essential and the adorning of it with ceremonies which enhance that for which it is intended, and the refusal to allow things indifferent to dominate either the church or the Christian life — these things, so carefully enunciated by Hooker, became integral to Anglican tradition.

Participation and the Christian Commonwealth

On the social level, Hooker's aim was the realization of the Kingdom of God in the Kingdom of England, a goal similar to that which in large part motivated Thomas Cranmer as he produced and revised the Book of Common Prayer.[82] The fifth book of the *Laws* is, as we have noted, devoted to explaining and defending the Prayer Book. It opens not with any direct reference to the Prayer Book, but with the assertion that true religion is the mother of all virtues and the "chief stay" of "all well-ordered commonweals" (V.1.5). The enemies of true religion, and thus the enemies of virtue and of the commonweal, are atheism and superstition. Hooker is concerned about the former,[83] but it is the latter that is at issue in the quarrel with the Puritans, who regard the Church of England as full of popish superstitions and out of tune with the Word of God. Hooker described the task he faced as being the examination of "the causes by you [Puritans] alleged, wherefore the public duties of religion, as our prayers, our Sacraments, and the rest, should not be ordered in such sort as with us they are" (Pref. 7.6). That is, Hooker was concerned to show that the laws governing the "public duties" toward God in England were such that true religion was publicly acknowledged and enforced by just laws to the benefit of church and commonwealth in the one society.

Hooker's understanding of the commonwealth at the beginning of Book V is linked to discussions in the first and eighth books. In Book I, following Aristotle, he described the genesis of government and its development from the family to the nation in terms of human necessity. In particular, government exists for protection against the wickedness and malice of others and for the promotion of human happiness (I.10.2–3). With Augustine, however, he believed that government is a result of the Fall, that human nature was "disabled," and that people stand in need of that supernatural law which teaches not only supernatural duties but also "such natural duties as could not by the light of Nature easily have been known" (I.12.3). True religion is necessary if the ends of the commonwealth are to be fulfilled.

In Book VIII there is recognition that the end or purpose for which societies exist is "living well," which involves putting spiritual things ahead of temporal, the chiefest of all spiritual things being "religion" (VIII.1.4). That which Hooker says here concerns all societies, but in that society where true religion is acknowledged and enforced the believers are the church, and where all persons are at one and the same time members of both church and commonwealth, then, while there remains a difference between them, they properly constitute one society and are not, as the Puritans argue, two distinct corporations (VIII.1.2).[84] Thus, in an argument drawing in part on Aristotle and political philosophy in general, in part on Augustine and the history of Christian doctrine and in part on Tudor political theory, Hooker asserts the necessary coinherence of true religion and "secular" society, church and commonwealth.

The Book of Common Prayer, according to this understanding, is a legal means whereby the commonwealth may more fully achieve its intended goal, "the happy life," "the life well lived," the life which is virtuous, realizing the Kingdom of God on earth. The Prayer Book, providing for the public devotions of the society, is approved because persons find in it the means "to help that imbecility and weakness in us" (V.25.1). The sacraments are moral instruments (V.57.4-5); they are causes instrumental for that participation in Christ whereby "such effects as being derived from both natures of Christ . . . are made our own," conveying "a true actual influence of grace whereby the life which we live according to godliness is his, and from him we receive those perfections wherein our eternal happiness consisteth" (V.56.10). Those who participate in Christ not only attain to perfection and happiness, but they do so together, all being "coupled every one to Christ their Head and unto every particular person amongst themselves" (V.56.11). The Eucharist is not, then, individualistic. Its end is participation in Christ, which involves the perfection and happiness of society, of people existing in many complex relationships, dependent upon one another.

It is of great importance to realize that Hooker's social views grew out of his basic theological principles, and out of fundamental philosophical and psychological understandings. All three ways of looking at life and interpreting experience — theology, philosophy and psychology — are involved in the Sermon on Pride as Hooker said: "God hath created nothing simply for itself: but each thing in all things, and of every thing each part in other have such interest, that in the whole world nothing is found whereunto any thing created can say, 'I need thee not.' "[85]

Hooker's well-known exposition of church and state in Book VIII, which provides a powerful defense of Royal Supremacy, grows out of basic convictions concerning creation, nature and humanity. That exposition, which some view as fundamental to Anglicanism, can be dispensed with as it has been through the course of events in Europe and America; but the fundamental belief in interdependence, mutual participation and coinherence, of which the church-state theory is but one possible expression, remains and has persisted in Anglicanism to provide one of its most characteristic elements. The Book of Common Prayer is a book of corporate devotion designed, not only for personal growth in participation, but for the formation of happiness in society. In more modern terms this means, not only that Christians may, but that they *must* "interfere" in the working of society — although that society be professedly "secular" or even anti-Christian — striving for justice and peace and for that love which is the fruit of mutual participation in the created order and in that redemption which is participation in Christ.

Critique: Pros and Cons

Hooker's theology was not without fault. He was prejudiced where Puritanism was concerned, too quickly categorizing Puritans of every shade with radicals and Separatists such as the notorious William Hacket (V.Ded.6) and the impatient Henry Barrow (V.12.1). Hooker did not seem to understand the difference between Thomas Cartwright and a Hacket or a Barrow or, if he did, he succeeded in convincing himself that the adoption of moderate Puritanism, such as that of Cartwright, led straight to the horror of Muntzer and the insanity of Hacket.[86] We know better than that now, although a political scientist of considerable repute has contended that Puritanism leads to modernism, to Hitler and Stalin, and the confusion of God with Man in the totalitarian state. For Eric Voegelin, Hooker is the champion of truth and goodness against the gnostic evil of Puritanism and modernism.[87]

Another way of looking at Hooker suggests that he failed to understand the value of moderate agitation for change and had no sympathy for civil disobedience when such was justified.[88] And yet he was himself critical of rapacious patrons and negligent bishops. Hooker's rather rigid attitude toward his opponents, his inability to listen and hear what Cartwright was saying and doing at crucial moments, contributed to moments of oversimplification, rigidity and unreasonableness in his writing. An example concerns the way in which he seized upon a statement of Cartwright's uttered in the midst of literary combat and labeled it *the* opinion of the Puritans.[89] But the remarkable thing is that the circumstances of his opposition to Puritanism did not make him even more rigid and legalistic than it did. That it did not is largely attributable to the fact that Hooker's mind generally operated on the theological level rather than in the gutter of contemporary controversy. At this juncture our concern is for certain problems encountered on the theological level.

First of all, there is Hooker's cosmology or world view. Hooker accepted without qualm or question the Hellenic-Jewish-Christian cosmology dominant at the end of the Middle Ages. The universe was for him an authoritarian system, rational but constantly reliant upon the authority of pagan and biblical antiquity. The universe as he understood it was geocentric rather than heliocentric. It was also thoroughly anthropological. During Hooker's lifetime human perceptions of the universe, of earth and of humanity were changing. Copernicus, in 1543, and Tycho Brahe, in 1573, contributed to the growing difficulty involved in viewing the universe as geocentric. But, even before Copernicus, the explorations of Columbus, landing on San Salvador in 1492, and of Magellan, circumnavigating the world in the first quarter of the sixteenth century, cast doubt upon the old views and the authorities which sustained them.[90] This is not to say that the "new cosmology" is simply true and relies on no authority. Like the old, it is a rational construct involving faith in a mathematical structure beyond mere appearance. The authority supporting the dominant cosmology is now neither Plato's *Timaeus* nor the Holy Bible; it is scientific method, but it also involves faith in a mathematical structure beyond mere appearance. Moreover, our perceptions continue to change. Kepler, Galileo, Newton and many others have contributed insights which further undermine the old views. Darwin and Freud have altered our understanding further, in terms of biological and social development and in terms of human nature. But Darwin and Freud have had their critics as their views have been tested, modified and sometimes refuted. Einstein, the atomic bomb, space travel, a revolution in communications — all are landmarks along the ever-changing way.

When viewed from the vantage point of the present, Hooker is seen to belong to the far distant past. In the seventeenth century John Donne was conscious of change and of the emergence of a somewhat frightening situation:

> *And new Philosophy calls all in doubt,*
> *The Element of fire is quite put out;*
> *The Sun is lost, and th' earth, and no mans wit*
> *Can well direct him, where to look for it.* [91]

The Aristotelianism basic to Hooker's understanding of the universe also contributes to his understanding of the divine and human in Christ. The two-nature model is derived from Aristotle's understanding of primary and secondary substance (*Categoriae,* c.5). Characteristics belonging to ourselves as individuals and as members of a species combine to make us who we are. The two-nature model as developed in the early church (*una hypostasis* and *duo physeis*) virtually identifies *hypostasis* with primary substance, or with the individual characteristics of the person, and *physis* with secondary substance, or the characteristics of the species or genus. The result, when applied to the second person of the Trinity, is, on the one hand, a dualism unknown to the New Testament, and, on the other hand, a depreciation of the human individuality of Jesus, depicting him as taking on what amounts to a vague but nevertheless important generality at the time of the Incarnation. [92] Granted that all christologies are in one way or another deficient and that, when we say "this coffee is weak," we are still involved in the basic Aristotelian distinction between primary and secondary substance; yet the two-nature model on which Hooker relied is not tenable now. Its view of substance is impossible and its understanding of human nature is altogether too static. The result is that Christ in Hooker's writing is often cold, distant, an abstraction in whom we participate not in the sense of participation as we know it with other persons, but rather as it is experienced in relation to attitudes, powers and principles.

Nor is Hooker's view of church and state tenable now. Here he seemed to have some qualms concerning absolute monarchy. F. D. Maurice indicated that Hooker often "failed in tracing the boundary line between" church and state,[93] but he did stop short of the theory of "divine right of kings." Given his understanding of the universe of laws, he could never countenance a ruler who said and believed: "I am above the law; I am the law." Nevertheless, the modern situation is far different from anything Hooker could have imagined. Most states are neither antagonistic to the church (as the state was in the two centuries before Constantine) nor overtly supportive of any particular religious groups (as states were in the sixteenth century). Separation of church and state characterizes the American situation — however much practice mocks theory. The same person is not always both a member of the church and of the body politic, and if a person is a member of both such membership does not mean the same now that it did in Hooker's day. Our relationships tend to be contractual. Hooker understood the relationship between church and state to be of divine origin and to be sustained by universal law.

And, finally, there may be something too ecclesiastical or "churchy" in Hooker's theology, at least where modern predelictions are concerned. For example, the ordained ministry seems, after all allowances have been made, to exist on a much higher level than the laity and to exist apart from the generality of the people of God. Furthermore, Hooker's way of expressing the superiority of the ordained ministry may seem sexist. For instance, priests are *"presbyters* of fatherlie guides" to whom "Christ has communicated *the power of spirituall procreation"* (V.78.3). Granted that such language reflects the age in which it was used and that Hooker could not be any other than a man of that age; even so some Anglicans will find Hooker hopelessly outmoded and his writings objectionable. The same could be said of Luther and Calvin. In the sixteenth century, church and society were hierarchical in structure and, with some exceptions, patriarchal and sexist.

It would be wrong to end on such a note, however. The theology of participation set forth by Hooker tends to rise above the culturally determined particulars which we have reviewed above. *Participation* is a term peculiarly suited to the modern age of globel interdependence and democratic ideals. *Participation* as a key term suggests ways of adjusting to new cosmologies. Hooker is at pains to avoid overdefinition, to admit that he doesn't *know* spiritual realities as he *knows* material things and to emphasize the importance of participation in the ultimate as saving grace. Christianity doesn't depend on the truth or falsity of its mythology, however such truth or falsehood may be determined. It depends upon participation as experienced through reasonable faith in the context of the holy community. This is the universe that ultimately matters, for here in participation is to be found the assurance needed concerning the unknown and the unknowable.

Furthermore, as the mode of Christ's presence is not the essential issue (that issue being the reality of participation in Christ), so the relation of the divine and human in Jesus Christ is not something we must logically understand, define and thus control, so much as it is something to be experienced in and through Word and sacraments and explained in rational, communicable terms. Christian experience is not irrational. As Hooker says, the working of the Spirit of God in us yields its reasons, reasons we must be capable of conveying lest we find ourselves indulging in private fancies. The person who participates in Christ, in that personal encounter which preserves individuality in community, knows that Christ is present and can speak of that knowledge rationally.

Then, too, participation in Christ takes place in the community which we know as the people of God. These people are citizens, hopefully active and responsible citizens engaged in political units ranging from the family to the nation, and beyond to the global community. Church and state intersect at many points, but nowhere more meaningfully than in the church itself as the affairs of state demand the church's prophetic judgment, and in the state itself when the course of events leads toward certain disaster without that prophetic judgment needed to alter its suicidal course. Both church and state are concerned for the happiness of the people and the preservation of the eco-system. As Christians we believe that the commonwealth needs the Gospel.

And, finally, participation is the key to the full ministry of the church. The purpose of the ordained ministry is to enable the participation of all the people of God in Christ as Savior working through the Spirit in Word and sacraments. The focus, as we have seen, is on the ministry of the people of God, of which people the ordained ministers are members. That ministry of the people is a ministry to one another and to the world for which Christ died. Hooker's theology of participation is modern because it partakes of that which is timeless.

Hooker and Present Anglicanism: A Conclusion

If Hooker has one clear message for modern Anglicanism, it concerns the necessity to locate and emphasize that which is truly essential in terms of ultimate ends and purposes. The foundation of the Christian faith, he tells us, is acceptance of Christ as Lord and Savior, with the faith which he has transmitted to us down through the ages, and baptism in his name. Or, to put it another way, the general aim is happiness, which is salvation through participation in Christ. To realize this end, there are God-given means, chiefly Word and sacraments, and the ordained ministry charged with responsibility for the preaching and administration of the same.

Such an understanding of salvation through participation by means of Word and sacraments stresses one end of a dialectic, that which Hooker indicates when writing of angels descending with doctrine. It seems evident, then, that at the heart of Anglicanism there will be the reading and preaching of God's Word, and thus a strong emphasis on God's gracious initiative emanating from his love. That the public reading and preaching of the Word have been neglected is altogether too evident and accounts for at least some of the weakening of Anglican churches in Great Britain and America. In the Third World and especially in Africa, Anglican churches have been growing rapidly. There the Word is read and preached with evangelical fervor and with openness to its power. Alongside the Word read and preached, there is at the heart of Anglicanism the administration of the sacraments, baptism as the beginning of saving participation in Christ and the Holy Communion as the means of continuance and growth in that participation. But, although the Eucharist has become the main means of corporate worship in the Anglican communion, too often its basic significance as a means of participation in Christ resulting in changed lives and a changed society is lost in a welter of secondary or even trivial concerns — sometimes a result of misunderstanding, sometimes a result of the deliberate avoidance of that which might be unpleasant.

The ordained ministry is emphasized in Anglicanism because it is responsibly engaged in essential matters — matters of the greatest importance to people as people and not only as church people. This responsibility is centered upon reading and preaching the Word and administration of the sacraments — they are central. From them there flow other tasks, such as pastoral care which is fundamentally concerned with that participation which is the chief end of Word and sacraments. The ministry of bishops, priests and deacons in Anglicanism is viewed primarily in the light of such fundamental responsibility. But the ministers must understand this and accept it. The laity must understand this and demand such responsible activity from their clergy. Hooker stresses the vital importance of the ordained minister leading the people in common prayer. "The authoritie of his place, the fervor of his zeale, the pietie and gravitie of his whole behavior must needes exceedinglie grace and set forward the service he doth" (V.25.3). Then too, according to the Anglicanism which Hooker represents, while the ordained ministry is honored, there is no place in it for pomposity or arrogance. This ministry serves the people of God. The fundamental order is that of deacon. Every priest, every bishop, is first of all and always a deacon. As such the ordained minister serves the needs of the people of God and of the world. Viewed thusly, the ordained ministry is subservient to the people and at its best it has always acknowledged that fact with gratitude. There is no greater honor than that which is shared by all who participate in Christ, and he in them. That the church is in trouble now is in large part due to the fact that ordained ministers and laity have forgotten the lessons which Hooker taught.

To be an Anglican is to await and receive God's Word and to attend and participate in the sacraments with conscientious care for their administration according to their proper ends. None should be ordained without having proven dedication and skill in preaching and administering the sacraments. In addition, the laity should understand that they are ill served if preaching and administration of sacraments are done in an off-hand, slovenly manner. Administration of the local church, counseling, social service and the like are all important, but secondary. And this is so because Anglicans believe that, if the essential matters are properly attended to, the rest will follow and be more meaningful and effective than they would otherwise be without the ministry of Word and sacraments.

Thus emphasizing essentials, Anglicans are not so wedded to their denominational identity that they find it a barrier to fellowship on a larger scale. They are first and foremost catholic Christians. The earliest Anglicans believed that the Church of England was not a denomination, but rather Christ's one, holy, catholic and apostolic church *in* England. True Anglicans have inherited that attitude and embrace it, working actively for the achievement of organic unity amongst all Christians. Anglicans exist to die, or rather to live in a larger context than they now know.

The other side of the dialectic — we have been considering doctrine, or the Word of God read and preached and the sacraments administered — is prayer, or the ascent of the angels back to God. Anglicans are a praying people, although their understanding of prayer may be so broad that to other Christians they may seem to pray not at all. Their prayer is a yearning, a thirst for God, for the Good which takes form in thoughts, words and actions. This prayer is enabled by divine inspiration working in the hearts of individuals as they are sustained in the holy community. Prayer as response to divine inspiration, and as the fulfillment of the most basic desire for the good, is expressed through what Hooker and his contemporaries understood when they wrote and spoke of the commonweal and every Christian's responsibility for the welfare of every other living being. We should speak now of social service or social action. For Hooker and Cranmer and others, such social action was not something apart from prayer or a mere extension of prayer; it was prayer itself. The Book of Common Prayer presupposed this fact, a fact which has been woefully neglected to the detriment of ourselves and those we are called to serve. The understanding and attitude so clearly expressed by Hooker is of vast importance for the present world as we strive to come to terms with our environment, learn to practice Christian presence in the midst of other world religions, and come to grips with the "new" cultural insights into human sexuality. God is merciful, desiring the salvation of all people and of all creation. To yearn for God and to desire the good is to participate in the divine mercy. This positive attitude toward God and the creation is characteristic of Anglicanism. Where it is lacking, there Anglicanism is diminished.

Involved in the Anglican attitude there is a sense of awe and wonder. This is expressed with considerable power by Hooker when dealing with the multiplicity of God's ways of communication with the creation and when explaining the essential nature of the Holy Communion. The holy, the beautiful, the good and the true are all highly valued by Hooker and by Anglicans in general. And this is so at least in part because, when confronted by the creation and by God in and through the creation, Anglicans are so often overwhelmed. As humans we are seemingly impelled to analyze and dominate that which we encounter. We are concerned to discover whether there is a God and if so what God is like and how God communicates to the world. The knowing is no idle exercise of natural curiosity, however, but involves an attempt to control that which is known. Likewise, when confronted by the Holy Communion, we want to know exactly how Christ is present, perhaps in anticipation that through such knowledge we shall be able to control his presence. Hooker's gift to Anglicanism, as one who highly respected reason, was the reminder that, if God is God and the Holy Communion a means of participation in Christ, we cannot know in the sense that we want to know or dominate that which is nothing less than God's grace. Anglicanism is not alone in inculcating awe and humility in its people, nor is it alone in neglecting such awe and humility, yielding to the aggressive, egocentric impulses of our kind. But Anglicanism is only true to its heritage when it glories in the holy, worshiping, loving, witnessing to the God beyond the gods we create and control.

There is much more that could and should be said here, but there is at least this much. Richard Hooker was the recipient of a tradition in process of formation, based upon the tradition which began with Jesus of Nazareth, and before. That he influenced Anglicanism is a fact beyond doubt, contributing to the development of a tradition which is, in its admittedly fallible way, faithful to the past and to the future in the present.

CHAPTER II

Frederick Denison Maurice

Frederick Denison Maurice

—II—
Frederick Denison Maurice

Frederick Denison Maurice has had a profound influence on English Christianity and has helped to shape the pattern of Anglican thought and practice to a greater degree than is commonly recognized. He expresses the spirit of Anglicanism. Centennial celebrations of his death both in England and in the United States revealed a steady growth in interest and in publications about him.[1] In America Maurice, more than any other theologian, influenced the early teachers in the founding of the Episcopal Theological School in 1867 at Cambridge. Much later, his thought was commended by H. Richard Niebuhr who, in his *Christ and Culture,* cited Maurice as a classic example of the theme "Christ the transformer of culture." More recently, Schubert Ogden has written: "Maurice may help us to understand that the responsibility of contemporary theology is to make clear that the hidden power, the inner meaning, the real substance, of *all* human happiness is the event of Christ . . . the *eschatological* event, or *eternal* word of God's unconditioned love."[2]

With Christology as the starting point of all Christian theology and ethics — a radical departure in his day — F. D. Maurice helped to establish a principle that has become a commonplace in our time.[3] He insisted that the Gospel be heard in terms of its universal message, an insistence which sounded dangerous to his contemporaries. Indeed, he was constantly accused of being a Universalist by those who prided themselves on their orthodoxy. Today this orientation is increasingly the context in which the Gospel is viewed.

Maurice's social concern gave rise to the Christian Socialist movement and to an Anglican tradition of the social gospel in which William Temple stood. Maurice's polemics against a sectarian approach to the church embodied the principles of an ecumenical theology that would later guide many of the early leaders of the ecumenical movement.

A quarter of a century after Maurice's death, Bishop Collins would observe: "Many elements in his [Maurice's] teaching have been so generally assimilated among us that this very fact stands in the way of our realizing our debt to him; we neither know whence we derived them nor who it was who brought them forth, but assume that our fathers were as familiar with them as we are. . . . It may be doubted whether we have yet begun to assimilate some of the most essential elements of his teachings."[4]

Stephen Sykes' *The Integrity of Anglicanism* (1978) faults Maurice as chiefly responsible for shoddy thinking about "comprehensiveness" and for lamentable Anglican disdain for systematic theology. His book, however, is seriously flawed by a curious misunderstanding of Maurice who actually is closer to Sykes' own positions than he apparently realizes. Sykes' knowledge of Maurice is largely second-hand and contains unfortunate misquotations.

Maurice's continuing influence has been due to the fact that he was not only the greatest Anglican thinker of the nineteenth century, but also one of the clearest examples to be found anywhere of a Christian prophet. He was extraordinarily aware of the unbelief that lay hidden beneath conventional religion and the popular orthodoxies of his day.

His period was one of upheaval when the injustices of early capitalism had yet to be challenged by Christians. Like a true prophet, Maurice saw that this social breakdown was rooted in a theological breakdown. It was the latter which became his real target. Hence, simply to give leadership to the Christian Socialists was, in his judgment, not enough. He felt it necessary also to challenge the popular notions of heaven and hell, which were considered by most churchmen of that day a necessary part of the apparatus of social control. Although his daring resulted in his dismissal from his professorship at King's College, London, he did succeed in making people realize that "eternity was not time extended."

Maurice was also an educator, very much aware that the seeds of a new era were being sown and that the narrow sectarianism then typical of Christianity was not adequate to meet the crisis. Few in his day were as sensitive as he to all that was going on in the hearts and minds of their contemporaries. To a remarkable degree he had the theological power to interpret these intellectual and social developments from a Christian point of view and to reconcile their truths with the Gospel. Nothing seemed to him to expose the bankruptcy of contemporary orthodoxies more than the constant vilification by the religious press of those whose opinions deviated from the editors'. Nothing seemed more calculated to drive all the important movements of the century into anti-Christian channels than the shallow dogmatism with which Christians resisted new truth. "The orthodoxy which covers our atheism must be broken through," he declared.

He approached the task not by joining the modernist or liberal abandonment of traditional Christianity; rather, he reasserted its forgotten depths. His christological orientation made it possible for him to recover biblical theology in a day when both catholic and protestant thought had obscured it with systems of dogmatic theology. "In reading Maurice," complained one of his most unsympathetic contemporaries, "one has to learn not so much a new set of facts as a new way of thinking."

Undoubtedly this orientation of Maurice's explains why his own generation had such difficulty evaluating him. There were those, like Julius Hare, who spoke extravagantly of him as the "greatest mind since Plato." A good many more agreed with the Tractarian J. A. Froude who wrote: "As thinkers, Maurice, and still more the Mauricians, appear to be the most hideously imbecile that any section of mankind has been driven to believe in."

His Early Life and Writing

John Frederick Denison Maurice, as he was christened, was born at Normanstone on the coast of Suffolk, England, on August 29, 1805. His father, Michael Maurice, was a Unitarian minister of the older English variety rather than of the modern anti-Trinitarian persuasion. He did not object to the doctrines of the creeds so much as to their use as a test for church membership. The simple biblical assertions of the Fatherhood of God were adequate for him. He had been a younger colleague of Joseph Priestly during the time a fanatical mob had burned Priestly's house. As a young man, Michael Maurice had given up a considerable estate rather than forsake his religious beliefs. In order to support his family he boarded pupils. Frederick, the only boy to survive infancy, had three older sisters (Elizabeth, Mary and Anne) and four younger ones (Emma, Priscilla, Esther and Lucilla).

The family was tightly knit and affectionate until serious dissentions began to rend its unity. Elizabeth became a member of the Church of England. Two other sisters and finally the mother joined Baptist fellowships with strict Calvinistic theologies. Young Frederick was bewildered at the quarrels these religious changes occasioned. Forbidden by their father to engage in religious discussions at home, members of the family wrote long letters to each other to explain their stands. Maurice's later drive to realize unity and to bring reconciliation to warring factions may have been rooted psychologically in these family confrontations or enforced silences that were so painful to the growing boy. Later he was to write: "I not only believe in the Trinity in Unity, but I find in it the center of all my beliefs: the rest of my spirit, when I contemplate myself or mankind. But, strange as it may seem, I owe the depth of this belief in great measure to my training in my home. The very name that was used to describe the denial of this doctrine is the one which expresses to me the end that I have been compelled, even in spite of myself, to seek."[5]

When he was not yet fifteen Frederick and a boyhood friend drew up and signed a resolution: "We pledge each other to endeavor to distinguish ourselves in after life, and to promote as far as lies in our power the good of mankind." To prepare himself for the study of law, Frederick lived for some time in London with a family closely allied to the Wilberforces and to evangelical circles in the Church of England. There is some indication from a letter that the sense of religious depression that he experienced at that time was much helped when a woman of his acquaintance introduced him to the writings of Erskine of Linlathen. Later a warm friendship developed between them. Maurice was undoubtedly influenced by Erskine's conception of Christ as dying not solely for the elect, but for all, thus making Christ the Head of the human race.

In 1823 Maurice entered Cambridge University, where he became a member of the Apostles' Club and developed skills in literary criticism. His tutor, Julius Hare, introduced him to Plato and to German thought. Hare later became his close friend and married his sister Esther. His most intimate friend was John Sterling who has been described so colorfully by Thomas Carlyle as "the noble Sterling, a radiant child of the empyrean, clad in bright auroral hues in the memory of all that knew him." Sterling shared Maurice's enthusiasm for Coleridge and helped him to overcome the great shyness that prevented him from participating in university life. Maurice took a First in civil law, but could not receive his degree because he would not at this time subscribe to the Thirty-nine Articles. With Sterling he moved to London in 1827 to write for literary journals and finally to edit one, the *Athenaeum.*

The dissatisfaction with Unitarianism that Maurice had been feeling since boyhood was resolved for him when he became a member of the Church of England by baptism on March 29, 1831. His affectionate letters to his father during this period articulate tenderly, but with great conviction, his joy in knowing God as the Trinity.[6] He returned to university study, this time to Exeter College, Oxford, to prepare for ordination. During this period he finished a long novel, *Eustace Conway.*[7] His mother transcribed the copy and read the chapters at the deathbed of his sister Emma. He was ordained in 1834.

From a country curacy in Bubbenhall, Warwickshire, he wrote *Subscription No Bondage,* a defense of the Articles as requirements at the universities. This first theological book drew praise from members of the Oxford Movement. His growing estrangement from them may be traced to his disagreement with a tract of Pusey's on baptism. Maurice thought Pusey undercut the scope of Christ's redemption by limiting it to a special infusion of grace given to the newly baptized but capable of being blotted out by subsequent sin. For Maurice baptism was "the sacrament of constant union" that declared Christ had redeemed all humanity. It was not the catholicism of the Tractarians that offended him, but their exclusiveness and utter failure to comprehend protestantism. In 1843 he wrote to Hare about W. G. Ward's inability to understand Luther. "The notion of Luther believing that the Gospel required a lower form of righteousness than the law! What havoc we must have made with his teaching before an intelligent and pious man could have produced such a conception of it. I am afraid we have to learn Protestantism again as well as Catholicism."[8]

Maurice's *Subscription No Bondage* deserves study today, quite apart from its dated controversy, as a thoughtful analysis of the theological foundations of education and culture. In 1870, as he drew near the end of his life, he indicated its importance in his own understanding of his work. "No book which I have written expresses more strongly what then were, and still are, my deepest convictions."[9]

At the request of an editor preparing an encyclopedia, Maurice began an article, "Moral and Metaphysical Philosophy," which continued to grow over the years until it ripened into two volumes. He was called in 1836 to become chaplain of Guy's Hospital in the Southwark slums of London, where his ministry to the ill brought out his pastoral warmth. Medical students were impressed with his lectures to them. His friendship with Sir Edward Strachey, who became a pupil in his household, also dates from this time. Maurice's letters to Strachey were, fortunately, preserved.

In 1837 Maurice married Anna Barton, sister-in-law of John Sterling. Two sons, Frederick and Edmund were born. Frederick, who would become a major general in the British

Army and a military writer, deserves the gratitude of all students for the wonderfully understanding and balanced two-volume biography of his father and collection of his letters which he published in 1883 and 1884. Unfortunately, most of the actual letters used and abridged at times by his son have been lost, impoverishing Maurician scholarship. Selections from the letters printed in the *Life,* together with some other letters, were published in 1964 under the title, *Toward the Recovery of Unity: The Thought of Frederick Denison Maurice.* [10]

The Kingdom of Christ

Maurice's masterpiece, *The Kingdom of Christ,* was written in his mid-thirties. He may well have derived the concept of the Kingdom of Christ from his curacy in 1833 under the Millenarian rector of Lympsham, Joseph Adam Stephenson, who also helped to bring him to ordination in the Church of England. In his memoir of Stephenson, Maurice wrote that his rector believed the events surrounding the destruction of Jerusalem actually brought the real establishment of Christ's Kingdom, the creation of a new heaven and a new earth. The evidence for a Millenarian origin for the phrase "the Kingdom of Christ" is that it does not occur in his writings before his association with Stephenson and that it is after this period his central organizing theological concept. Maurice expressed his gratitude in a letter to Stephenson on July 24, 1834.

I have often desired to express to you how much more lively my impressions of your kindness and of the truths which I heard from you are now than when I was in the neighborhood of Lympsham. . . . But since I have been engaged in preaching myself, I have found the advantage of your instructions in a degree that I could scarcely have believed possible; especially as they have led me, almost unawares, into a method of considering many subjects, and of setting them forth, which I should not have naturally fallen into . . . but I have found myself in all my private meditations, as well as in preaching, drawn to speak of Christ as a King, and His Church as a Kingdom; and whenever I depart from this method, I feel much less clearness and satisfaction, much less harmony between my own feelings and the work of God. I am sure you know how much lively gratitude may be excited in a person's mind by feeling that he has been directed into a clearer course wherein it is possible to make continual progress, and you will not refuse to accept my thanks on this behalf.[11]

Shortly after this letter, Maurice became aware through his sister Elizabeth of a controversy that was threatening to divide the Society of Friends. As a result of the deism and rationalism of the eighteenth century, the older body of Quaker divinity had been largely reduced to a universalist emphasis upon the spirit in everyone with a loss of the evangelical understanding of incarnation and atonement. In direct opposition to this development and inspired by the rising evangelical movement in England, a group of Quakers began to interpret Quaker doctrine in terms of personal salvation from sin. They organized separate worship with reading from the Bible, evangelical witness and even sacramental ordinances. Maurice became fascinated with the controversy as illustrating for him a hunger in the sect for the reality of church and yet as also showing the preservation by the sect of a truth needed in the church. He connected these thoughts with his continued reflection upon Pusey's views on baptism and saw a way of addressing both controversies in a larger context. At the urgent request of Samuel Clark, a Quaker publisher who was in later years to become ordained in the Church of England as a result of Maurice's influence, Maurice began in January 1837 a series of twelve "Letters to a Member of the Society of Friends" published in monthly installments by Darton and Son. The second letter was really Maurice's answer to Pusey. Other topics treated were Quaker, sect and church principles, eucharist, Scriptures, unity, liturgy, church and state, education and family relationships. We have Maurice's own testimony as to the genesis and development of *The Kingdom of Christ*.

Reflecting much on this controversy and connecting it with what was passing in the English Church, it seemed to me that the old Quakers were affirming a most grand and fundamental truth; but that it had become narrow and contradictory, because they had no ordinance which embodied it and made it universal; that we on the other hand, forgetting their Quaker principles, or rather the words of St. John, necessarily made baptism a mere ceremony or a charm. The two being united expresed to me the reconciliation of the High Church Baptismal regeneration with the Evangelical demands for personal faith. Starting from this text, I wrote a series of tracts addressed to Quakers, but really concerning ourselves more than them. They formed the book called the "Kingdom of Christ," of which a second edition, much altered appeared in 1841. In the second of these tracts I commented on Dr. Pusey's theory of baptism. Nothing I have written had so important an effect on my life. It set me in direct antagonism with his school, to which I had many attractions, and by some members of which my "Subscription No Bondage" had been partially approved.[12]

The letters were collected and published toward the end of 1838 in three volumes by Darton and Clark as *The Kingdom of Christ: or Hints on the Principles, Ordinances, and Constitution of the Catholic Church in Letters to a Member of the Society of Friends.*[13] Maurice was urged by many to turn the book into a treatise on the church by reducing its discussion of the Quaker controversy and by enlarging its scope to survey all the churches and sects of the Christian West, together with a critique of philosophical and social movements. He accepted the latter advice, but rejected the former, feeling that to keep its context with the Quaker controversy better illustrated his conception of doing theology by digging down to foundations than by constructing systematic theologies. It also justified his comprehensive apologetic as he explained in an advertisement prefixed to the second edition in 1842 as "the circumstances which induced me to attempt a comparison between our own position and that of those who seemed to be at the greatest distance from us." The second edition, moreover, contained a dedication to the Reverend Derwent Coleridge with an acknowledgement of the influence of his father Samuel Taylor Coleridge upon him.[14] Maurice, writing confidentially to his friend Strachey on September 10, 1841, revealed his own evaluation of the second edition: "I like my own alterations in it, but I question if that portion of mankind which read the first edition will. As it expresses more of what I really think and believe, it is better *quoad me*, and if the universe don't approve it, the universe must write a book for itself."[15]

The first part of the book consists of an analysis of Quakerism, Pure Protestantism (Lutheranism, Calvinism, Zwinglianism and Arminianism), Unitarianism and, later in the book, Roman Catholicism. There are many historical flashbacks in this survey, particularly one on the early Luther which communicates Maurice's deep sympathy with him. Maurice describes Luther's need to speak out on issues in language identical with statements elsewhere of his own need to speak out. If it can be said that the Tractarians rediscovered the catholic heritage, Maurice rediscovered the Reformation and reclaimed it from the contemporary evangelical deformation of it and the Tractarian contempt for and ignorance of it. Seeking to counter a widely held view that religious views and churches were dying out and that what was really valuable in them was preserved in philosophical theories (Carlyle), Maurice added a rambling section, refuting the view by showing that these philosophical ideas became contradictory and untenable once severed from their religious rootage. The material on religious, philosophical, historical and social movements is probably more confusing to a modern reader because of a lack of clear identification of the persons or movements discussed than it would have been for Maurice's contemporaries who shared the consciousness of the age with its conventional short-cut allusions and coded references. There is discussion, seldom clearly interrelated or convincingly organized to promote his purposes, about Locke, Hume, the Romantic school, American sectarianism, Kant, Rousseau, Hegel, Bentham, Saint-Simon and Owenite socialism. A far more responsible wrestling with the history of philosophy can be found much later in his two-volume *Moral and Metaphysical Philosophy* (1873). Maurice's basic conclusion is that nearly every one of these movements is right in its positive assertions, but wrong in its negations. These negations are compounded into systems that further divide people and shatter the unity of Christ's Church. When Maurice is at his best in describing alternative Christian positions, he shows an imagination and appreciation of the beliefs of others, living and thinking himself into their ways of experiencing reality. He becomes a Christian Socrates almost without a rival trying to meet other Christians on their own ground.

The second half of *The Kingdom of Christ* describes the "hidden hunger" of the previous sects and systems and interprets the Bible as the progressive manifestation of covenantal relations between God and humanity in the given institutions of family, of the nation and, finally, of the church as the Kingdom of Christ. The Catholic Church is for Maurice not just a theological idea or a Platonic universal, but a concrete, historical reality, unfortunately obscured by systems that have been forced upon it. The six "signs of a spiritual society" are then analyzed in the usual order in which people are drawn into living communion with Christ: baptism, the creeds, the forms of worship, the eucharist, the ordained ministry and, undergirding and interpreting them all, the Bible. Maurice's usual method is to describe the sign and its true meaning in the Bible or in tradition. Then he discusses and disposes of the various sectarian and philosophical objections to the sign. Lastly, he acknowledges the presence of the sign in the Roman Catholic Church, but argues that it has been corrupted there.

Maurice is convinced that the Roman Catholic Church has become the "sworn enemy of nations and national churches" and that the Reformation rightly restored the principle of national churches. The long and rambling section on church and nation is of more interest to the Victorian specialist than to the general reader today. Maurice believes that if the New Testament discloses the principles of the universal society which is the church, then the Old Testament reveals chiefly through the Ten Commandments the basic institutions of national life. He could not really conceive the separation of church and state in a Christian nation. The church was required as a conscience to keep political institutions from becoming instruments of internal oppression or of external imperialism. The state was needed to keep the church from becoming a worldly despotism. In a letter to Ludlow, who developed the principle of democracy from the sovereignty of the people and found a way of adjusting monarchy to this analysis, Maurice wrote in protest:

Twist the word as you will it must imply a right on the part of the people to choose, cashier, and depose their rulers. It must imply that power proceeds from them that it does not find them. . . . Do they make Christ their King? Might they choose another if they liked? . . . I must have Monarchy, Aristocracy and Socialism, or rather Humanity, recognized as necessary elements and conditions of an organic Christian Society.[16]

Depending on whether one finds Maurice emphasizing monarchy and aristocracy or socialism, he can be described as a conservative or a revolutionary. His interpreters have often followed either one of these options. The significant reality, however, is that he is both at the same time because he holds paradoxically the two poles together as "necessary elements and conditions of an organic Christian society."

Behind Maurice's analysis there is a basic presupposition: the contrast and correlation of church and world. This relationship is related to the contemporary theology of secularization in its many forms. It is important to establish just what Maurice means here, for there is a radical development today beyond Bonhoeffer's *Letters and Papers from Prison* which is content to collapse church into world without remainder, just as there are right-wing denominationalists who completely devalue the structures of the world to concentrate totally upon the church. For Maurice the church must remain a distinct society, but this is held alongside the conviction that "the State is as much God's creation as the Church." In the same passage Maurice adds: "I have been most anxious to rescue the idea of a national society from those who would make it out to be something cruel and devilish. . . ."[17]

His clearest statement of the correlation of church and world occurs in the *Theological Essays*.

The world contains the elements of which the Church is composed. In the Church, these elements are penetrated by a uniting, reconciling power. The Church is, therefore, human society in its normal state; the World, that same society irregular and abnormal. The world is the Church without God; the Church is the world restored to its relation with God, taken back by him into the state for which He created it. Deprive the Church of its Center and you make it into a world.[18]

The last section of Maurice's *The Kingdom of Christ* discusses the Church of England, particularly its party structure, with respect to the previous problems and concerns. The Prayer Book becomes the key for understanding the views of the Church of England on the six signs of the Catholic Church. Maurice understands the political forces which shaped the Anglican reformation, but beyond that he finds the English character itself to be politically oriented. English literature exhibits this tendency as seen in Shakespeare's historical dramas, Spenser's *Faerie Queene* and Milton's writings on government and much of his poetry. This political orientation, with its political metaphors to describe religion, meant that the English would naturally look upon Christ's Church as a kingdom rather than a system. Elsewhere differences in theology would lead to varying schools of thought responsive to great theologians, but in England differences would be expressed politically as parties in church life. The great Anglican classic, Richard Hooker's *The Laws of Ecclesiastical Polity,* reveals in its very title this political concern and orientation. Maurice's own classic incorporates the political image into its title as *The Kingdom of Christ.* Maurice's tribute to Hooker is evidence for a continuing sense of identity in Anglican history and for a deep feeling of kinship with him.

> Hooker's work is the specimen of a class, though certainly the highest specimen. And when one considers it, and the whole life and character of the man who wrote it, I think we must feel how very little excuse lies in that habit of mind which God has bestowed upon us, for any defect in meekness and gentleness, its superiority to the low notions and canons of this world, in converse with the hierarchies of heaven.[19]

Maurice's book has commonly been misunderstood, although there is some evidence for the charge, as an apology for the Church of England, whereas his theological principles, despite his failure at times to apply them fully, are the basis for a Christian ecumenism that has yet to be recognized and accepted in the churches. Maurice clarifies his intention in these words:

> I am not ignorant, also, that the hints which I have offered in opposition to systems, may, themselves, be turned by myself or by others into a system. . . . On the other hand, if

there be anything here which may help to raise men above their own narrow conceptions and mine, may lead them to believe that there is a way to that truth which is living and universal, and above us all, and that He who is Truth will guide them in that way — this which is from Him and not from me, I pray that He will bless.[20]

Later Life and Writing

John Sterling's wife died suddenly on Easter Tuesday in 1843, leaving him with six small children for whom the Maurices assumed much responsibility. Then Sterling himself began a losing battle with tuberculosis. Mrs. Maurice took Sterling into their home and nursed him, with her husband's help, until his death in September 1844. In the process she too contracted the disease. Maurice watched by her bedside until the end in 1845. Four years later he married Georgiana Hare, half-sister of his friend Julius Hare who had married Maurice's sister Esther. Maurice gave up the chaplaincy at Guy's Hospital to become a chaplain of Lincoln's Inn, a center for law students. Earlier he had been appointed professor of English literature and of modern history at King's College, London. In 1846 he accepted the chair of divinity in its newly established theological college.

Scholarly recognition came to him in 1845 with his appointment by the Archbishop of York and by the Bishop of London to the Boyle Lectureship. The lectures developed into *The Religions of the World*, a pioneer work in the field and one that enjoyed immediate popularity. So much more is now known about the world's religions, and Maurice so frequently employs an inadmissible style of asserting what the Buddhist or Hindu "will have thought" (Leslie Stephen called this tense "the conjectural preterite" in Maurice), that little attention is usually paid to the book today. It has, however, a surprising relevance for the continuing discussion of the Christian attitude toward the world's religions. It anticipates in some measure positions about the world's religions suggested in the documents of the Second Vatican Council and would add a dimension of understanding to the growing interest in the West in the non-Christian religions and in mysticism. Professor H. G. Wood has caught the highly dialectical method of Maurice.

His task ... is to discover the element of truth in other religions, to show how Christianity, rightly understood, can do justice to them, to admit that in actual fact Christianity has needed the corrective contained in the insights of other faiths, to suggest that Christianity, again rightly understood, can supply what is lacking in other faiths. Throughout he has in mind the theory that the religions of the world are but so many products of man's wishful thinking, and also that kind of speculation about religions which blurs all the distinctions between them and so misses their true significance.[21]

In 1845 the Archbishop of Canterbury invited Maurice to give the Warburton Lectures. These were to develop into his *Epistle to the Hebrews*, which contains an important preface that is longer than the book itself. It is a careful reply to the *Essay on the Development of Christian Doctrine* written by John Henry Newman just as he entered the Roman Catholic Church. With the contemporary interest of Roman Catholicism in Newman it would greatly enrich the current ecumenical dialogue to have Maurice's evaluation of Newman's seven tests of development republished. Maurice agreed with Newman about the need for authoritative guidance on the part of the contemporary church, but he denied that an infallible authority had been given. What was given was the historical actuality of Christ and the abiding presence of his Spirit in the entire Christian community. God's judgments were more to be heard in historical events, he believed, than in oracular ecclesiastical authority.

Maurice is often described as the founder of Christian Socialism. This description may actually be the source of more confusion than light because Maurice's socialism bears no resemblance to the modern, post-Marxian varieties. He was not interested in government ownership of the means of production, but in producers' cooperatives, a radical innovation in his day. More important to him than a specific set of social goals for which legislation should be sought, was the theological analysis of political and economic reform. He wanted to challenge his theological students to a concern for the social implications of the Gospel. He was as committed to provide educational opportunities for working men and women by founding colleges for them as he was to improve social conditions. In fact, he saw the first helping to bring about the second. If Christ had redeemed all, then all human life must express this redemption.

Further, the real founder of the Christian Socialist movement was J. M. Ludlow, an English social critic who had been born in India and educated in France. He interested Maurice in the cooperative movement and originally proposed the formation of an association dedicated to the reform of English society along Christian lines. After the revolutionary events of 1848, a group of outstanding young men gathered around Maurice and Ludlow, meeting weekly for Bible study. They promoted producers' cooperatives, conducted classes in a slum section of London and published *Tracts on Christian Socialism*.

The name "Christian Socialism" had been seized upon by Maurice because, as he put it, "It will commit us at once to the confict we must engage in sooner or later with unsocial Christians and unChristian socialists."[22] "Competition is put forth as the law of the univese. That is a lie. The time is coming for us to declare it is a lie by word and deed. I see no way but by associating for work instead of for strikes. . . . This is my notion of a Tailors' Association."[23]

Within one year of the *Communist Manifesto*, Maurice opened his first *Tract on Christian Socialism* as follows:

> *Somebody* (a person of respectability): Christian Socialism! I never saw that adjective united to that substantive before. Do you seriously believe that a Socialist can be a Christian, or a Christian a Socialist?
> *Nobody* (the writer): I seriously believe that Christianity is the only foundation of Socialism and that a true Socialism is the necessary result of a sound Christianity.[24]

Though it made a great impact on English society, the movement did not achieve all that Ludlow envisaged for it, partly because of dissension among the members. Maurice quickly became the real head of the movement and dominated it according to his own understanding that society was already constituted in Christ. His interest was not in social revolution, but in the regeneration of English society by reasserting its foundation in Christ. This regeneration involved, in Maurice's eyes, raising the laboring classes up to take their rightful place in the social order, but it did not involve the formation of a new society by revolutionary force. Consequently, he ultimately turned the energies of the Christian Socialists from producers' cooperatives to Workingmen's College, founded in 1855.

The history of these developments has been examined afresh by the Danish scholar, Torben Christensen, and told in his *Origin and History of Christian Socialism, 1848-54*.[25] Christensen reveals that there were tragic depths in the conflict between Maurice and Ludlow of which neither was fully cognizant. Of the two, Maurice sounded the more prophetic note. In a sermon for Advent in the turbulent year 1848, he asked the question: "Do you really think the invasion of Palestine by Sennacherib was a more wonderful event than the overthrowing of nearly all the greatest powers, civil and ecclesiastical, in Christendom?"[26] His repeated references to current events seen under a Christian prophetic interpretation of history bring to mind the preaching of Reinhold Niebuhr.

Thus, Maurice is one of the sources of that concern for social redemption that has characterized Anglican theology in the modern period and which, through men like Headlam and Temple[27] has been a tributary stream to the Life and Work movement of modern ecumenism.

Maurice's discussions with the radical Chartists and revolutionaries of his day may be seen as a daring anticipation of the Marxist-Christian dialogue of our day which can be as dangerous to contemporary participants on both sides in terms of the security of their jobs and standing as it proved for Maurice. In 1889 Bishop Stubbs wrote of Maurice what would become even more true as time went on:

> It was the doctrine of Maurice which . . . kept the whole forward movement in the social and political life of the English people in union with God and identified with religion, a doctrine which, idealized and transfigured in the two great poets of the century, Tennyson and Browning, dominant in the Cambridge schools of Lightfoot and Westcott and Hort, assimilated almost unconsciously by the younger Oxford theologians of the *Lux Mundi* school, has during this decade turned the current of our English Christianity to the consideration of the great social problems of the age. . . ."[28]

Maurice held the religious press responsible for exacerbating party strife. It seemed as if the press had only to attack someone to have Maurice rise to that person's defense. Sanders writes: "Maurice was undoubtedly one of the most important forces which caused English journalism in the last half of the nineteenth century to insist more and more on the use of the signed article."[29] Attacked on all sides by the politically conservative papers of both low and high churchmanship, Maurice gave his enemies the opportunity they were seeking to impugn his orthodoxy when in 1853 he published his *Theological Essays*.[30] In his book he criticized the popular equation of eternity with endlessness in reference to future punishment. His own understanding of the word *eternal* was drawn from such Johannine texts as "This is life eternal that they might know thee the only true God and Jesus Christ whom thou hast sent." He denied that he was a universalist, but to the self-consciously orthodox of his generation any weakening of the traditional picture of hell seemed to subvert the sanctions for morality and social control.

After much controversy he was dismissed by the Council of King's College for undefined opinions on eternal punishment "of dangerous tendency, and calculated to unsettle the minds of the theological students." Four years before his dismissal he had taken time to write a long answer to a letter from F. J. A. Hort (then a student unknown to him), who was troubled by the conventional picture of eternal punishment. This letter remains his clearest statement on the issue.[31]

His earlier writing on education and his conviction that the church had a primary responsibility to educate the nation led to the founding of Queen's College, London, in 1848. Started at first as a school for governesses, it quickly became a pioneering agency for the higher education of women. From 1848 to 1854 Maurice served as its principal. After his expulsion from King's he founded the Workingmen's College, giving a set of six subscription lectures to raise funds for it. These were published later as *Learning and Working*. Maurice's grandson, Major General Sir Frederick Barton Maurice, who was Director of Military Operations, Imperial General Staff, 1915–18, later served as principal of the Workingmen's College.

Maurice made the Gospel the foundation of his educational philosophy. His prophetic role in this field is gradually being recognized.[32] His lectures in defense of Britain's system of ecclesiastical education were published in 1859 under the title *Has the Church, or the State, the Power to Educate the Nation?* He found that three major types of education were emerging in Western culture: The Spartan system which cultivated discipline; the Athenian which encouraged self-expression; and the modern type which disseminates scientific information. Each type, he notes, fails when it is made the sole guide to educational practice. Self-expression alone destroys discipline. Discipline alone stultifies self-expression. The mere dissemination of information loses any central meaning in life. The Gospel, however, furnishes a foundation for the creative combination of all three. Because it brings information of the highest kind, knowledge that people are made children of God in Christ, it can furnish a productive foundation for the pursuit of scientific information. Yet this higher revelation also reveals human self-centeredness which is at war with one's true standing and which must be disciplined if one is to realize it. Finally, because the Gospel reveals the ground of our being in Christ, it reveals to us our true self and brings it to full self-expression. Hence only the church as the custodian of the Gospel has within itself the foundation for true education. The church, in other words, is the school God has appointed for the race.

The critical question Maurice puts to state education is whether it can ever have the universality to call forth the highest potentialities of its students. "The maxim of a state education must always be, how much nobler a thing it is to make shoes than seek for principles." Since the state must of necessity concern itself with vocational training, Maurice did not believe it could ever offer any corrective to the commercial spirit which he believed the ruin of any nation. Compartmentalization would so fragment the educational system that it must fail to impart any sense of meaning to the whole of life or to elicit any universal loyalty. It could teach theology only as another specialty among the various specialities, rather than as the ground of unity for all. Thus Maurice believed that the true life of the intellect would be dried up under a state system. Consequently, the professions (by which Maurice means the occupations dealing specifically with the person as person, such as law, medicine, teaching and the ordained ministry) must inevitably be lowered to the level of trades (by which Maurice means those occupations dealing with our material wants). What the nation requires, however, is the exact opposite — that the tradesmen and the laborer discover in their callings the same dignity originally attached to the professions. To this end he proposes specific courses of subjects for each. Much of this theory was tested at the Workingmen's College in interesting experiments in adult education. Many of the questions he raised about the adequacy of state conducted schools have become burning educational issues today.

Maurice fiercely attacked Dean Mansel's Bamptom Lectures, *The Limits of Religious Thought*, in *What Is Revelation?* (1859). He returned for a second round in *The Sequel to What is Revelation*. Mansel was skeptical about our ability to know God. In some ways he anticipated the approach of linguistic analysis and has been defended in modern times as an "incomparable theologian and philosopher . . . shamelessly misrepresented by F. D. Maurice."[33] The asperity of Maurice's attack on Mansel is surprising, considering his usual ability to see much truth in positions opposed to his own. The explanation is that Mansel's "Christian Agnosticism" cut to the very root of Maurice's faith and actual relationship with God.[34] Mansel was a gifted logician and witty lecturer who pulled down the opposition with such irreverent mirth that Maurice considered him a baleful influence on the undergraduate mind. Mansel argued that there could be no philosophically certain knowledge of God and that therefore the Bible must be accepted as a divinely given but purely arbitrary authority for the regulation of thought and conduct. Christianity was commended precisely because it was impossible to know God. The Bible was a substitute for any real knowledge of God. Maurice saw in this view the essence of all that he opposed in the religion of his day, for to him the Bible was treasured for the opposite reason. It offered a genuine relationship to the living God in intimate union with his Son. Professor A. V. G. Allen, in *The Continuity of Christian Thought*, described the conflict between Mansel and Maurice as "perhaps the most significant one in the whole history of the Church since Athanasius stood up to resist the Arians on a similar, if not the same identical issue."[35]

Maurice was appointed to St. Peter's, Vere Street, London, in 1860. The Colenso controversy brought to a head the question of biblical criticism in England. Bishop Colenso published his *Commentary on the Pentateuch* in 1862, just two years after the appearance of *Essays and Reviews*. The situation was particularly difficult for Maurice because he abhorred the outcry and the proceedings against Colenso. Yet he could not sympathize with his point of view. Colenso represented the negative phase of biblical criticism. He seemed to delight in exposing mathematical inconsistencies in the text and believed that this somehow wholly discredited the Pentateuch as history. He proposed the reorganization of religion along rationalist lines. Yet Colenso was a friend who had dedicated a book to Maurice during the controversy over eternal damnation in order to demonstrate his support. It was painful to write against him.

At the same time, Maurice found that the defenders of the Bible did not express his convictions either. He never liked to call the Bible the Word of God as such. It was always the history of God's Word, by which the Word was to be discerned in life. *The Claims of the Bible and of Science*, published in 1863, is Maurice's contribution to resolving the issue.

One can only lament Maurice's lack of training in historical methodology, because his approach to the Bible is genuinely prophetic and is dependent upon regarding it as the actual history of the people of God. He was prevented, unfortunately, from giving great leadership in his time by his naivete in the exegesis of questionable passages. Before the insights of Maurice could come into their own, purged from their precritical limitations, the battle for the freedom of scientific and historical study of Scripture had to be won.

In 1866 he became Knightbridge Professor of Moral Theology and Moral Philosophy at Cambridge. His books,

The Conscience and *Social Morality*, are the fruits of his Cambridge lectures.[36] The remainder of his life was spent in these university surroundings, where he also accepted the unpaid cure of souls at St. Edward's Church. Maurice died on Easter Monday, 1872, as he prepared in his sickbed to receive the Holy Communion. His last words were the Trinitarian blessing.

Most of Maurice's books were developed from sermons he delivered on the Scriptures. Some of his outstanding books on biblical theology are: *The Prophets and Kings of the Old Testament, The Patriarchs and Law Givers of the Old Testament, The Doctrine of Sacrifice, The Unity of the New Testament, The Gospel of the Kingdom of Heaven, The Gospel of St. John, The Epistles of St. John, The Acts of the Apostles* and *The Apocalypse.* Liturgical theology today would be enriched by his biblically oriented sermons on *The Prayer Book, The Lord's Prayer* and *The Church a Family*, twelve discourses on the occasional services of the Book of Common Prayer.[37] The extent of his writing throughout an active life is amazing. One estimate runs to more than 16,300 octavo pages.[38]

Maurice as a Person in Christ

Two things about Maurice seem to have attracted people to him wherever he went and to have given him a certain fame. One was his encyclopedic mind and the other his Christlike character. Even his enemies, once they met him face to face, admitted that they had never known so good a man. He knew how to reach out to others in deepest sympathy and he constantly chose to work with the ignorant, the suffering and the poor of English society. Friends liked to parody his frequent references to a bedridden old woman as the criterion of truth. Yet he was a shy person at the beginning of his life and was always filled with self-doubt and self-reproach. The sense of unworthiness and of sin displayed in his correspondence strikes the modern reader as morbid. Apparently it did not so strike those who knew him best. R. H. Hutton attributes it to his intense sympathy with others, claiming that Maurice literally felt the sins and the shame in others as his own, yet constantly accused himself of not having entered more generously into their doubts and feelings. He felt himself implicated in the sins of the age. Hutton, considering this the secret of his sense of inferiority, said:

> His confessions must be taken as the outpourings of the conscience of a race rather than as the outpourings of the conscience of an individual, or they will seem artificial and unreal. Once catch the perfect simplicity with which he pours the humiliation of the heart of man, rather than the humiliation of the heart of an individual man — though, of course, it is the experience of the individual man which justifies him in that confession — and you see how truthful and genuine it is, how wonderful was the ardor with which Maurice entered into the social tendencies of his day.[39]

In theological discussion his aim was not to defeat, but to find the point of reconciliation between various truths. In this he lived out personally his understanding of the vocation of Anglicanism, which was "to hold together things which were never meant to be separated."

All this, however, grew out of his understanding of the Christian life. It was a life of repentance, if repentance is understood as constant dependence upon God-in-Christ. He was a living embodiment of the righteousness which he felt the Scriptures revealed. He trusted in a deliverer. Though it is fashionable to call him a Johannine thinker, the principle of his life was Pauline. He trusted in a justifier. His understanding of John opened his eyes to the meaning of Paul's phrase, "Christ in you." He considered Christ both the Word who confronted him and the person at work in his life actively giving him sympathy with others, strength in temptation, true thought and good intention. These things, he believed, were first found in Christ, then distributed to humanity. Christ united each individual and all humankind to the Father. The Christian life was trust and nothing but trust; yet the trust produced certain fruits — sympathy, understanding, the sense of oneness with others and self-control — all that Paul calls the fruits of the Spirit. Trust, if it was real, involved obedience. Thus faith in Christ enabled him to overcome his shyness and to enter into genuine relationships with others despite his sense of sin. Maurice put it this way:

That truth, of Christ being in us the hope of glory . . . I have found most necessary to sustain my own spirit when it has been sinking with the sense of its own unworthiness; for it shows that we can have no goodness apart from Him, that all our goodness must be by union with Him who is perfectly good.[40]

His Method and Style

There is an inner consistency in Maurice's thoughts from the time he sought ordination in the Church of England until his death. Very few changes are to be recorded. He remained loyal to the basic principle of Christ as King, which he had accepted very early. He found, however, ever more fascinating ways of illuminating the cultural task in its light.

Many times Maurice made clear his opposition to system-building. While he modestly described his vocation as "metaphysical and theological grubbing," this phrase really expressed his deliberate choice of the method of laying bare the theological presuppositions of culture and of dogma. In *The Kingdom of Christ* he observed:

Now to me those words [system and method] seem not only not synonymous, but the greatest contraries imaginable: the one indicating that which is most opposed to life, freedom, variety; and the other that without which they cannot exist.[41]

Behind this opposition to the system is something comparable to Kierkegaard's existentialist protest. The note of struggle in finding "the truth-for-him" can be discerned in one of his letters: "I can say, I did not receive this of man, neither was I taught it. Every glimpse I have of it has come to me through great confusions and darkness."[42] His chief opposition to systems of doctrine, however, was founded on his respect for the facts of historical existence. In this Maurice expressed both English empiricism against the conceptualism of continental thinkers and the Anglican's respect for historical institutions as points of departure for theological analysis.

> When once a man begins to build a system the very gifts and qualities which might serve in the investigation of truth, become the greatest hindrances to it. He must make the different parts of the scheme fit into each other; his dexterity is shown, not in detecting facts, but in cutting them square.[43]

One of his letters provides this insight into his understanding of the theologian's task:

> Theology is not (as the schoolmen have represented it) the climax of studies, the Corinthian capital of a magnificent edifice, composed of physics, politics, economics, and connecting them as parts of a great system with each other — but is the foundation upon which they all stand. And even that language would have left my meaning open to a very great, almost an entire, misunderstanding, unless I could exchange the name theology for the name *God*, and say that He Himself is the root from which all human life, and human society, and ultimately, through man, nature itself are derived.[44]

Maurice's style presents a hurdle for the reader. It is often opaque, gristly and confusing. This is partly the result of Maurice's extensive use of the Socratic method of inquiry in which it is not always clear whether Maurice is stating his own argument or that of his imaginary interlocutor. In spite of all this he frequently exhibits a gift of epigrammatic utterance that more than compensates for the difficult task of reading him.

The Basic Christological Principle

Though it may be said of almost any theologian that Christology is central to thought, with Maurice Christology furnishes in a unique way the underlying principle of all that he said and did. It is the element that gives unity and coherence to his thought, yet saves him from constructing a system. He saw the unifying power of Christology more clearly, perhaps, than any other Christian thinker.

In a letter to his son he wrote: "I was sent into the world that I might persuade men to recognize Christ as the center of their fellowship with each other, that so they might be united in their families, their countries, and as men. . . ."[45]

The basic principle of Maurice's theology is that God has created and redeemed the whole race in Christ. The heart of the Gospel, as he understood it, is that Christ, the Eternal Son of God, is "the Head and the King of our entire race." He believed this to be the witness of the creeds and behind them of the biblical revelation. He interpreted every Christian doctrine, and the human situation as well, in the light of the doctrines of the Incarnation and Atonement, placed in a Trinitarian setting. The cosmic Christ of Ephesians, Colossians and Hebrews and the Logos Christ of the Fourth Gospel became for Maurice the key to understanding both the scriptural revelation and the human situation. Maurice made this insight into his fundamental ontology. Unlike many Christians who have an independent concept of reality and then try to describe Christ as somehow fitting within or expanding or judging these categories, Maurice defined reality itself in terms of the Christ of the creeds through whom all things were made. The obviously organic nature of the conception grounded human solidarity and ethics in a christological ontology. Specifically, this meant for Maurice a closing of the gap between creation and redemption, a definition of the human person through Christ and not through Adam, and priority for the Incarnation over the fall.

> My desire is to ground all theology upon the name of God the Father, the Son, and the Holy Ghost, not to begin from ourselves and our sins; not to measure the straight line by the crooked one. This is the method I have learned from the Bible. There everything proceeds from God; He is revealing himself; He is acting, speaking, ruling.[46]

Maurice felt that the theology of his day, whether Roman Catholic or Protestant, whether Anglo-Catholic or Anglican Evangelical, had wrongly oriented itself around human sinfulness as the actual (even if not the explicit) starting point. He proposed instead the early divinity of the creeds which do not mention the fall. Although he took a literalistic view of Genesis and thus believed the fall as historical fact, he maintained that we know Adam and humanity through Christ, and not *vice versa*.

Protestants and Romanists, even while they denounce and excommunicate each other, yet appear to recognize the fact of depravity, of Evil, as the fundamental fact of divinity. The fall of Adam — not the union of the Father and the Son, not the creation of the world in Christ — is set before men in both divisions of Christendom as practically the ground of their creed.[47]

Such a passage reveals to us what Maurice meant when he called himself a theological digger. Using the revelation of God in Christ, the union of all in the Head of the race, he probed into every problem and every area of human life, tracing every abuse or evil in Christendom to an inadequate faith in Christ. This is why, in his book *Christ and Culture*, H. Richard Niebuhr cites Maurice as expressing more clearly than "any other modern Christian thinker and leader" the position that Christ is the transformer and converter of culture.[48]

Maurice, however, never leaves in isolation the principle that Christ is the Head of all. It is always correlated with the nature of the church and its function in the world. To Miss Williams Wynn he wrote in 1858:

I do anticipate a very deep and searching reformation, one which cannot be attended with less trials, one which I trust is to issue in greater blessings than the Reformation of the sixteenth century. . . . I feel very strongly that the ascension of our Lord into the heavens, and the glorification of our nature in Him with the corresponding truth that the Church exists to witness of Him, not only as her Head, but as the Head of every man, will be the battle-cry that will rally Protestants and Romanists, hungry seekers after wisdom, lonely tatterdemailions without bread, about the one standard. . . ."[49]

Maurice held his understanding of the concept *Christus Consummator* in close association with that which Archbishop Ramsey has called *Ecclesia Consummatrix*.[50] It remains to underline the significance of this fundamental christological principle for such other doctrines as revelation, sin and atonement, the church and sacraments, and for the principle of ecumenism.

Revelation and Scripture

In spite of his largely precritical attitude toward biblical study, Maurice anticipated many of the theological commonplaces today about revelation and its modes. For Maurice revelation is not a set of dictated propositions, but is given in events particularly in relationship to the person of Christ. "The revelation which the reason demands cannot be one of merely moral principles or axioms — it must be the revelation of a living Being. It cannot therefore be one in which events are merely accidents that can be separated from some idea which has tried to embody itself in them."[51]

He distrusted the scholastic distinction between natural and revealed theology on at least two grounds. He could not accept the notion that there were two distinct pathways to the knowledge of God, especially that there could be one initiated from the human side by something called "unaided reason." In today's terminology we should say that he believed in general revelation: "I hold that all our knowledge may be traced ultimately to Revelation from God."[52] In the second place, he refused to class the Gospel as one among the religions of the world. The Bible is not about religion, but about the acts of the living God: "We have been dosing our people with religion when what they want is not this but the living God."[53]

Maurice's use of the Bible has sometimes been criticized as "Platonizing eisegesis." There is no question about the impact of Plato on his thought. Yet the influence is often more in terms of a method of inquiry than in substantive propositions. Maurice's method in *The Kingdom of Christ* will remind the reader at once of Socrates' method when seeking the definition of justice by questioning conflicting schools of opinion. Maurice, of course, is leading his respondents on to the admission that there actually is a Catholic Church in their midst and that to it each bears a partial witness. The problem of Platonism is rooted in the recognition that, for Maurice, the Johannine writings are very much the clue to his understanding of the Bible as a whole. It might even be permissible to limit the field further by saying that, within the Fourth Gospel, it is the prologue which is the key. Careful study, however, reveals that Maurice integrated Pauline and Johannine Christianity. What may partially explain the persistent charge of Platonism is more the form than the substance of his exposition. Maurice asserts that what God had intended things to be and has made them through redemption is the real though unseen world. What the world has become through rebellion is the false though seen world. Torben Christensen's detailed study of Maurice's theology has led him to formulate the problem of his Christian Platonism in the following way:

> Maurice's idea of revelation represents a fusion of the Platonic idea of reality and the Biblical history of salvation. . . . With extraordinary systematic talent he, so to speak, set out to unite Plato and the Bible, and by appropriating leading ideas from both of them he constructed a new, fundamentally coherent and consistent view of totality. The success of his achievement is indicated not least by the fact that it is a most difficult task to point out precisely where Plato gives way to the Bible and vice versa.[54]

Christensen has here overstated his case. Maurice, to be sure, expresses biblical realities on the base of a Platonic ontology, but Christensen exaggerates when he speaks of Maurice "appropriating leading ideas" from Plato. The leading ideas are biblical, but they are expressed on a Platonic base, a Platonic view of reality. H. Richard Niebuhr has a different way of describing the same problem in Maurice. Maurice may be said to have had a peculiar version of realized eschatology.

> With universality Maurice mated the idea of eschatological immediacy. Eternity meant for him, as for John, the dimension of divine working, not the negation of time. As creation was the eternal, not the pretemporal, work of God, so redemption also meant what God-in-Christ does in that eternal working that ever stands over against man's temporal action. The eternal does not cancel man's past, present, and future; neither is it dependent on one of these: God was and is and is to come; He reigns and He will reign. . . . The kingdom of God is transformed culture, because it is first of all the conversion of the human spirit from faithlessness and self-service to the knowledge and service of God. This kingdom is real, for if God did not rule nothing would exist; and if He

had not heard the prayer for the coming of the kingdom, the world of mankind would long ago have become a den of robbers. Every moment and period is an eschatological present, for in every moment men are dealing with God.[55]

Yet it would be incorrect to say that Maurice has translated all New Testament eschatology into a "realized" form. He preserves, for example, the tension between the "already" and the "not yet" in a passage soon to be quoted on his view of Atonement from his *Doctrine of Sacrifice*. This quotation will also show his use of Platonic ontology as a base.[56]

The Bible is the witness to the Kingdom of Christ, and that Kingdom is the real theme of the Old Testament and the source of truth in other religions and philosophies. In interpreting any passage, Maurice tried to understand its simplest and historical context. Then he sought to show how the historical facts therein narrated also were pointers to God's universal kingdom and, in particular, to the constitution of all in Christ. He believed that the Holy Spirit would reveal the relevance between these insights and the situation of the preacher or reader of the Bible. He believed deeply in the self-authenticating character of revelation.

> I use them [the Scriptures] because I conceive they set forth Christ as the Son of God and the Lord of every man. I do not use them because I think they set forth some standard which is good for a set of men called Christians, who are different from other men, and who have not the same God with other men. I use the Scriptures to show us what I believe is the law and the life for all of us, that law and life of which men in the old world had only a partial glimpse. I should not use them if I thought them less universal and more partial than the books of heathens or of later moralists.[57]

For Maurice the Bible is not a solitary fact. He seeks to lay bare the organic connection that actually exists between church, creeds and Bible. His Anglican heritage, with its respect for Bible, tradition and reason interpreted in a pastoral way, received a creative evaluation in depth. The following passage of his about these relationships is genuinely illuminating and relevant in view of the discussion at the Second Vatican Council.

He who dwells with us and governs us, the Ever-blessed Word, has formed us to be one in Him; He seeks to make us one by bringing us to a knowledge of Himself; for this end He has revealed Himself to us, and has preserved the revelation in a book; this revelation He has entrusted to His Church, that she may impart it to men, and train men to apprehend its contents; the Church, in the exercise of her functions, has from Scripture formed a creed which is the first step in her scheme of education; when men were awakened by this creed, it became her duty to use the Bible, that they might know the certainty of those things wherein they have been catechized; with this Bible, she is able to cultivate the reason, which is the organ wherewith we apprehend spiritual matters; the Church tried what she could do without the Bible, and she became weak; the Bible has been set up against the Church, and has been dishonored; the Reason has been set up against both Church and Bible, and has become partial, inconsistent, self-contradictory. Finally, bitter experience must lead us at least to a conviction, that God's ways are higher than our ways; that a universal Church, constituted in His Son, and endowed with His Spirit, is the proper instrument for educating the universal reason.[58]

Sin and Atonement

Maurice's method of evaluating the human situation flows quite logically from his basic christological principle. Christ precedes Adam in the order of being. When it is written in Genesis that man has been created in the image of God, Maurice at once understands that the human being has been created by the Eternal Son and that this image can therefore not be destroyed by sin. We are "not to think that the world was created in Adam, or stood in his obedience for the Scriptures of the New Testament, illustrating those of the Old, teach us that it stood and stands in the obedience of God's well-beloved Son; the real image of the Father, the real bond of human society and of the whole universe, who was to be manifested in the fullness of time, as that which he had always been."[59] This means that Christ comes not as an alien intruder into the world, but as the redeemer of his own creation. While Christ brings us the utterly new gift of redemption, he does not extricate us from the race, but restores us to our true life as persons created in his image.

It is clear that such a premise will entail a different understanding of sin from the traditional one which speaks either of a total loss of the image of God or only of certain aspects of the image. Maurice does not understand sin prospectively as the prelude to redemption. He sees it retrospectively, in the sense that we are now members of a race that has been redeemed by the incarnation of the Word, by Christ's bearing the sins of the whole world, and by his resurrection from the dead on the plane of our history.

There is no minimizing of the Atonement in Maurice. Indeed, the opposite is the case, for his firm convictions about the work of Christ in overcoming sin led him to demote the doctrine of sin from its too dominant place in popular theologies. Maurice's view of the Atonement, as set forth in his *Theological Essays,* has been characterized as one close to the moral-influence theory. This is only a partial description, although perhaps justified because of the obscurity of expression in that work. His own view of the Atonement is best set forth in *The Doctrine of Sacrifice*, one of the clearest of his writings. Tracing the sacrifices of the Old Testament in a way that would need correction today from newer historical perspectives, Maurice holds that the New Testament asserts sacrifice as the great principle of the divine obedience of the Son before the world existed. What is new here is the careful linking of the Trinity and the idea of creation with the concept of Atonement.

> We see beneath all evil, beneath the universe itself, that eternal and original union of the Father and the Son . . . which was never fully manifested till the Only Begotten by the eternal Spirit offered Himself to God. The revelation of that primal unity is the revelation of the ground on which all things stand, both things in heaven and things in earth. It is the revelation of an order which sustains all the intercourse and society of men. It is the revelation of that which sin has ever been seeking to destroy, and which at last has overcome sin. It is the revelation of that perfect harmony to which we look forward when all things are gathered up in Christ . . . when the law of sacrifice shall be the acknowledged law of all creation.[60]

In terms of Christ's accomplished work, Maurice does not underestimate the power of sin, as he has often been accused of doing. Sin, for him, is defined as self-willed isolation from the true constitution of humankind as created and redeemed by Christ. Sin is the refusal to acknowledge our true center in Christ and the desperate effort to establish a false independence. Maurice accepted the reality of the devil, but refused to grant that the world was properly his possession.

Maurice criticized Calvinism for misinterpreting God's election and predestination in a narrowly individualistic and exclusivistic way. It made a travesty of the biblical witness that Christ was himself the elect One and that the whole race, not just a favored few, was included in him. This perspective is quite close to Barth's criticism of Calvin. Maurice claimed that the constitution of the race in Christ was the proper background for appreciating the power of Luther's concern for justification by faith and of keeping that cardinal insight uncorrupted. But protestantism found it almost impossible to submit its doctrine of justification by faith to the experience of justification by faith, with the result that, as Maurice shrewdly observed, "when assent to the doctrine of justification was substituted for belief in the Justifier, Protestantism went into the lean, sickly and yet contentious stage of its existence only to emerge from that into indifference — a mere denial of Romanism."[61]

The Church and Its Six Signs

For Maurice the church was organic to the Gospel. The church is the body of Christ, given life by its Head. It exists to show the world its true center and to support, by articulating the law of mutual sacrifice, the unity of both nations and families. Maurice held that the church was really the world when the christological principle was rightly understood.

It was not customary in Maurice's time to develop the idea of the church as the Israel of God. With a thoroughly scriptural analysis he traced a series of covenants between God and Abraham and the Israelite nation to show that family and nation are preliminary manifestations of church structure. *The Church a Family* continued consideration of this theme. The ultimate pattern of unity is God who as the Trinity expresses the ground of the family principle. He described his fundamental position in *The Kingdom of Christ* as follows:

> There rose up before me the idea of a *Church Universal,* not built upon human inventions or human faith, but upon the very nature of God Himself, and upon the union which He has formed with His creatures; a Church revealed to man as a fixed and eternal reality by means which infinite wisdom had itself devised.[62]

Just as the church had a history in Israel and in the New Testament period, so it has today. It is to be recognized by concrete facts of historical existence, not just in theological ideas. The theologian does well to accept the historical givenness of the signs of the church. As facts of history they are more impressive in their witness to the "Universal Society" than in the views entertained about them.

The fundamental sign of church life is baptism, wherein we are forgiven our sins, are incorporated into Christ and realize our status as children of God in the power of the racial atonement effected by Christ. Maurice liked to call baptism "the sacrament of constant union." He stressed the importance of sacraments as demonstrations of the free grace of God in Christ and as salutary checks to any excessive preoccupation with our own feelings or faith:

> Outward signs and tokens have a great worth. They attest the reality and universality of God's gifts, as in the case of the water in Baptism and the bread and wine in the Lord's Supper. They prevent men from fancying that their thoughts, and impressions, and beliefs, create the blessings which are bestowed upon us by God's free grace.[63]

Baptism interprets the human situation. Maurice has a way of bringing all his previous insights together when he seeks the depth of his next point. Notice the themes, hitherto separately developed, now focused on baptism.

> I have maintained that Christ, by whom, and for whom all things were created, and in whom all things consist, has made reconciliation for mankind; that on the ground of this atonement for mankind, God has built His church, declaring men one family in Christ. . . . And (we believing) that the

mark of that universal body or fellowship, appointed by God Himself is Baptism, do, without fear or scruple, asseverate of ourselves, and of all others who will come to this holy Baptism, of all who bear the marks and impress of that nature which Christ took, in His birth, of the blessed Virgin; that they are admitted into these high and glorious privileges; that they are brought into a state of salvation; that they are made sons of God and heirs of everlasting life. . . . And in saying this, we contend that we give faith . . . a ground upon which to stand, and which otherwise it cannot have.[64]

The second sign, which he elaborated in *The Kingdom of Christ*, is the two creeds which confess the triform name into which we are baptized. The creeds are not digests of doctrines; they are our protection against theological systems. To say the creed is to confess the Name, to make an act of allegiance to a person. Baptism is the sign that we are saved by grace, the creed that we are saved by faith.

The third sign of the church is the existence of set forms of worship, such as are collected in the Book of Common Prayer. Maurice is a profound interpreter of liturgics. He rejoiced that ordinary English people expressed their worship in forms derived from the Hebrews, the Greeks and the Latins. It was evidence to him that the church transcended space and time. Like many engaged today in the liturgical movement, he held the prayers written in the first ages of Christianity to be "in general more free, more reverent, more universal, than those which have been poured forth since."[65]

The eucharist is the fourth sign. It testifies that, because of Christ's sacrifice once and for all perfected on Calvary, a "living and perpetual communion" has been established between God and humanity. It expresses Christ's "continual presence with His universal family." More significant than the debates over the manner of Christ's presence, Maurice maintained, was the reality of that presence as sheer fact. There was, moreover, social meaning to the eucharist and an eschatological anticipation of the new age. Maurice felt personally that the eucharist expressed a depth and a practicality that one could not find elsewhere. "Ask yourself then solemnly and seriously — 'Can I find Christianity for men of all countries and periods, all tastes and endowments, all temperaments and necessities so exhibited as I find it in this Sacrament?' ''[66]

The ordained ministry is the fifth sign of the Catholic Church. It testifies that there is a permanent structure in the life of the church, a representative office of sacrificial service. Unless it serves faithfully it may congeal into a hierarchy of power and become only another expression of the world. Maurice wrote that the four gospels might be described as "the Institution of a Christian Ministry." The historic episcopate, he believed, expressed the reality of universal communion in the church and was the order that stood in succession to the apostolate. He expresses the idea in these words:

> I believe that He meant His Church to stand in certain permament and universal institutions . . . in a permanent ministry through which He should declare his will, and dispense His blessings to the whole body, and the main office in which should be that apostolic office, which belongs characteristically to the new dispensation, seeing that it expresses the general oversight of Him, who no longer confines himself to any particular nation, but has ascended upon high that He might fill all things.[67]

Although he considered the episcopate necessary, he did not, as the Tractarians did, unchurch those who lost it. This bond of communion might be broken and yet many ties with the universal church might still stand. He refused to define the limits of the church. "I cannot answer the question; I believe only One can answer it. I am content to leave it with Him."[68] The sixth sign, the Bible, has already been discussed. For Maurice, it is the reality behind all the previous signs.

The Relevance of Maurice's Thought for Contemporary Ecumenism[69]

Maurice's *The Kingdom of Christ*, and many other writings and letters of his, set forth a theology of Christian ecumenism that has yet to come into its own. As the Protestant Churches see beyond pan-Protestantism to an ecumenism that is genuinely catholic and as the Roman Catholic

Church comes out of its isolationism and loses what one of its own theologians has called its "anti-Protestant face," Maurice's modestly offered "hints" will become increasingly central to ecumenical discussion and action. A surprising number of studies on the nature of the church by Roman Catholic ecumenists follow a methodology similar to Maurice's. One of these theologians, Louis Bouyer, explicitly mentions Maurice's work in these sympathetic and perceptive words well before Vatican II.

[Maurice's work], at first misunderstood, is seen now to have been of greater influence in the Church of England than any other of the nineteenth century. A contemporary of the Oxford Movement, Maurice never joined it, revolted as he was by the deliberate scorn and ignorance shown by most of the Tractarians for all that was best in Protestantism. Having come to Anglicanism from Quaker [sic] surroundings, he never ceased to uphold the validity of the fundamental principles of the Reformation. At the same time, he constantly maintained that the logic of these principles, far from requiring the overthrow of the Church of tradition, with its sacramental and doctrinal structure, ought to lead to a completely fresh understanding of them, and could not be followed out fully outside that framework or, rather, outside the living organism willed by God. His principal work, *The Kingdom of Christ*, dedicated to this thesis, is certainly of capital importance in the evolution of Protestant thought. That is not to say that it is exempt from prejudices or misunderstandings in detail, both in regard to the ultra-Protestantism it starts from and to the Roman Catholicism it stops short of; in fact, it abounds with them. This only makes the depth and sureness of his thought all the more remarkable. If there is anyone within Protestantism who saw with clarity and depth into the principle needed to resolve the crisis endemic within Protestantism, it is certainly Maurice.[70]

With this awareness of the universal applicability of Maurice's ecumenical principles, it may be well to illustrate just how he saw the vocation of his own communion as a reconciler. Anglicanism, he maintained, had never defined itself in sectarian terms. The word sect represents one of Maurice's basic distinctions in ecclesiological analysis. The real opposite of catholicism, in his mind, was not protestantism, but sectarianism. The sect principle was opposed to the principle of catholicism in that a sect built itself upon some human formula of truth. To paraphrase his own words, the Church Catholic is a community united in the acknowledgment of a living person, Christ. Every sect is a body united in the acknowledgment of some notion or system of divinity. The sect invariably considered Christianity as an ecclesiastical organization to which one must adhere.

True catholicism, however, looked upon Christianity as the bestowal of a relationship with God. The relationship was given by God to all. The church existed to bear witness to it in the world. It was, one might say, the necessary means by which God proclaimed people his children and heirs and invited them to receive their heritage. Thus the church could never be conceived as simply a human organization pitted against the organizations of the world. It was part of the "constitution of the race." The sect, on the other hand, always saw itself pitted against the world. It could make no peace with those outside its confines. Its only approach to unity was to demand agreement with or submission to itself.

All of this analysis is common enough today. For a variety of reasons modern Christians are much aware of the sect type of Christianity. Maurice's concern, however, was the manner in which the sect principle had infected all of Christendom, whether originally sectarian or not. The tendency of church bodies to identify themselves with "the true church" meant that the sect principle triumphed almost everywhere in Western Christianity. The ecumenical movement is a sign that responsible Christians have now become aware of these evils and are seeking a way out of the impasse. Though he came long before the movement had established itself, Maurice too felt the impasse and thought Anglicanism had something to contribute toward its solution.

Many Anglicans today fail to let the depth of Maurice's distinction between church and sect judge their understanding of the Anglican Communion. They seem never to question whether they are members of a church. From this uncritical assumption they look down their noses in scorn or pity at the historic Protestant churches as "sects" because, for example, they may not exhibit all the points of the Lambeth Quadrilateral. It has been ironic that the points of the Quadrilateral which were really "principles" or "signs of the Catholic Church" for Maurice have been converted by many latter-day Anglicans into a sectarian system. Maurice speaks today to this element of self-righteousness and legalism in the Anglican system. Often we have prided ourselves since the formation of the Anglican Communion on being delivered from being a national or regional sect when all that we have really become is a world sect.

> I can well conceive how galling it is to a Dissenter to be told that he is the member of a Sect, and that we are not members of one. Moreover, the words seem to me unjust. I think he claims to be a member of Christ's Church as I do. I think I am as liable to sink into a Sectarian, and to be only that, as he is.[71]

Maurice made his point clearly in his criticism of the Episcopal Church of Scotland: "They have stood too much upon their ecclesiastical dignity, that they have seemed too much mere anti-presbyterians."[72]

Anglicanism, he contended, was an important expression of Christianity precisely because it did not have a "system of divinity" or a confessional formulation. It was not a church that insisted upon an official point of view, but embraced warring factions within itself dedicated to catholic, protestant, or liberal principles. This holy pandemonium might be the despair of the strict Roman Catholic or of the pure Protestant, but it did emphasize the fact that the church was founded not upon a humanly contrived system, but directly upon God.

> Our Church has no right to call herself better than other churches in any respect, in many she must acknowledge herself to be worse. But our position, we may fairly affirm, for it is not a boast but a confession, is one of singular advantage. If what I have said be true, our faith is not formed by a union of the Protestant systems with the Romish system, nor of certain elements taken from the one and of certain elements taken from the others. So far as it is represented in our liturgy and our articles, it is the faith of a Church and has nothing to do with any system at all. That peculiar character which God has given us, enables us, if we do not slight

the mercy, to understand the difference between a church and a system better perhaps than any of our neighbors can, and, therefore, our position, rightly used, gives us a power of assisting them in realizing the blessings of their own.[73]

Maurice did not attribute the advantages of the Anglican position to human wisdom and foresight. Rather he contended that the events of the English Reformation had prevented the Church of England from formulating its understanding of itself in sectarian terms. The result was a church body in which the catholic constitution of the church was united to a Protestant protest against the papacy. In her insistence upon national freedom, in her emphasis upon justification by faith, in her refusal of a human, visible head for the church, the Church of England was thoroughly a church of the Reformation. Yet none of the classic marks or "signs" of the church, he believed, were abrogated. The apostolic ministry, the catholic creeds, Scripture as the Word of God, the two dominical sacraments and liturgical worship all remain. It is interesting to note that these very items, which Maurice treats at great length in *The Kingdom of Christ*, were later also affirmed in the Chicago-Lambeth Quadrilateral as essentials of church life.

It is not usually recognized that Maurice's writings were the real source of the Chicago-Lambeth Quadrilateral since most commentary on its development stops on this side of the Atlantic with William Reed Huntington's *The Church Idea*, published in 1870. Huntington telescoped Maurice's six signs of the Catholic Church into four by bracketing baptism and holy communion into one point and by omitting Maurice's forms of worship. Huntington compared his four points to the foursquare City of God in the Apocalypse and unfortunately borrowed the name "Quadrilateral" from the four Lombard fortresses. The liturgical setting within Anglicanism is so dominant that a "pentelateral" might have been more realistic and possibly more productive than the Lambeth Quadrilateral. Gone also from the Quadrilateral was much of the spirit of Maurice, the replacement of Maurice's view of principles and process by a somewhat legalistic and static ultimatum about "this sacred deposit."[74] The Lambeth Conferences of 1920 and 1968 in their commentary on the Quadrilateral have come closest perhaps to Maurice's spirit, whereas, in general, Anglicanism has been fairly stodgy, defensive and myopic in its use. *The Decree on Ecumenism* of the Second Vatican Council comes much closer to the spirit of Maurice.

Maurice was not an especially accurate prophet of what would happen to the religious systems of his day. He saw them headed for a speedy dissolution but in a way that history simply has not confirmed. Also, he was not without a certain anti-Roman bias that may largely be accounted for in the dismal condition of the Italian church in his day. On most points he has been vindicated since the renewalist theologies of Vatican II have often taken positions surprisingly similar to his.[75]

The Kingdom of Christ gives us an indication of Maurice's views on the unity of the church. As indicated above, he tries to show that in the positive witness of each sect some basic living Christian principle is recognized, but not the whole of Christian truth. In constructing a system to embody and defend its partial truth, each sect denied other truths and excluded other Christian bodies from its fellowship. In the process, it betrayed the truth it set out to enshrine. The trouble lay in the sectarian conviction that it must construct the church anew to purify it from error. There was no remedy for this trouble, Maurice contended, unless the church already existed, built upon the foundation of the living Christ, reconciling all the fragments of truth which the various sects had championed, liberating them from the distorted shapes into which their defenders had forced them. Maurice joined the Church of England because in it he saw the partial fulfillment of this vision.

Far from claiming anything for itself, Anglicanism simply witnessed to the living foundation underlying all sects. Far from excluding all those who disagreed with it, Anglicanism claimed for itself and others membership in Christ's one, holy, catholic and apostolic Church. Its role was to affirm and defend major catholic truths denied by Rome or by protestant churches. Thus, Maurice saw the ideal of Anglicanism to be just as concerned to defend justification as the Lutheran, just as occupied in proclaiming election as the

Presbyterian, just as zealous for the inner light as the Quaker, just as insistent upon the preservation of catholicism as the Roman Catholic. Precisely because it had no system of its own except, of course, this very formula itself, it was in a better position, he believed, to champion the truths others had perceived.

> Let us make the members of sects to understand that we are setting up no opinions of ours against theirs, no leaders of ours against their leaders; that we desire to justify all that they and their fathers have clung to in their darkest and bravest hours, all that their leaders have taught them when they were inspired with most indignation against our indifferences to Christ and His Gospel; that what we preach is Christ the One Head of a body which time and space cannot bound, Christ the source and object of their faith and ours. Christ is the destroyer of all sects, inasmuch as He joins man to God. Let us make Spaniards, Frenchmen, Italians understand that we do not ask them to leave their churches for ours, to accept any single English tradition which is not also theirs, or to travel through the path by which God led the Teutonic nations in the sixteenth century.[76]

From the perspective of its ecumenical vocation, the parties of Anglicanism could be of considerable value. The Tractarians preserved the catholic witness to a constitution and order for the whole race and to the reality of the Church Catholic in the world. Evangelicals witnessed to the fact that there was a real bond for all in Christ's sacrifice. The liberals or broad churchmen insisted that the church must be comprehensive and throw off all partial truths. Each party, unfortunately, became as narrow and as divisive as any sect in the defense of its principles. But between them they outlined the things to which any branch of the church must witness. The fact that they stayed together in one communion testified to the divine union which the church was meant to proclaim to the world. It has often been remarked that Anglicanism itself is a microcosm of the ecumenical movement. This is precisely Maurice's point.

Maurice's opposition to parties within the Church of England is well known. Although he had been influenced by each of the three parties of his day, he never joined one. He also saw the dangers of a "no-party" and even of a Maurician party. His insight into the tendency within the Church of England to form parties is quite profound. This tendency has characterized Anglicanism far beyond its first homeland. "Elsewhere the defenders of a system may merely form a school. In England because by constitution we are politicians and not systematizers, they must form a party."[77]

Episcopalians in the United States have tended to take pride in the last few decades at the diminution of party strife, but it would be premature to pronounce the death of party division. Today it is resurfacing in a new and particularly complex and self-contradictory way. It may be illustrated by a certain yawn which often appears, for example, when Episcopal churches are asked to study the Consultation on Church Union (COCU), and in a certain eagerness in the press and on the local scene when some new statement of the Anglican-Roman Catholic International Commission (ARCIC) is announced. Many in the Episcopal Church are in danger of forgetting that their ecumenical relations with the Roman Catholic Church and the protestant churches must be of a "both/and" rather than an "either/or" nature. In other words, the old party system reappears as a division about whether one wants union with Rome or with the protestant churches. Every agreement whether in COCU or ARCIC ought to be mutually productive and in a wider ecumenical context rather than bilaterally isolating. The Consultation on Church Union specifically writes the purpose of wider union with Rome into its plan, although the purpose should be strengthened in any revision. The ARCIC statement on the Eucharist may be helpful in a wider reconciliation in the first section on the sacrificial work of Christ and the sacrificial nature of the eucharist, but in the section on presence it fails here to communicate the rich diversity of Anglican views on presence. Nor does the international statement acknowledge the still more fundamental need to confess in Maurice's spirit that the very fact of the eucharist is a far richer reality than any of our attempts to define it.

The point to be made here is that Maurice's "ecumenical" ecumenism is still needed by us and that we need to listen to his warnings about party divisions within. The fine quality of Maurice's spirit breathes through this well-known passage as he concludes *The Kingdom of Christ.*

> But if shame and humiliation are needful for English clergymen generally, they must be especially needful in those who have presumed to speak of our sins, and to offer any suggestions for our amendment. . . . I have in this book attacked no wrong tendency to which I do not know myself to be liable. . . . I am not ignorant, also, that the limits which I have offered in opposition to systems may, themselves, be turned by myself or by others into a system; and that neither its weakness and inconsistency, nor the insignificance of its originator, may prevent it from connecting itself with some new party. . . . But since a school, which should be formed to oppose all schools, must be of necessity more mischievous than any of them, and since a school, which pretended to amalgamate the doctrines of all other schools, would be, as I think, more mischievous than that, I do pray earnestly that, if any schools should arise, they may come to nought.[78]

How was the ecumenical vocation of Anglicanism to be carried out? This would not be done by calling other groups to unite with it as one possessing all the essentials of church life. That would be a return to sectarianism. Yet neither would it do to propose indiscriminate mergers with other groups. Few of the religious bodies in Maurice's day understood the truth he was driving at. His approach was to invite those of sectarian views to see that they were not really members of a sect at all, but of the church. On this ground he justified refusal of the Church of England to permit itself to be called a sect. Though this seemed pretentious to nonconformist churchmen, its purpose was to preserve a witness against their own view of themselves. "We will not submit to be called an episcopalian sect, because we do not want you to consider yourselves as sects. We want you to feel that you are members of a Church, members of Christ, children of God."[79]

Thus Maurice stumbled across the very principle which has made the ecumenical movement possible — the recognition that somehow all Christians are already united in Christ and members of his Church. He was perfectly willing to associate with other Christians on the grounds of "common membership in Christ." But he sharply rejected any sort of union based on the lowest common denominator of belief. Such a union would only be the dead residue of all sectarian systems.

The ecumenical vocation of Anglicanism, on the other hand, was to be carried out by claiming for others the privileges and the position Anglicanism claimed for itself. Rather than unchurch those who disagree with it — which is, in effect, the approach of sectarianism — it is to "church" them. It is to insist that what is true of itself is also the truth about them. Maurice even approached the thorny question of apostolic orders in this way. The doctrine of apostolic ministry, he insisted, was not held in order to cast doubt on the validity of other ordained ministries, but to testify to the fact that every minister is more than a denominational official. God himself had brought the pastoral office into being. The nonconformist minister, it was granted, could stand in a deeper, more organic relation to his congregation than he himself recognized or admitted. The intention of Anglican insistence upon apostolic orders was in part to enable such a minister to see the real validity of the ordained ministry and the catholicity of the given communion.

Can we be more concrete about what Maurice would urge us to do for church union if he were here today? I believe we can, although any extrapolations from his circumstances to ours is hazardous. First, I believe he would take a dim view of the procedure followed in COCU's *A Plan of Union*, which turns out to be a crypto-constitution, and of the statements on the Eucharist and on Papacy and Authority by ARCIC. There is too much here about joining together on the basis of "agreed opinion" as he would call the procedure. He did not "feel much sympathy with experiments for restoring Church Unity by arrangements or concessions among divines about points which have been in dispute for many centuries between them."[80]

This does not mean that Maurice is indifferent to truth. He would place primary emphasis upon church union as incorporating institutional elements not by describing them theologically, but by somehow providing for a process of growing together that would be primarily liturgical. "Our object is clear; we are to aim at entering into communion with all Christian people, so far as we can do so without sacrificing any of those principles upon which communion itself rests."[81]

We may say that for Maurice the formula of *lex orandi, lex credendi* was developed into *lex orandi, lex unitatis*. This deep conviction of his is expressed in his statement that the eucharist "keeps doctrines from perpetual clashing with each other and men from being slaves of doctrine."[82]

Maurice readily accepted theological and devotional pluralism as the way to union, even apparently the polemical statements of the past. Such an approach today would be a more honest and realistic program for both COCU and ARCIC than their attempts to bypass controversy with some newer phraseology.

> It is a very weighty consideration, that men, if they be honest, cannot throw aside old forms of thought and expression; they are intertwined with the dearest and holiest mysteries to which their hearts pay homage . . . under pretense of removing a falsehood, you are almost sure to destroy a truth. It is therefore more than a kindly act, it is a solemn duty to bear with things which seem to us dangerous in language, and even in practice, provided we do not ourselves conform to them.[83]

Maurice would undoubtedly hold that intercommunion far from being simply the sign of an already achieved oneness would be by God's grace his very means of achieving oneness. He imagines bishops of the Roman Catholic Church addressing Anglicans:

> We do not hold you excommunicated because you assert the dignity of your Bishops, and their direct subjection to Christ; we believe that you have the Sacraments, the Creeds, the Episcopacy, all those institutions which are the bonds of a common life, and are not merely connected with particular congregations or particular nations; we can and will meet you upon the basis of these institutions. We will not ask you to tell us what your theory of the Sacraments is, neither will we tell you what ours is; we will receive them together as witnesses and bonds of Christ's continual presence with us.[84]

What I believe Maurice is trying to point to here and elsewhere is the role of liturgy in fostering and moving toward union. "It is my protection and the protection of the Church against Anglicanism and Evangelicanism and Liberalism and Romanism and Nationalism."[85] Worshiping together testifies to the given union with each other in Christ the Head of all.

If this is a legitimate interpretation of Maurice and not too fantastic an extrapolation from his second letter to Palmer, then it would seem that Anglicanism, in omitting Maurice's fifth point — liturgical worship — from its Quadrilateral, has somehow lost the dynamic process that Maurice believed would lead toward union. In the theologizing about the four points of the Quadrilateral, especially about "the historic episcopate" in such a way to make it less available or acceptable to the non-episcopal churches, Anglicanism has pursued more of an ecumenism of "notions" or of "a system."

The acid test for my theoretical projection of Maurice would be the question of how he concretely would achieve communion with the non-episcopal churches. Here Maurice usually underestimates the difficulties for the non-episcopalian. He would somehow communicate episcopacy as a liturgical act and not as a series of theories or theological opinions. The process might be roughly comparable to what was done in the Church of South India in which previously non-episcopally ordained clergy were without further ceremony simply placed in communion with previously consecrated Anglican bishops or with newly consecrated bishops drawn from the non-episcopal churches in the union. Or the process might be roughly comparable to the services of inauguration held for the Church of North India and the Church of Pakistan in which all ordained ministries of the uniting churches were reconciled in a series of initial services. Maurice in 1842 supported the quite pragmatic and open-ended plan for a Jerusalem bishop who would oversee both Anglican and Prussian congregations in Turkish-ruled Jerusalem, with the implication that this local act might be a stage in restoring episcopacy in Prussia itself. Negotiations between the Prussian king and the Church of England were carried through to the indignation of the Reverend William Palmer and with the support of Maurice. In a sense, this plan, approved by the Archbishop of Canterbury and the Bishop of London, was a hundred-year and much bolder anticipation of the Church of South India. The arrangement later lapsed.

> Supposing that he [the Lutheran King] should therefore ask us to unite with him in conducting this work by means of a Bishop; suppose he should submit the whole ordination of this Bishop to the direction of our Church, requiring only that we should perform it according to our own Catholic principle.

Maurice then imagines the English bishops replying: "Here is the most satisfactory recognition of Episcopacy as a permanent institution, and yet as one especially adapted to this day." Maurice wishes to comprehend in a united church very divergent protestant interpretations of episcopacy on the principle he mentioned before with Roman Catholics.

> But what, if this . . . [non-episcopalian] . . . after performing this act, should continue to use language which seems to import that the religious bodies of his country may preserve their existence, without that institution to which in this way he has been doing homage; nay, what if he should interpret this very act into a quasi recognition of them under their old character? Why, Sir, I should apply precisely the same principles in this case, which I applied in both the others.

Maurice transcends both his Anglicanism for a higher catholicism, and traditional catholicism for a more comprehensive one in the following passage near the end of the second letter to Palmer.

> Shall I require the German, or the Helvetian, or the Dutchman to say, I have had no Church, not even the dream of one, I come to ask one from you? God forbid. If he can say such words, he does himself a deep moral injury. . . . No, if we would bind him to the Church Catholic . . . let us allow him to lay fast hold of every portion of truth which he possesses, of every institution which belongs to him. . . . [Otherwise] . . . it is as much as saying, that we want him to be an Anglican, which he cannot be, and not a Catholic, which he can be.[86]

Maurice did not share the timidity of many contemporary Anglicans about making episcopacy readily available. He worried about the guilt of not doing this.

But whether there be, or be not, a capacity in the Prussian nation for receiving this gift, we must not have to accuse ourselves of being the means of withholding it. We must be able to clear the consciences of the guilt of not having embraced every opportunity, of not having watched every indication of the will of Providence which might enable us to further so great a design.[87]

It would, however, create a wrong picture if we try to torture Maurice's positions into a rationalized process for achieving union under our circumstances today. Often he spoke almost apocalyptically about a fearful smashing of sects, and of the sufferings of a new reformation or renewal.

To whichever it come first, the faith, the faith [that leads to union] will pass rapidly, as by an electrical chain, from one to another. It will break through all barriers of opinion and circumstance. None will know how he has received it, because all will have received it from that Spirit who bloweth where He listeth.[88]

Maurice did not feel that the vocation he envisaged for Anglicanism could be undertaken with any sense of self-righteousness. Essentially he was contending that the Church of England was to call others to repent the sectarian temper which led them away from Christ and divided them from each other. Such a call could only come out of a like repentance from the Anglican. Maurice was extraordinarily aware of the sins of his own church, of the way it had treated its catholic structure as a pretext for a sectarian temper, of its treatment of both the Bible and Prayer Book as a "series of inspired sentences" and of its neglect of the poor in England. There was no sin in any church that was not also a sin of the Church of England. Only out of repentance could a call for unity come. But come it must, for God was "a destroyer of sects." On the horizon of the nineteenth century Maurice saw a "fearful crushing of sects"; this made him hopeful for the unity of the church, but not optimistic about the future. "Permitted destroyers of faith" would force the church back to its oneness in Christ.

Maurice's understanding of the ecumenical vocation of Anglicanism and of the much larger focus, the reconciliation in depth between catholicism and protestantism, is the message of the Spirit to the churches in our day. Maurice many times described his whole ministry and authorship as a search for unity. He expresses in his life and thought the spirit of Anglicanism. He knew, however, that its deepest ground was there all the time, in the given unity of the Triune God:

> The idea of the unity of the Father and the Son in the Holy Spirit, as the basis of all unity amongst men, as the groundwork of all human society and of all thought, as belonging to little children, and as the highest fruition of the saints in glory, has been haunting me for a longer time than I can easily look back to.[89]

CHAPTER III

William Temple

William Temple

—III—
William Temple

William Temple has been described as the most "various-ly distinguished" of the Archbishops of Canterbury since Anselm. He was undoubtedly the first churchman since the Reformation to be a national leader and a world figure. In 1963 two political scientists stated: "William Temple was the most significant Anglican churchman of the first half of the twentieth century. By the sheer power of his mind, the depth of his faith, the seeming tirelessness of his vitality, and the force of his personality, he dominated the Church of England. No comparable figure has arisen since his death to eclipse him either within his own church or as a religious spokesman in the wider world."[1]

Temple's main public distinction was that of a great Christian leader and statesman, especially in the areas of social concern, the ecumenical movement and Christian thought. Less public but more fundamental was the fact that he affirmed and practiced the Christian faith and life in the Anglican tradition with the utmost seriousness and that he manifested in his life, work and thought the fruit of the Spirit to a remarkable degree. Reinhold Niebuhr said of him: "It is safe to say that not only in public characters but also in private individuals few if any of us have known any person whose life and personality were so completely and successfully integrated around love for Christ as their focus and source and crown."[2]

Temple's personality was at the same time richly comprehensive and uniquely unified. His knowledge was immense, and he wrote about poetry, music, painting, banking, unemployment, democracy and education, as well as every area in philosophy and theology. But all this richness of thought and experience was integrated and illuminated by his devotion to Christ and his Kingdom.

Many have remarked on Temple's astonishing simplicity and humility. He spent himself without reserve for innumerable individuals and human causes. He was on terms of affectionate intimacy with men and women of all classes, schools of thought and nations. Ordinary people looked to him as their trusted leader, advocate and spokesman. One of his vicars in York described him this way: "It was the simple intense humanity of the man William Temple that made many say how gladly they would give all they had, their very lives if they could do him service. It was the man in the Archbishop that drew out all the love and devotion in us."[3]

Temple was a superbly happy man with "immense laughter." His faith was deep and tranquil, untroubled by serious doubts. He was a once-born Christian and the very opposite of a skeptic. It occasionally troubled him that he did not share the painful doubts of many of his contemporaries. The one time he was remembered to have failed in speaking to young people was an address sponsored by the Student Christian Movement on "Why I believe in God." When he was asked later what had gone wrong, he replied: "I have never known what it is to doubt the existence of God, and I felt I had no right to be speaking to that audience of young people."[4] In this connection W. R. Matthews wrote of him: "Some of the greatest philosophers and theologians convey to us a deep sense of the profound mystery and tragedy of the being and destiny of man; we feel that it is this which has stirred them to think; I do not find this in the writings of Temple."[5]

In spite of this or perhaps in part because of it, Temple was a superb popular preacher and teacher. He was a thinker rather than a scholar. Although his thrity-seven books and innumerable essays would have been more than a respectable harvest for a scholar, Archbishop Ramsey described him as an "amateur" in theology. Temple was in fact a "lover" of theology, and he put Christianity on the map for many in the twentieth century. W. R. Matthews again: "I doubt if any other writer has done as much to convince the general public that the Christian faith has a claim to be seriously considered by rational men and that it has something important to say on the problems which confront contemporary society."[6] And Joseph Fletcher wrote of him: "Temple's is far and away Anglicanism's most creative and comprehensive contribution to the theological enterprise of the West."[7]

Life, Work and Writings

William Temple was born in 1881 in the Bishop's Palace in Exeter, and he lived most of his life in bishop's palaces in the heart of the English Establishment. After schooling at Rugby, he studied classics, literature and philosophy at Oxford. He was deeply influenced by the philosophy of idealism through Edward Caird, the Master of Balliol, to whom he later dedicated the Gifford Lectures. His election to the presidency of the Oxford Union, the famous debating society, brought out his gift of stating issues clearly and working out a consensus of opposing views. Upon graduation he was offered a great many positions but chose the post of Fellow and Lecturer in Philosophy at Queen's College, his only academic position.

As an undergraduate, Temple was a Conservative with a bad conscience. He became concerned with social and political issues through his friendship with R. H. Tawney, among others. He was elected president of the Workers' Educational Association in 1908, and because of this and his new socialist convictions he was placed on a list of dangerous characters by the government during the First World War. He thus entered the tradition of Christian socialism which had been championed by F. D. Maurice. His concern for the ecumenical movement at this time is evidenced in his attendance at the 1910 Edinburgh meeting of the International Missionary Conference as a representative of the Student Christian Movement.

Temple had intended to seek ordination in the Church of England since his boyhood. But in 1906 the Bishop of Oxford declined to ordain him because Temple stated that he was not certain about the virgin birth of Jesus or his bodily resurrection. But by 1908 he had come to accept these doctrines and was ordained by the more liberal Randall Davidson who had succeeded his father as Archbishop of Canterbury. Later Temple became quite certain about these doctrines. The general tendency of his faith and theology was toward a more catholic or orthodox position. But this was always balanced by his concern for freedom in doctrine and by his generally liberal attitude of mind.

It was at this time that Temple published his first book, *The Faith and Modern Thought* (1910), which was originally given as a series of lectures to a university group in London. It is a consideration of the grounds in experience and reason for belief in God and an outline of Christian faith expounded in relation to modern science and philosophy.

In 1910 Temple became headmaster of Repton School. Although he became beloved there, his interests were too broad to be focused on this kind of work. This period saw the publication of *The Nature of Personality*, which was an elaboration of the fundamental category in his philosophy and theology, and essays on the church and the divinity of Christ in *Foundations: A Statement of Christian Belief in Terms of Modern Thought: By Seven Oxford Men*. With these essays Temple became an important figure on the English theological scene, holding what can be described as a moderate liberal position.

After four years at Repton, Temple became rector of St. James' Church, Piccadilly, in London, his one parochial post. Here his strength lay in clear and forceful preaching, and his involvement in social and political issues increased. His editorship of the shortlived weekly, *Challenge*, and the quarterly, *Pilgrim*, was a vehicle for his interpretation of Christian social principles and their application to the issues of the day.

In 1915 Temple met Frances Anson, who worked for *Challenge* and was also secretary of the Westminster branch of the Christian Social Union, of which he was the chairman. They were married in 1916. Although they had no children, it was a very happy marriage. Her intense social concern matched his, and her natural friendliness and vivacity made her a perfect companion in his busy life.

In 1916 Temple was appointed to a commission to propose a plan for a National Mission of Repentance and Hope whose purpose was to get the church to address the social and spiritual crisis brought about by the First World War. The results of the Mission were disappointing. It became clear, however, that the Church of England desperately needed autonomy from Parliament in managing its own affairs. Thus was born the Life and Liberty Movement. Temple resigned his living at St. James, took a sixty-five percent cut in salary and accepted leadership in the Movement. It was mainly through his prodigious efforts that the Movement achieved its main goal in the Enabling Act of 1919 which established the Church Assembly.

It is worth noting, in view of contemporary interest, that Temple fought hard and successfully for the inclusion of women in the Assembly. He believed that deaconesses were ordained ministers, and he believed that women should be ordained to the priesthood, but that this should be postponed for strategic reasons. In 1916 he wrote to a priest's wife: "Personally I want (as at present advised) to see women ordained to the priesthood. But still more do I want to see both real advance toward the reunion of Christendom, and the general emancipation of women. To win admission to the priesthood now would put back the former and to moot it would put back the latter."[8]

During this period of intense activity Temple continued to produce a series of small books including *Church and Nation* and *Plato and Christianity*, and his first major treatise, *Mens Creatrix* (1917). In the latter his method is first to show that the sciences of knowledge, art, morality and religion present four converging lines of evidence which do not meet, and that this incompleteness threatens their security. Then, beginning with the Christian hypothesis, he shows that the Incarnation supplies the central point at which the four converging lines meet and find their unity. In the first part he calls his method philosophical, in the second part theological.

After turning down two academic posts, Temple accepted a canonry at Westminster. In 1921 he was consecrated Bishop of Manchester, the midland industrial diocese in Lancashire and one of the largest in the Church of England. He succeeded Bishop Knox, an autocratic and militant Protestant and Conservative. This post was a great test and proof of his administrative, pastoral and leadership abilities. He accomplished the long-needed division of the diocese and won the hearts of the people through his warmth, humility and devotion.

His years at Manchester deepened his interest and involvement in the social witness of the church. He was chairman of a group which planned the Conference on Politics, Economics, and Citizenship (Copec), which was held in Birmingham in 1924. Preparatory study for the conference extended over four years. Its goal was to seek the will and purpose of God in political, social and industrial life. It was an international conference which drew 1,500 delegates and had an important impact on the direction of the ecumenical movement. One observer described Temple's chairmanship of the conference as his greatest service to the church and the Kingdom of God.

In 1926 there was the coal stoppage which led to a general strike. Temple served on a committee of churchmen which mediated between the mine owners and the labor unions. Although the committee's intervention failed, and the Conservative Prime minister Stanley Baldwin rebuked the committee for interfering in something which was not the church's business, Temple held that it was a proper activity, in fact a duty, of the church to mediate between conflicting parties while not making technical proposals. His views on these and related matters were published the next year as *Essays in Christian Politics*. One result of these events was a remarkable change in the attitude of organized labor to the churches. The churches had appeared to the working class to embody the conservative spirit of the privileged, but now they appeared capable of an independent outlook which indeed seemed to favor the point of view of working people.

In 1924 Temple published his most extended theological study, *Christus Veritas*, which he described as a sequel or companion volume to *Mens Creatrix*. Whereas the latter was mainly philosophical, the new book was mainly theological. Although Temple writes with the Christian revelation in full view from the outset, his method is again to "work in from the circumference to the heart of the Christian position and then out again."[9] He notes that the intellectual atmosphere of the day is dominated by a philosophy which, although it is theistic, leaves no room for a specific Incarnation. But he believes that a very slight touch to the intellectual balance may make the scales incline toward such an act of God. Therefore his aim is to present a "Christo-centric metaphysics." His procedure is again to treat the major metaphysical problems, the structure of reality, value, religious experience, humanity, history and God, from a metaphysical point of view, then to elaborate the central Christian affirmations and finally to consider the metaphysical issues again in the light of the Incarnation. (We shall return to parts of this volume below.)

The failure of Parliament to ratify the Prayer Book revision of 1928 was a great disappointment to Temple. He had labored on the revision and argued successfully for it in the Assembly and in his own diocese which was inclined to be in opposition. This defeat in Parliament caused him to conclude that disestablishment was not too great a price to pay for the church's freedom.

In January 1929 Temple was enthroned as Archbishop of York, succeeding Cosmo Gordon Lang who had been appointed to Canterbury. His thirteen years in the Northern Primacy was his longest service in one post and it was jammed with activity. Temple was at the height of his powers and quickly became a world figure. He chaired the Council of the youthful B.B.C., was a member of the Privy Council, preached at the disarmament conference in Geneva in 1932, wrote a dozen books, delivered the Gifford Lectures, lectured in the United States, presided at the Malvern Conference and led the ecumenical movement — all the while visiting almost all of the 457 parishes in his diocese.

Temple was the first archbishop ever to deliver the famed Gifford Lectures. He did not complete them beforehand but wrote them, one by one, prior to delivery, in the odd half hours snatched from his extremely busy life. This was possible only because Temple remembered and ordered everything he had ever read or thought, and this massive knowledge was always at his fingertips. In the preface to the published lectures he gave a revealing glimpse into his mental processes.

> All my decisive thinking goes on behind the scenes; I seldom know when it takes place — much of it certainly on walks or during sleep — and I never know the processes which it has followed. Often when teaching I have found myself expressing rooted convictions which until that moment I had no notion that I held. Yet they are genuinely rooted convictions — the response, not of my ratiocinative intellect, but of my whole heart, to certain theoretical or practical propositions.[10]

Nature, Man and God is Temple's fullest statement of his philosophy of religion or natural theology. It consists of an extended argument for theism beginning with the picture of the world offered by science and concluding with the demand for a special revelation of the transcendent and immanent God. He considered subtitling it "A Study in Dialectical Realism," and it represents his movement from the idealism of his early teachers toward the realism of Whitehead. It incorporates a complete value theory, and its underlying vision is that of the "Sacramental Universe." The chapter titled "Revelation and Its Mode" has been widely influential in modern theology.[11]

Temple's most effective apologetic presentation of the Christian faith was *Christian Faith and Life*, which was published from a shorthand report of his addresses at the Oxford University Mission in 1931. A trip to America in 1935 was the occasion for lectureships at Harvard and the College of Preachers, which resulted in the volumes *Christianity in Thought and Practice* and *The Centrality of Christ*.

In 1925 Temple had succeeded to the chairmanship of the Archbishops' Commission on Christian Doctrine. It had been appointed in 1922 because the tensions between different schools of thought in the Church of England were impairing its effectiveness. Its charge was to explore the extent of doctrinal agreement and disagreement within the

Church of England. Its final report, *Doctrine in the Church of England* (1938), is a monument to the gifts and wisdom of its chairman, and it served to promote that spirit of mutual understanding and cooperation which he so diligently sought. (A recent criticism of his role in the Report will be discussed below.)

In the Chairman's Introduction to this Report, Temple refers to a transition in the minds of the Commission which is reflected in the minds of theologians all over the world, a transition from a theology of the Incarnation toward a theology of redemption.

> A theology of the Incarnation tends to be a Christo-centric metaphysic. And in all ages there is need for the fresh elaboration of such a scheme of thought or map of life as seen in the light of the revelation in Christ. A theology of Redemption (though, of course, Redemption has its great place in the former) tends rather to sound the prophetic note; it is more ready to admit that much in this evil world is irrational and strictly unintelligible; and it looks to the coming Kingdom as a necessary preliminary to the full comprehension of much that now is.
>
> If the security of the nineteenth century, already shattered in Europe, finally crumbles away in our country, we shall be pressed more and more towards a theology of Redemption. In this we shall be coming closer to the New Testament. We have been learning how impotent man is to save himself, how deep and pervasive is that corruption which theologians call Original Sin. Man needs above all else to be saved from himself. This must be the work of Divine Grace.[12]

In an essay in *Theology* in 1939, in the shadow of war, Temple returned to this theme, but with greater emphasis. After quoting his call for a Christo-centric metaphysics in *Christus Veritas*, and also the above passage from the Doctrine Report, he remarks on the sad state of the world.

> The world of to-day is one of which no Christian map can be made. It must be changed by Christ into something very unlike itself before a Christian map of it is possible. . . . Our task with this world is not to explain it but to convert it. Its need can be met, not by the discovery of its own immanent principle in signal manifestation through Jesus Christ, but only by the shattering impact upon its self-sufficiency and

arrogance of the Son of God, crucified, risen and ascended, pouring forth that explosive and disruptive energy which is the Holy Ghost. . . . One day theology will take up again its larger and serener task and offer to a new Christendom its Christian map of life, its Christo-centric metaphysic. But that day can hardly dawn while any who are now already concerned with theology are still alive.[13]

Temple's labors and travels for the ecumenical movement were a prime concern during the York primacy. He had learned the ropes at the Faith and Order Conference at Edinburgh in 1910, in Lausanne in 1927 and at the International Missionary Conference in Jerusalem in 1928. In 1929 Temple succeeded Bishop Charles Brent as chairman of the Faith and Order Continuation Committee, which laid the groundwork for the founding of the World Council of Churches. In 1937 he chaired the second Faith and Order Conference in Edinburgh. In that same year two of the branches of the ecumenical movement — Faith and Order and Life and Work — were merged, and Temple became chairman of the provisional committee charged with writing a constitution for the World Council of Churches. In 1939 he opened discussions with Roman Catholic theologians. In 1942 he helped established the British Council of Churches and became its first chairman. The next year he sent Archbishop Garbett to reopen relations with the Russian Orthodox Church in Moscow. In all this work his passion for Christian unity and his gifts for reconciling differences came to full flower.

Temple had supported the novel and creative scheme of union of the Church of South India from its beginnings in 1919. It brought together Anglicans, Presbyterians, Methodists and Congregationalists for the first time in Christian history. In 1930 he chaired the Committee on the Unity of the Church of the Lambeth Conference and drafted its report, which gave measured support to the scheme. His vision and labors helped to make possible the consummation of the Scheme in 1947 after his death. His successor in York said of him: "Archbishop Temple probably did more than any one man had ever previously done for Christian unity."[14]

Temple's involvement in the social witness of the church came to a climax in the Malvern Conference of 1941. It had been planned by the Industrial Christian Fellowship, with the purpose of exploring social reconstruction and the ordering of a new society on Christian principles. As usual, Temple presided and drafted the final report which supported a moderate socialist approach to economic issues. The Conference produced a storm of controversy, and conservatives on both sides of the Atlantic denounced Temple as a confused and dangerous radical. The English genius was demonstrated the next year when the Conservative Prime Minister sent Temple's name to the King as the next Archbishop of Canterbury. George Bernard Shaw commented: "An Archbishop of Temple's enlightenment is a realized impossibility."

Temple was enthroned at Canterbury in January 1942 in the midst of war, and many of his activities as Primate were involved in the wartime struggles of his compatriots. He was already a national leader and the chief spokesman for the Christian conscience. He visited and preached to the armed services and in industrial plants. He supported a negotiated peace and opposed the policy of unconditional surrender. At the same time he managed to complete his last and perhaps best known book, *Christianity and Social Order*, which argued the church's right and duty to interfere in social issues and the principles upon which such intervention should be made. The gout which he had suffered since he was two years old increased in severity during the war years, but he did not let it interfere with his heavy schedule. His continuous labors for church and nation ceased only in September 1944, and he died the next month. The overarching theme of his life and work are summed up in some of his last written words:

> Our need is a new integration of life: Religion, Art, Science, Politics, Education, Industry, Commerce, Finance, — all these need to be brought into a unity as agents of a single purpose. That purpose can hardly be found in human aspiration; it must be the divine purpose. That divine purpose is presented to us in the Bible under the name of the Kingdom (Sovereignty) of God, or as the summing-up of all things in Christ, or as the coming-down out of heaven of the holy city, the New Jerusalem.[15]

The Incarnation

At the center of Temple's faith, theology and philosophy is the Incarnation of God in Christ. In 1913 he wrote: "The whole of my theology is an attempt to understand and verify the words: 'He that hath seen me hath seen the Father.' "[16] He addressed the doctrine of the Incarnation in one of his essays in *Foundations* (1912), in a chapter in *Mens Creatrix* (1917), in a long sermon titled "the Philosophy of the Incarnation" (1918), as well as in many of his shorter works. But his fullest statement is in two chapters of his most extended theological work, *Christus Veritas* (1924).[17]

In surveying the New Testament evidence for the divinity of Christ, Temple notes the "spiritual law" that religious experience always precedes theological interpretation. This is what makes Christian theology "a veritable science" (p. 108). Furthermore, this theological interpretation is usually expressed in the language of function.

> They become aware that Jesus Christ does what only God can do. The functions which he discharges are functions of God. Now functions, that is actions and reactions, are all we know. If Jesus Christ performs the acts of God, then Jesus Christ is God in the only sense in which any name can justifiably be attributed to any object. The method by which in the New Testament the supreme affirmation is reached is the only method by which any such affirmation could be scientifically justified (p. 113).

Temple concludes on the basis of the New Testament testimony that the life of Jesus Christ was a real human life subject to all the limitations and temptations that are the lot of humanity, with the exception of those deriving from past sin. Yet because of Jesus' perfect union and communion with God, it can be asserted that in him God has a real experience of human life, suffering and death.

Temple elaborates his view of the Incarnation on the basis of his view of the structure of reality. In his philosophical theology he presents a view of reality in grades: matter, life, mind and spirit. Every grade finds its fulfillment only when it is possessed by a higher grade, and each grade uses those which are lower for its expression. Temple's basic thesis is that, since Jesus Christ is fully human and also fully possessed by God, in him we have the one adequate presentation of both God and humanity. The attempts of the early church to interpret this were hampered by the inadequate notions of Godhead and humanity which then existed. In terms of these notions it is clear that the claim that the same being should be both divine and human was a demonstrable impossibility. "Therefore, the theory or doctrine of the Person of Christ will not be found by merely stating His nature and works in terms of God and Man, but will involve restating God and Man in terms of the revelation given in him" (p. 127).

Temple surveys the attempts of the early church to formulate an intelligible Christology and comes to this conclusion about the formula of Chalcedon:

> The truth is that this great formula derives part of its value from the clearness with which it refuses to explain. It does in one sense represent "the bankruptcy of Greek patristic theology" [as he had stated in *Foundations*, p. 320]; it marks the definite failure of all attempts to explain the Incarnation in terms of Essence, Substance, Nature, and the like. It is content to reaffirm the fact. But that is all an authoritative formula ought to do. Interpretations will vary from age to age, according to the concepts supplied to the interpreters by current thought. It would be disastrous if there were an official Church explanation of the Incarnation (p. 134.).

Temple's own interpretation of the Incarnation is based on his view of the grades of reality. When life supervenes upon matter, it takes direction of it, and when mind supervenes upon life it takes direction of it. "We shall expect, therefore, to find that when God supervenes upon humanity, we do not find a human being taken into fellowship with God, but God acting through the conditions supplied by humanity" (p. 138).

The testimony of Christian experience that fellowship with Christ is in itself fellowship with God coincides with what we are led to expect by "the analogy of the whole creation" (p. 138).

> Now this is exactly the culmination of that stratification which is the structure of Reality; far therefore from being in-

credible, it is to be expected, it is antecedently probable. Even had there been no evil in the world to be overcome, no sin to be abolished and forgiven, still the Incarnation would be the natural inauguration of the final stage of evolution. In this sense the Incarnation is perfectly intelligible; that is to say, we can see that its occurrence is all of a piece with the Scheme of Reality as traced elsewhere (p. 139).

Since, however, we do not understand the levels of reality above our own, in another sense the Incarnation is beyond our understanding, and we cannot find solutions to problems arising from belief in it.

First, there is the Nestorian difficulty: Can we call a child God? What is necessary is that "human experience as conditioned by the sin of men should become the personal experience of God the Son" (p. 140). This does not require that God is active only in Jesus, but only that God the Son, without ceasing his creative and sustaining work, added to this the human experience of Jesus. This poses a difficulty with regard to the mode of consciousness of God the Son, but we can have no knowledge whatever about that.

Temple believes that his solution to the Nestorian difficulty alleviates the problem which theologians have sought to solve by the Kenotic theory, which asserts that God the Son emptied himself of his divine attributes in assuming human nature in the Incarnation. He argues that the problems with the latter are intolerable. It is mythological in character and raises the difficulty that the creative Word has no being except in the infant Jesus. The Kenotic theory makes the Incarnation essentially episodic. In Temple's interpretation the Incarnation is revealingly episodic but essentially eternal.

> Certain attributes or functions incompatible with humanity are, in this activity of the Eternal Son, not exercised; but what we see is not any mere parable of the Life of God, not an interval of humiliation between two eternities of glory. It is the divine glory itself. . . . The limitations are the means whereby the Eternal Son, remaining always in the bosom of the Father, lays bare to us the very heart of Godhead (p. 144).

Temple next takes up the relation of the human experience of Jesus to God the Son. There is real growth and real temptation, but there is no danger of defeat in the face of temptation, and obedience is deepened. "This human life is the very life of God. It is both human and divine in every detail. If we know what we are about we may rightly say that the unity of God and Man in Christ is a unity of Will, for Will is the whole being of a person organized for action" (p. 149). (Temple states in passing that perfect humanity is in no sense identical with divinity. "But if the question means, 'Is Perfect Man *eo ipso* God?' the answer is, 'No. Nothing that happens to a creature could possibly turn him into his own Creator. At that point the gulf between God and Man is plainly impassable" [p. 147n].)

Temple holds that the view of Paul of Samosata that the union of divine and human in Christ in terms of will had been condemned because it made a sharp distinction between will and nature. This made will indeterminate and nature unspiritual, which led to the failure of the orthodox Christology. The identity of will and nature in regard to personhood in modern thought makes it possible to speak of the unity of God and humanity in Christ as a unity of will. But in our imperfect humanity, will is still departmental; it does not cover the whole of our personal being. Therefore it is better to say that in Christ God and humanity are personally one. "The Person of the man Christ Jesus is God the Son" (p. 149).

Does this mean that Jesus' humanity is impersonal, or does it find its personhood in God the Son? Here Temple notes the important point made in the orthodox doctrine of the two wills.

> Therefore the Will in Him, while always one with, because expressive of, the Will of God, is not merely identical with it. ... Consequently, though there is only one Person, one living and energising Being, I should not hesitate to speak of the human personality of Christ. But that personality does not exist side by side with the divine personality; it is subsumed in it. Will and personality are ideally interchangeable terms; there are two wills in the Incarnate in the sense that His human nature comes through struggle and effort to an ever deeper union with the Divine in completeness of self-sacrifice. And it is only because there is this real human will or personality that there is here any revelation to humanity

of the divine Will. Thus I do not speak of His humanity as impersonal (p. 150).

Temple takes note of the fact that the doctrine of the impersonal humanity of Christ is used to support the idea that, when Christ assumed human nature, he assumed the nature of all of us and united us all to God. This involves the difficulty of implying that all people are united to God whether believers or not. So Temple offers his own reinterpretation of this doctrine. He affirms the theory of real universals on which the doctrine is based, but he states that they are concrete rather than abstract. "There is no such thing as human nature apart from all individual human beings. But there is a perfectly real thing called Mankind or Humanity which is a unit and not a mere agglomeration" (p. 151). Each person is a focusing point for reality and is largely made what he is by the character of his fellows.

> Therefore Mankind or Humanity is a close-knit system of mutually influencing units. In this sense the humanity of every one of us is "impersonal"; and the greater the man, the less merely "personal" is his humanity. He is more, not less, individual than others; but he is individual by the uniqueness of his focus for the universe, not by his exclusion of all that is not himself. He more than others is Humanity focussed in one centre. Into this system of mutually influencing units Christ has come. . . . He inaugurates a new system of influence. . . . So He is a second Adam. . . . Thus in a most real sense Christ is not only a man; He is Man. . . . All the significance and destiny of the human race is summed up in Him. He is the Head of the Body (pp. 151–53).

The Church

The church is second only to the Incarnation in Temple's theology. His treatment of the doctrine of the church followed from and paralleled his explication of the doctrine of the Incarnation in *Foundations, Mens Creatrix* and *Christus Veritas*. "The Church, then, is the direct outcome of the divine act of the Incarnation and the continuance of its principle" (p. 166).

The fundamental result of the Incarnation in human history was a group of men and women who were imbued with a new spiritual power.

This society is a veritable Fellowship of the Holy Spirit. It is definable in terms of the Spirit; and the Spirit is definable in terms of it. To be a Christian is to confess Jesus as Lord, to have the Spirit, to be a member of the Church; it is all of these or any of them, for no distinction has arisen between them in experience, and none or scarcely any had yet been drawn in thought. Here, in the company of the personal disciples of Jesus, is found an activity of the Divine Spirit so plainly identical with the activity of the same Spirit in Jesus of Nazareth, that St. Paul . . . finds it natural to speak of it as His body and of its constituent individuals as His limbs or members (p. 155).

Temple argues that the fundamental task of humanity is inner and outer unity: "The inner unity of complete personality and the outer unity of a perfected fellowship as wide as humanity. . . . Towards this human nature is impelled by the Creator's act at the Incarnation, and the consequent activity of His Spirit at work upon humanity from within. Thus the Church's task is defined for it. It is the herald and foretaste of the Kingdom of God. For that it exists, and for service to that end it must be organised and equipped" (p. 158).

Because of the danger of secularization, the church developed four means of keeping alive the knowledge of the end which the church exists to serve: the canon of Scripture, the creeds, the sacraments and the ministry. These means help to secure the principles of transcendence and catholicity. Nothing human can become a power capable of uniting all peoples and nations in fellowship. Only a transcendent power can do that. "It is the fact that in Christ God Himself intervened in human history, and that in the Church the Spirit of God and Christ is actively imparting the life of God to man, which gives any hope that mankind may be actually drawn together, whether on this planet or elsewhere, in realised and universal fellowship" (p. 164).

The secularization of the church after Constantine led to the weakening of its spiritual power, but this was accompanied by the permeation of society outside the church by the Holy Spirit.

Today the Holy Spirit speaks through many who stand aloof from the Church as truly as in the Church itself. But it remains true that the Church is His normal channel, and by the reading of the Scriptures, by the recital of the Creeds, by the maintenance of an historic ministry as a living symbol of God's transcendence and man's fellowship, by the witness of the same truths in the sacraments, the Church supplies the chief instruments of the Spirit's agelong activity (p. 166).

The ideal church does not exist now nor did it in the past, but it will exist in the future.

The church only exists perfectly when all its members are utterly surrendered to Christ and united to Him. . . . The true Church is still coming slowly into historic existence; that process is the meaning of History from the Incarnation onwards; it consists both in the drawing of men and nations into the fellowship of the Holy Spirit, and in the completion of His work upon them in perfecting their surrender to Christ and their union with Him (pp. 167-68).

The outbreak of World War II led Temple to place greater emphasis on the distinctiveness of the church in contrast to the world. In an article in *Theology* in 1939 he stated that the Gospel was not so much the clue to a universal synthesis as the source of world transformation. He noted the emphasis in contemporary New Testament scholarship on the central place of the church in the apostolic experience and teaching. He concludes: "We did not fail a quarter of a century ago to insist on the necessity and claim of the Church. But this was secondary and derivative; now it is primary and basic."[18]

Social Witness

Temple's assertion that the task of the church is "to win this world for the Kingdom of God"[19] is an expression of the great social concern which dominated his life. He formulated this concern in many different ways: theologically and philosophically, in terms of love and justice, the sacraments, church and state, personality and community. But the basic thrust was always the same: to move the world toward the Kingdom of God.

Robert Craig suggests that the root of Temple's view of the relation of Christian faith and the social order lies in his sacramental understanding of the relation of spirit and matter.[20] We have noted that the underlying vision of Temple's world view is that of the "sacramental universe." In the light of this vision he makes his well known assertion that Christianity is "the most avowedly materialist of all the great world religions,"[21] a phrase which an American theologian has described as "one of the most original and daring and at the same time germinal statements in modern theological literature."[22]

On the basis of the Incarnation the working out of this sacramental principle means that the total being of humanity — material and individual, social and historical — falls within God's plan of redemption. "By the very nature of its central doctrine Christianity is committed to a belief in the ultimate significance of the historical process."[23] *"It is in the sacramental view of the universe, both of its material and of its spiritual elements, that there is given hope of making human both politics and economics and of making effectual both faith and love."*[24]

We have seen that Temple believed firmly in the right and responsibility of Christians and the church to act in the light of Christian principles in the life of the world, in the sphere of politics and economics, in order to move the world toward the Kingdom of God. It is fitting that in his last book, *Christianity and Social Order* (1942), Temple outlined his mature understanding of these principles. He offers four grounds for the right of the church to make its voice heard in matters of politics and economics: the claims of sympathy for those who suffer, the educational influence (for better or worse) of the social and economic system, the challenge to the existing system in the name of justice and the duty of conformity to the "natural order" which represents the purpose of God.[25]

But how should this responsibility for action in the social order be carried out? Here Temple deals sensitively and out of a great wealth of experience with the complex issue of the social action of the church. He points out that the main work of the church in this area is usually overlooked. "Nine-tenths of the work of the Church in the world is done by Christian people fulfilling responsibilities and performing tasks which in themselves are not part of the official system of the Church at all" (p. 17). Thus the most important work of the church in this area as in all others is to "make good Christian men and women" who will manifest the Spirit of Christ in their personal, family and social relations, in their work in the world and in their responsibility as citizens for the political processes which shape the national life. To these ends the church must supply its members with "a systematic statement of principles to aid them in doing these two things, and this will carry with it a denunciation of customs or institutions in contemporary life and practice which offend against those principles" (p. 21). However, the church acting corporately should not commit itself to any particular policy or interfere on any particular issue. "A policy always depends on technical decisions concerning the actual relations of cause and effect in the political and economic world; about these a Christian as such has no more reliable judgment than an atheist, except so far as he should be more immune to the temptations of self-interest" (p. 18).

In regard to the principles of Christian social action, Temple believes that the church needs to recover lost ground. In the past the church had developed a complete system of principles, but the rise of individualism since the Reformation caused the church to retreat from this area. Temple distinguishes primary and derivative Christian social principles. The primary ones are God and his living purpose as creator, judge and redeemer of humanity, and the dignity, tragedy and destiny of humanity as created in the image of God, fallen into sin and destined for God's Kingdom. The derivative social principles are richly elaborated under the headings of freedom, social fellowship and service. "Society must be so arranged as to give to every citizen the maximum opportunity for making deliberate choices and the best possible training for the use of that opportunity." This means "the widest possible extension of personal responsibility. . . . Freedom is the goal of politics. . . . For it is in and through his freedom that a man makes fully real his personality — the quality of one made in the image of God" (p. 45).

Freedom is actual only in society and social groupings, for "man is naturally and incurably social" (p. 47). This is realized mainly in the groupings intermediate between the individual and the state: family, school, college, trade union, guild, professional association, parish and city. Most modern political theory and especially revolutionary theory tends to ignore or aim at abolishing these intermediate groupings and thus to vacillate between individualism and collectivism. But Temple argues that the "real wealth of human life" consists in these intermediate communities, associations and fellowships. This had made British democracy more a "democracy of persons" and thus more stable and fulfilling than its continental counterparts.

The combination of freedom and fellowship as social principles issues in the obligation of service. Service includes unpaid voluntary activities in the community, but it also includes the obligation to see one's occupation as a divine vocation in obedience to God and in service of one's fellows. Vocation to service must apply to groups as well as to individuals. And the principle here is that we must use our wider loyalties to check the narrower.

According to Temple these principles of Christian social action are to be regulated by the principles of love and justice. Love is the predominant principle, and the primary form or expression of love in social organization is justice.

> These two great principles then — Love and Justice — must be rather regulative of our application of other principles than taken as immediate guides to social policy. But they must constantly be borne in mind as checks upon policy. As we must use our wider loyalties to check the narrower, so we must use these highest principles of all to check our application of the lower. Freedom must not be pursued in ways which offend against Love, nor must service be demanded, or fellowship in any actual instance promoted, in ways that offend against Justice (pp. 57-58).

Temple interprets justice in the traditional sense of what is due a person, and he appeals to the notion of natural law or natural order in the sense of the proper function of a human activity as apprehended by a consideration of its own nature. This is task for human reason, but since God is the creator, the natural order or law discovered is God's order or law.

In Temple's view, the advantage of the idea of natural law is that it holds together the two aspects of truth: the ideal and the practical. He offers the example of economic production.

> Production by its own natural law exists for consumption. If, then, a system comes into being in which production is regulated more by the profit obtainable for the producer than by the needs of the consumer, that system is defying the Natural Law or Natural Order. . . . There is nothing wrong about profits as such. . . . But it is possible none the less for these two to get into the wrong order, so that the consumer is treated, not as the person whose interest is the true end of the whole process, but only as an indispensable condition of success in an essentially profit-seeking enterprise (p. 58).

Furthermore, natural law teaches that economic life cannot be isolated from the rest of life. "According to Natural Law the economic process is not an end in itself; it and all its parts are primarily a means to something that is much more than economic — the life of man" (p. 59).

In the light of these principles Temple concludes this book with an assessment of British social and economic life and a statement of what should be the objectives of government policy in the areas of housing, education, employment security, voice in the conduct of business, leisure and civil liberties. "The aim of a Christian social order is the fullest possible development of individual personality in the widest and deepest possible fellowship" (p. 76). In an appendix he explains how he personally believes a beginning should be made on these objectives. Here he recommends "a Christian social programme" which includes the functional and regional devolution of the responsibilities of the House of Commons, the accompaniment of limited liability by a maximum rate of dividends, the principle of "withering capital" or the reduction of capital invested according to the amount of interest received, the making of credit into a public utility, the public ownership of urban land and the taxation of land rather than buildings.

Reunion

Temple knew that the greatest weakness of the church in its witness to the social order is in its disunity. He believed deeply in the motto of the 1937 Oxford Conference on Life and Work: "A divided Church cannot lead a divided world." So, along with the social mission of the church, the overriding concern of his life and work was the reunion of the church. No one felt the pain of Christian disunion more than Temple. The "calamities" which result from it are the hindrance of the fulfillment of the prayer of Christ that we may all be one, the paralysis of witness, the perpetual hampering of practical action and the injury to our apprehension of truth.[26] In his sermon at the opening service of the 1937 Edinburgh Conference on Faith and Order he described the answer of the world to the proclamation of the church that the divisions of the world may be healed through fellowship in Christ.

> Have you found that fellowship yourselves? Why do your voices sound so various? When we pass from words to actions, to what are you calling us? Is it to one family, gathered round one Holy Table, where your Lord is Himself the host who welcomes all His guests? You know that it is not so. When we answer your united call, we have to choose for ourselves to which Table we will go, for you are yourselves divided in your act of deepest fellowship, and by your own traditions hinder us from a unity which we are ready to enjoy.[27]

Temple responds to this answer as follows:

> Here is a matter for deep penitence. I speak as a member of one of those Churches which still maintain barriers against completeness of union at the Table of the Lord. I believe from my heart that we of that tradition are trustees for an element of truth concerning the nature of the Church which requires that exclusiveness as a consequence, until this element of truth be incorporated with others into a fuller and worthier conception of the Church than any of us hold today. But I know that our division at this point is the greatest of all scandals in the face of the world; I know that we can only consent to it or maintain it without the guilt of unfaithfulness to the unity of the Gospel and of God Himself, if it is a

source to us of spiritual pain, and if we are striving to the utmost to remove the occasions which now bind us, as we think, to that perpetuation of disunion.[28]

Temple's concern for Christian reunion was rooted in his doctrine of God and the church.

But the unity of the Church is precious not only for its utility in strengthening the Church as an evangelistic agent. It is itself in principle the consummation to which all history moves. The purpose of God in creation was, and is, to fashion a fellowship of free spirits knit together by a love in all its members which answers to the manifested love of God — or, as St. Paul expresses it, to "sum up all things in Christ" (*Ephesians* i,10). The agent of that purpose is the Church, which is therefore called the Body of Christ. . . . The unity of the Church is something much more than unity of ecclesiastical structure, though it cannot be complete without this. It is the love of God in Christ possessing the hearts of men so as to unite them in itself — as the Father and the Son are united in that love of Each for Each which is the Holy Spirit. . . . It is therefore something much more than a means to any end — even though that end be the evangelisation of the world; it is itself the one worthy end of all human aspiration; it is the life of Heaven.[29]

In his enthronement sermon at Canterbury, Temple described the ecumenical movement as "the great new fact of our era," and no one had contributed more to the emergence of this new fact than himself. He approached the question of Christian reunion with four fundamental convictions. First, the unity of the church is a fact and the basis for our seeking to exhibit it, and therefore it is not our task or accomplishment but the gift of God in Christ.

The unity of the Church of God is a perpetual fact; our task is not to create it but to exhibit it. Where Christ is in men's hearts, there is the Church; where His Spirit is active, there is His Body. The Church is not an association of men, each of whom has chosen Christ as his Lord; it is a fellowship of men, each of whom Christ has united with Himself. . . . We could not seek union if we did not already possess unity. Those who have nothing in common do not deplore their estrangement. It is because we are one in allegiance to one Lord that we seek and hope for the way of manifesting that unity in our witness to Him before the world. . . . It is not by contrivance and adjustment that we can unite the Church of God. It is only by coming close to Him that we can come nearer to one another. And we cannot by ourselves come closer to Him. If we have any fellowship with Him, it is not by our aspiration but by his self-giving; if our fellowship with Him, and in Him with one another, is to be deepened, it will not be by our effort but by his constraining power.[30]

Second, the divisions among Christians are divisions within the church and do not cause separation from it. All Christian churches are in schism from one another, and all share responsibility for this.[31] The burden of guilt lies both on those churches which have maintained the historic order and failed to commend it as well as on those who have separated themselves for conscience' sake.[32]

Third, faith and order are not equally essential in Christian reunion.

In regard to the matter of Reunion I find myself quite unable to agree with the proposition that has been advanced that as foundations of the Church, faith and order stand on a level. Faith seems to be perfectly indispensable and about that there must be agreement on the vital points, before union and communion are possible. But that we should agree about any necessary order in the Church for maintaining that seems to me, at any rate, less important and, I am inclined to think, not essential at all. That we must agree what order is in fact to be adopted is plain, for Reunion means the adoption of a common order. But we know quite well that it makes all the difference in the world in our approach to our Free Church brethren whether we say that the Church order which we recommend — and which many of them after all are ready to adopt — is the best for achieving the purpose which the Church has in view and therefore is to be adopted; or that it is the only one which constitutes the Church as a Church at all and that, therefore, as long as they do not adopt it they forfeit all right to that name.[33]

Fourth, Temple believed that those who participate in ecumenical gatherings should be more concerned to appropriate what is true and valuable in other traditions than to explain to others what they are lacking.

In our dealings with one another let us be more eager to understand those who differ from us that either to refute them or to press upon them our own tradition. . . . Wherever there are divisions which persist, there is sure to be something of value on both sides. We ought always to be eager to learn the truth which others possess in fuller degree than ourselves, and to learn why some give to various elements in our common belief a greater emphasis than we are accustomed to give. . . . And yet with both of these there must be full loyalty to the truth as we have been enabled to apprehend it. . . . The united Church must bring together all the elements of truth in all the several traditions, each unblunted as regards its definition and consequently as regards its cutting edge. But with that let us recognise that the drawing together of the elements of truth in the sundered traditions must also certainly involve modification in the expression of the truth that has been traditional and familiar. In a certain sense what is required is that every existing Christian communion should die in order to rise again into something more splendid that itself.[34]

The Ministry

Temple believed that the problem and task of Christian reunion centered on the ministry. He was convinced that the churches discussing reunion were fundamentally agreed on the other three points of the Chicago-Lambeth Quadrilateral: scripture, creed and sacraments. In his presidential address to the Synod of Canterbury in 1943 he made "a personal confession of faith" concerning the ministry.

When we go back to the first records of the Church we find neither a Ministry which called people into association with it, nor an undifferentiated fellowship which delegated powers to a Ministry; but we find a complete Church, with the Apostolate accepted as its focus of administration and authority. When the Lord's earthly ministry was ended, there was found in the world as its fruit and as means of its continuance this Body, in which the distinction of Ministry and Laity is already established. The Apostles were in no sense ministers of the laity; they were ministers of Christ to the laity, and to the world waiting to be won. They took steps for the perpetuation of the Ministry, and it has descended to ourselves. So when I consecrate a godly and well-learned man to the office and work of a Bishop in the Church of God, I do not act as a representative of the Church, if by that is meant the whole number of contemporary Christians, but I do act as the ministerial instrument of Christ in His Body the Church. The authority by which I act is His, transmitted to me through His Apostles and those to whom they committed it; I hold it neither from the Church nor apart from the Church, but from Christ in the Church.[35]

On the basis of this high doctrine of the ministry and the episcopate, Temple came to certain conclusions on this central question in Christian reunion. In a lengthy essay in 1931 he addressed himself to the question of why the Church of England insists on the historic episcopate as a condition of full intercommunion. First of all there must be some perspective on this issue.

> I am convinced that the Anglican Communion is right to maintain its insistence on the Historic Episcopate, but I am equally convinced that Anglicans think far too much — not necessarily too highly, but assuredly too often and too long — of that same Episcopate. It would be far better for us if we could take it for granted and give our undistracted thought to other matters.[36]

The importance of the historic episcopate rests on the fact that the Church is a sacramental organism. The supreme sacrament is the Incarnation, and Christ now acts in the world through his body the church. Because the response of the members of the Church of Christ has always been imperfect and corrupt, it is most important for the church to maintain those elements which express its basis and purpose. "The possibility of corruption in the earthly Church is one ground for insisting on those elements — the distinctively Catholic elements — which witness to the transcendence of Him whose Body it is" (p. 108).

Sometimes it is asserted that only episcopal ordination confers the power to make sacraments, and without it there are no real sacraments. Temple holds this view to be magical, untenable and unintelligible. In this connection he affirms the possibility of lay celebration of the sacraments.

> What is conferred in Ordination is not the *power* to make sacramental a rite which otherwise would not be such, but *authority (potestas)* to administer Sacraments which belong to the Church, and which, therefore, can only be rightly administered by those who hold the Church's commission to do

so. The objection to lay celebration is not that it is in its own nature inoperative, but that it is a usurpation by one member of what belongs to the whole Church. Strictly speaking, I submit, we should not say that a layman cannot celebrate, but that he has no right to celebrate, and it would therefore be wrong for him to do so (pp. 110–11).

Temple acknowledges the reality of the sacraments in at least some non-episcopal communions, but the ministries in these communions may be in varying degrees irregular or defective. "Though real ministries within the Universal Church, they may still not be ministries *of* the Universal Church with a commission from the whole fellowship to all its members" (p. 114). This is assured only through episcopal ordination.

It is sometimes argued that the strong feeling of fellowship with members of other churches and the desire to express this in the meal of fellowship should be honored by intercommunion between episcopal and non-episcopal churches. But Temple's response is that "a large part of the value of sacramental worship is its independence of 'feeling,' or present consciousness of gifts received" (p. 120). Also the eucharist is not primarily a fellowship meal but rather "our incorporation into the One Body in which Christ made His eternal self-oblation to the Father. The bonds across time and space are here definitely more important than the realised fellowship of the present congregation" (pp. 124–25). Thus he affirms his agreement with the Report on the Unity of the Church (which he wrote) of the 1930 Lambeth Conference: "The general rule of our Church must therefore be held to exclude indiscriminate Intercommunion, or any such Intercommunion as expresses acquiescence in the continuance of separately organised Churches" (pp. 126–27).

Temple concludes: "If it be said that this is all very complicated and the ways of Christ are simple, I answer that His way indeed is simple, but these complications are not of His making; they are part of the entanglement of sin — that sin of disunion of which the guilt rests on us all, not less on those who have maintained the historic order and failed to commend it than on those who for conscience' sake broke away from it" (p. 129).

Anglicanism

There was not doubt as to Temple's "full loyalty to the truth as we have been enabled to apprehend it" in the Church of England nor to his conviction about the mediating function of Anglicanism on the ecumenical scene. In conclusion, let us turn to Temple's understanding of Anglicanism. He spelled this out in three essays in the later twenties.[37] He speaks primarily of the Church of England but indicates that his words apply to Anglicanism as a whole.

In Temple's view the distinctive characteristic, vocation and responsibility of the Church of England (and Anglicanism) is that it holds together and comprehends in one communion the catholic, evangelical or protestant and liberal traditions in Christianity. It combines in one fellowship the faith, order and worship of the ancient and continuous traditions of the church with the characteristics of the new birth of the sixteenth century and the freedom of intellectual inquiry.

Temple's interpretation of these three elements is not unique. The Church of England has retained the creeds and traditional ministry of the Catholic Church and made its Prayer Book out of the old liturgies. It is also heir to the great spiritual movement of the Reformation. Temple sees the Reformation as a movement toward spiritual purity whose form was determined by the appeal to Scripture as the test, by what he calls "nationalism in religion" and by the assertion of the duty of private judgment. He stresses the fact that the Church of England affirms the supremacy of Scripture. Nothing is to be taught as necessary for salvation but what is grounded in Scripture.

The phrase "nationalism in religion" falls strangely on American ears. By it Temple means the rejection of any foreign dictation in religious matters. He saw this as a manifestation of religious freedom on the national level; national tradition and individual religious freedom reinforce each other.

Temple's view of nationalism in religion is closely associated with his views on establishment, which is equally strange to the American situation. Although he opposed any merger of church and state, he also opposed any divorce or complete separation of them. This was based on his view that both church and state are divine orders concerned with the well-being of the people. They should cooperate: The state should give the church freedom in the preaching of the Gospel, and the church should admonish the state. Therefore, he favored the establishment of the Church of England so long as its freedom was preserved. But his labors for the Church Assembly and his dismay over the denial by Parliament of the Prayer Book revision led him to see that disestablishment might be necessary for the freedom of the church.

Temple sometimes explains the Reformation idea of the duty of private judgment in terms of the immediacy of access to God which is offered to all in Christ, but more often in terms of spiritual liberty of the individual. He saw liberty as the only indispensable condition for a truly spiritual response. Everyone is called upon to exercise conscience and to appropriate the truth of revelation. To this private judgment the Church of England offers the whole treasury of the catholic tradition, and it calls upon each member to determine how he will use this tradition.

Temple is not very clear on the meaning of the liberal tradition and its relation to that of the Reformation concept of the spiritual liberty of the individual. He mentions it only in the last of the three essays where he quotes from the Report on the Unity of the Church which he drafted at the Lambeth Conference of 1930. The report states:

> Our special character and, as we believe, our peculiar contribution to the Universal Church, arises from the fact that, owing to historic circumstances, we have been enabled to combine in our one fellowship the traditional Faith and Order of the Catholic Church with that immediacy of approach to God through Christ to which the Evangelical Churches especially bear witness, and freedom of intellectual inquiry, whereby the correlation of the Christian revelation and advancing knowledge is constantly effected.[38]

Temple refers to this latter point specifically as the liberal element in Anglicanism. But he interprets it in terms of freedom in two senses: the freedom of the federation of the churches in the Anglican Communion and the freedom of the individual inquiry and individual response to the leading of the Spirit.

This is elaborated in a somewhat different form in the Introduction to the Report of the Commission on Christian Doctrine. This statement refers to "those whose attitude to the distinctively Christian tradition is most deeply affected by the tradition of a free and liberal culture which is historically the bequest of the Greek spirit and was recovered for Western Europe at the Renaissance."[39]

In an important recent study, S. W. Sykes erroneously attributes this statement directly to Temple and criticizes it for its confusion about liberalism.[40] (Sykes has apparently confused the Chairman's Introduction, which was signed by Temple, with the general Introduction to the Report, which Temple may well have written but for which he had no more responsibility than the rest of the Commission. Sykes also misquotes the statement by omitting a key line.) Sykes interprets Temple to be implying that any kind of liberal theology can be comprehended within Anglicanism. It is clear, however, from the little that Temple does say about liberalism that he is referring to an attitude and a way of approaching theology rather than to a particular theological position. This seems to be the view that Sykes himself is advocating.

The attempt of the Church of England and of Anglicanism generally to hold together and combine these three diverse traditions is beset with difficulties, but Temple notes that they are the difficulties of the ideal itself. It is relatively easy to develop one virtue to the exclusion of others, but the Christian life requires the development of a number of virtues in balance. Likewise, it is relatively easy to affirm one aspect of religious truth, but much more difficult to hold together the many aspects of truth. Just this, however, is the special mission and responsibility of Anglicanism. This leads inevitably and properly to the development of schools or parties in the church which see the importance of certain aspects of these traditions and affirm them. What is to be avoided is the spirit of partisanship in which different groups see others as opponents rather than as colleagues in a common enterprise.

Thus, according to Temple, the particular vocation of Anglicanism requires that it be slow to answer such questions as to whether it holds this view or that and whether it regards its institutions as necessary in the church or only as spiritually valuable or convenient. This means that Anglicanism loses some sharpness of definition and allows a variety of interpretation of its common faith and order. Temple wrote to Ronald Knox in 1913: "I don't believe in the ideal of a Church with sharply defined boundaries; its unity . . . is like that of a ray of light — bright in the centre (?Rome) but ending none knows exactly where."[41] This, of course, creates an impression of vagueness and indecisiveness in thought and practice which has often been noted by critics who have argued that Anglicans thus prefer peace to truth. To this Temple responded: "We have learnt from a full experience that nearly always peace is the best way to truth."[42] Because Anglicans are called to put the peace of the church before their personal convictions, the latter are modified by the influence of others. Each side of a controversy learns to value what is true in the contentions of others. This rather than partisanship is the way to the fullness of truth. The vocation of Anglicanism is to hold together different sides of a truth which is so rich that no individual or group can appropriate it fully.

How does William Temple stand in relation to his own view of Anglicanism? From what has been explored in this chapter there can be little doubt that Temple strongly affirmed the catholic tradition of faith, order and worship. This we have seen especially in his teaching on the Incarnation, the church and the ministry. It is also clear that in the tradition of the Reformation he asserted repeatedly the spiritual liberty of the individual and felt perfectly free to criticize the catholic tradition in the light of the teaching of the Bible. This we have seen, for example, in his assessment of the christological teaching of the early church councils. One of his greatest gifts and concerns as an heir of the Reformation was his ability to place the church and the world under the judgment of God and the Gospel of Christ so that their idolatries and injustices could be brought to light.

Temple sees spiritual freedom as a fundamental element of both the protestant and liberal traditions, and his passionate concern for it pervades all his writings and actions. He sought it constantly for himself and for others. There is also little doubt that, as one standing firmly in the liberal tradition, Temple was quite open to the new truth and insights of the modern world and to the critical and constructive use of reason in Christian faith and life. This can be seen clearly in his commitment to philosophic truth. His only academic post was in philosophy. His three major works were in large measure philosophical in approach. His openness to the insights of modern science can be seen in the fact that the beginning point of the argument in the Gifford Lectures is the view of the world offered by modern science. Moreover, he argued in these lectures that the only way we can understand anything today is through its history, and he described the use of the historical method as "the main distinguishing characteristic of our own modern thought."[43]

Yet if there is one area of modernity in which Temple did not participate fully, it was in the historical critical study of the Bible. It was not that he was opposed to or suspicious of biblical criticism. It was that he was simply not much interested in it, and when he turned to it, his conclusions were quite conservative. For example, he affirmed the historical reliability of the Fourth Gospel and held a traditional view of its authorship.[44]

William Temple's importance for modern Anglicanism lies in his being a living exemplar of the best in the spirit of Anglicanism and in his strong emphasis on the ecumenical vocation of Anglicanism and on the fundamental importance of Christian social witness and action. In a time of considerable confusion about the nature and vocation of Anglicanism the witness of Temple's life, work and thought can be an important inspiration and guide.

It has been asserted that we are in a post-ecumenical era. Many Christians have become bored with the problems of reunion. If they are doing anything about it at all, they are assuming the unity of the church and are worshiping, studying and acting together with little concern about the divisions of the church. It also means that the most significant divisions in the church today are not those between the traditional communions but between Christians who are colored and white, rich and poor, liberal and conservative, Third World and Western. If this means that the task of the church is to heal the old divisions while not allowing the new tensions to divide the church further, then the testimony of Temple's life is sorely needed.

Since World War II, with some important exceptions, there has been a tendency in American life and in the churches to retreat from the vast and complex issues of the modern world into the private concerns of family, career and recreation. This has been accompanied by a notable increase in religious individualism and a resulting decrease of concern for the social order. Again the witness of Temple to the centrality of Christian social witness and action can be a needed inspiration.

All these themes of Anglicanism which were exemplified in the life, work and thought of William Temple are summed up in his enthronement sermon in Canterbury Cathedral in 1942.

> So let us set ourselves to gain a deepening loyalty to our Anglican tradition or Catholic order, Evangelical immediacy in our approach to God, and liberal acceptance of new truth made known to us; and let us at the same time join with all our fellow Christians who will join with us in bearing witness to the claim of Christ to rule in every department of human life, and to the principles of His Kingdom.[45]

CHAPTER IV

Anglicanism
and Its Spirit

–IV–

Anglicanism and Its Spirit

Hooker, Maurice and Temple illustrate ways of meeting institutional challenges and responding to the Gospel in three very different historical periods. Each has contributed significantly to the long historical development of an Anglican sense of identity and spirit. One would hesitate, however, to assign to this impressive Anglican triumverate anything more than the word *classic,* for they must stand or fall on their merits, certainly not as authorities for the communion. They are, however, major tributaries of the stream we call contemporary Anglicanism. Unlike some other Christian churches, the Anglican Communion sets aside no special authoritative place for a great reforming figure such as Luther or Calvin for the Lutheran and the Reformed Churches or Thomas Aquinas, somewhat less dominant in Roman Catholicism since the Second Vatican Council. To attempt to give to Thomas Cranmer, the leading Anglican reformer and architect of its two early Prayer Books, the exalted place of a Luther or even of an Aquinas would provoke laughter and impatience. It may be questioned whether Anglicans really appreciate the positive qualities and martyr's death of their chief reformer. He deserves more than he has received from the Communion he so helped to shape. Chillingworth's statement that we call no man master partly explains this pervasive characteristic of Anglicanism. The Communion has unfortunately produced no systematic theologians of the first rank comparable with Aquinas, Calvin or Barth, although it has produced major constructive

137

theologians in the persons of Hooker, Butler, Maurice and Temple. The theological system has always seemed somewhat foreign or "Continental" to it. At times this tendency has encouraged laziness of thought and amateur theological analysis, but at its best it has been grounded in a perception of the historical nature of the Gospel and of the inevitability of the institutional element in the Christian religion. Another way this Anglican tendency expresses itself is through the group method of doing theology. Anglicans of the same theological orientation like to cooperate in articulating a common platform in a joint book. Among the many symposia that have been produced are *Essays and Reviews, Lux Mundi, Foundations, Essays Catholic and Critical, Anglican Evangelicalism, The Apostolic Ministry, The Historic Episcopate in the Fullness of the Church, Soundings* and *Essays in Anglican Self-Criticism.* [1] The multiple authorship of this book obviously continues the trend.

The group approach may also be related to Maurice's insight that, while in most churches "schools" of theology tended to be formed around some dominant theologian, in Anglicanism this feature was replaced by the forming of "parties" in the political sense of like-minded people with a special platform and program to communicate. This Anglican characteristic can be traced back further to its roots in the historical situation of the English Reformation which was a movement over a long period of time. It was dominated therefore by no single individual, but became a corporate enterprise undertaken by king and parliament and sometimes, when they were allowed, by the convocations of the Church of England. The often asked question whether the reformation in the Church of England was political or theological is wrongly phrased. It was both, but intensely political because of the institutions involved. Those very institutions, however, were responding to new theological pressures and liturgical developments. There is no understanding of the nature of contemporary Anglicanism without a feeling for the historical process that was originated under Henry VIII, intensified under Edward VI and given classic shape under Elizabeth I. The so-called "Elizabethan settlement," however, is a misnomer because the process of adjustment continued through the Caroline and Cromwellian periods to the restoration of Charles II and culminated with the Prayer Book of 1662. The "comprehensiveness" of contemporary Anglicanism, about which much more will be said later, is partly derived from the earlier political-religious struggle of the Church of England to remain the national church of the English people in spite of separations from it on the right in Roman Catholicism and on the left in the free churches.

It is not the task of this chapter to discuss in depth the history of reformation in the Church of England. Enough must be said, however, to establish the fundamental reality of historical events and institutional forms for all subsequent Anglican theological analysis. It is nearer to the truth, although an oversimlification, to say that Anglicanism has been more productive of Anglican theology than that Anglican theology has produced Anglicanism. However complicated the details of reform within the Church of England, there emerged at least three centers of commitment (catholic, protestant and liberal), usually overlapping in practice but capable of separate identification and definition. In any historical movement that aims to preserve continuity with the past but at the same time to be responsive to change, there are bound to be the conservatives who hold out for continuity with what has been and the progressives who are prepared for basic, even revolutionary, change.

The Catholic Group

The conservative wing of the English reformation emphasized the catholic tradition and respect for ecclesiastical authority, having seen papal authority replaced by that of the bishops under the English monarch as supreme head or governor. This catholic group would always continue within Anglicanism sometimes identified with "high church," with "non-jurors," with "Tractarian" or with "Anglo-Catholics." The place of the English monarch as authority within Anglicanism would tend to be diluted by the political transition from the absolute theory of kingship in the Tudor and Stuart dynasties to the later symbol of a constitutional figure.

Parliament would become increasingly the real ruler. Within the Church of England bishops have been appointed by the crown through the prime minister, an anomaly that has often produced abler episcopal leadership than that elected by the other Anglican jurisdictions that are free of any establishment. The historic practice within the Church of England has been modified recently to allow dioceses more control in elections. Early in the English reformation the appeal to authority was seen to go far beyond any contemporary group of Anglican bishops under an English monarch back to the consensus of the supposedly "undivided church," before what we today call Eastern Orthodoxy and Western Catholicism became separated from each other. Actually this perception of the unity of the first five centuries was romantic because it ignored or was unaware of the early divisions within Christianity; its result was to "de-institutionalize" somewhat and to render more amorphous and multifaceted, but not less real, the Anglican feeling for authority. Lancelot Andrewes codified a typical Anglican commonplace on authority: one canon, two testaments, three creeds, four general councils, five primitive centuries of patristic agreement. Keble's Assize Sermon of 1833 was a protest against Parliament's abolition of some Irish bishoprics. The early Tractarians were urged not to place their emphasis upon the state as authority, but upon the apostolic succession of Anglican bishops from the apostles under Christ. This increased emphasis upon episcopal authority, supervening upon the previous struggle of Anglicanism to maintain its episcopal succession under Elizabeth's Archbishop Parker, then intensified by a civil war during which the commonwealth fought partly against the very institution of episcopacy, and finally traumatized by Pope Leo's Bull of 1896 declaring Anglican orders "absolutely null and void," has become a characteristic in the modern period of Anglicanism as a whole and especially of the catholic party. Anglicans agree about the retention of the episcopate and its necessity for union, but differ strongly among themselves about the theological significance of episcopacy. Unfortunately, in union negotiations Anglicans have tended to ask of the others a higher theology of episcopacy than they required of themselves.

A representative statement of the catholic party in recent times was the 1947 publication, by a group of Anglo-Catholics, at the instigation of Archbishop Fisher, of *Catholicity, a Study of the Conflict of Christian Traditions in the West.* The Archbishop also commissioned a reply and critique from the evangelical wing of the Church of England entitled *The Fulness of Christ.* [2] The revival of monasticism throughout Anglicanism in the nineteenth century marked another strong advance of Anglo-Catholicism. Participation in a ministry in slum parishes in England and concern over social justice characterized another branch of this catholic group down to the present century. One has to be very careful in delineating a supposedly "pure" form of any of these groups because each has modified its view by accepting some of the perspectives of the others. For example, *tradition* is the key word in describing the contemporary catholic group, but there are also very evangelical ways of presenting tradition as when Roman Catholic George Tavard calls tradition simply the act of passing on the Gospel. Also, the perspectives of the liberal group, with its respect for the critical use of reason and the right of the individual to search without restraint for the truth as he or she sees it, are reflected in a quotation from Temple. It begins as a seemingly flat-footed endorsement of tradition, but ends on quite a different note: "There is always an initial presumption in favor of the tradition for it represents the deposit of innumerable individual apprehensions. None the less it must be remembered that it is by fresh individual apprehensions that the tradition has been developed, and to reject the new intimation may be, not the suppression of human aberration, but a quenching of the divine spirit."[3] A chapter on Bishop Charles Gore, who greatly influenced Temple, would be useful here to express the spirit of the catholic wing of Anglicanism.

The Protestant Group

The progressive group in the Church of England during the Reformation was responding to the imact of the continental reformers, Luther and Calvin. It produced through Cranmer and Parker a confession in the Thirty-nine Articles that would become officially authoritative for the Church of England, but would never play the role within Anglicanism-at-large that the classic Reformation confessions would for Lutheranism and Calvinism and that the Decrees of Trent would for Roman Catholicism. Maurice held that the Articles were not a system of divinity, but rather the catholic foundation (first eight Articles) and then the principles of the Reformation (Articles 9–19), "not as necessary qualifications, but as indispensable conditions of the great Catholic truths."[4] The protestant emphasis would also continue within Anglicanism sometimes identified as "low church," sometimes as "literalist" or "evangelical." In the United States the word *protestant* would become part of the official title of the Protestant Episcopal Church in the United States of America. For this evangelical wing of Anglicanism, the primary authority remains the Scriptures or more concretely the Gospel as definitive for the church. The Articles of Religion assigned a normative role to Scripture. It contained "all things necessary to salvation." Nothing outside of Scripture or that could not be proved by it was to be required as an article of saving belief. The creeds should be believed because they could be proved by Scripture. General Councils were not infallible, but required also the acid test of Scripture. In ordination the solemn handing over of the Bible to ordinands emphasized the primary duty to preach the Word of God and deliberately eclipsed the medieval handing over of the sacramental vessels. Lengthy Bible reading formed the skeleton of the services of morning and evening prayer. Scriptural quotation and paraphrase were woven into the Book of Common Prayer. "Justification by faith through grace," as the watchword of Luther was expressed in reformation Anglicanism, has remained as a positive expression of response to the Gospel and as a prophetic criticism whenever it was felt that too much emphasis was being placed by catholics on the sacramental system or upon ecclesiastical authority. One of the tragedies of the Church of England was its inability, because of its spiritual aridity, to contain within itself the evangelical thrust of the Methodist movement initiated by John Wesley and later alienated from Anglicanism against the intentions and desires of its founder. Mention has already been made of the evangelical response in the Church of England to the Anglo-Catholic statement in *Catholicity*. As a counter to tradition, the evangelicals appropriately chose as their title *The Fulness of Christ*. There has been in the Church of England and throughout many of the branches of the Anglican Communion since World War II a revival of biblical evangelicalism strongly Christocentric in orientation. In England in 1977 a very large conference of conservative evangelicals at Nottingham symbolized a vital and growing wing of Anglicans who see themselves in the tradition of Ryle, Moule, Simeon and the sixteenth-century reformers. A chapter on Charles Simeon at this point would express the spirit of this party which today claims some five of the seminaries of the Church of England and some forty-five percent of the ordinands in training.

The Liberal Appeal to Reason

A number of interpreters have limited their analysis to the catholic and protestant wings of Anglicanism, for these two have obviously produced the basic two-party system that has been characteristic of Anglicanism. This two-factor analysis, while true as far as it goes and theologically tidy by including within it the two basic sources or authorities for belief in Bible and tradition, oversimplifies a very much more complex situation. "The Anglican synthesis is the affirmation of a paradoxical unity, a prophetic intuition that Catholicism and Protestantism, though in the past they have encased the Gospel in mutually antagonistic systems, are not ultimately irreconcilable."[5] Such a statement raises more questions than it solves. It really presupposes an unassigned role for "reason" as an authority in stating a "paradoxical unity" and in making a "synthesis" of what looks to be "antagonistic" and "irreconcilable."

The bipolar analysis, however, is far too simplistic, for there exists a third and even a fourth type — the commitment to reason and to experience — that may not have produced actual parties, but have been and are movements or positions exerting considerable influence on the first two. The emphasis upon reason found classic expression in the

Cambridge Platonists and especially in a famous aphorism of Whichcote, one of their number. "To go against reason is to go against God: it is the self-same thing, and to do that which the reason of the case doth require, and that which God himself doth appoint. Reason is the Divine governor of man's life. It is the very voice of God."[6] At a later time and in an America newly freed from England, Bishop White of Pennsylvania, one of the statesmen and architects of the newly organized Episcopal Church, developed a rational theology partly influenced by deism and partly an answer to it that has been called a "common-sense" theology. Behind these developments, however, was the humanist influence of the renaissance as a dynamic factor in the Anglican reformation. The scholastic reason of the Middle Ages was yielding to the critical reason of an evolving historical consciousness with its scientific methods of inquiry. Renaissance learning as typified by Dean Colet, Thomas More and Erasmus with an interest in classical literature and culture has been an important and perennial contributory stream. Canon Howard Johnson, in an address before the Anglican Congress at Toronto in 1963, accurately delineated three of the factors that must define Anglicanism, but allowed himself to be swept along by his own rhetoric into an Anglican chauvinism that grates upon readers.

> Catholic we are; Protestant and Reformed we are. Yet also the Renaissance is in our blood, and this made for a saving dose of skepticism, for an openness of mind, for a willingness to suspend judgment until we have more data. . . . More important than any formal statement of that consensus of the faithful, more significant than any kind of confessional declaration, is the appearance of a type of human being the world doesn't otherwise see. He is the Anglican. He creatively synthesizes within his own being the best that is in Catholicism, the best that is in Evangelicalism or Protestantism, the best that is in Liberalism.[7]

Since this third factor, reason, has been somewhat muted in analyses of Anglicanism, it deserves some further characterization. Father Van de Pol, A Roman Catholic scholar pursuing a phenomenological method, claims that moderation is the distinctive characteristic of Anglicanism. He quotes from the Preface to the 1662 Book of Common Prayer a sentence of Bishop Sanderson that was also paraphrased in the first Prayer Book of the American Church: "It hath been the wisdom of the Church of England, ever since the first compiling of her Publick Liturgy, to keep the mean between two extremes, of too much stiffness in refusing, and of too much easiness in admitting any variation from it." What would happen in the development of Anglicanism would be that this "mean" for coping with liturgical change would be expanded into a principle applicable even to doctrine. The *via media* is really the classical Greek dictum of "nothing too much." It is the Aristotelian principle of the golden mean in ethics transformed and defended by scholastic reason and made into a theological principle for the expression of truth. The *via media* requires constant disciplining by all the resources of clear and careful thinking available lest it degenerate into a magic phrase in which rhetoric substitutes for thought. An infamous example would be Bishop Patrick's "virtuous mediocrity ... between the meretricious gaudiness of the Church of Rome and the squalid sluttery of fanatic conventicles." Sometimes the *via media* hovered like a mirage in the desert air as an ideal for the future, not the recognition of a given historical reality. Such was Newman's vision of the *via media* in his most explicit Anglican writing. For him it was not an apologetic defense for the Church of England as presently constituted, but an ideal for the future to be reached only by painful mending of its ways. The sense of tolerance for opposing theological views that can characterize the *via media* today is well illustrated by *Doctrine in the Church of England*, a report commissioned by the archbishops and prepared over a period of years with Temple as the final chairman.[8] The orthodox creedal view of the Virgin Birth is well described, but the denial of its historicity on historical-critical and even theological grounds is also given place. There is a clear implication that on this creedal issue Anglicans are prepared to live in a church that allows both views. This latitude, however, would not be extended to disbelief in the Incarnation (despite the flurry created by a discussion recently of the Incarnation as "myth") to which the biblical witness is far more central than the peripheral witness to the Virgin Birth. (This issue will be discussed later in greater detail.)

The appeal to reason as a moderate course between Rome on the one hand and Geneva on the other characterized the method of Richard Hooker who, in analyzing Genevan polity, referred to historical circumstances thereby suggesting a critical use of reason for historical methodology. Hooker also used God-given reason as competent to deal with problems of polity and as an authority in theology in such phrases as "in defect of proof infallible the mind doth rather follow probable persuasions" and "such as the evidence is ... such is the heart's assent thereto." More and Cross, in their anthology of the religious literature of the seventeenth century, saw another dimension of the *via media:* the difference between things essential for belief and those that are secondary, a principle that would be later developed ecumenically by the Second Vatican Council.

> [The Caroline Divines] manifest intention was to steer a middle course between the excesses of Romanist and Radical Protestant. Clearly also such a middle course was not in the nature of a compromise or of hesitation to commit themselves to conviction, but was governed by a positive determination to preserve the just balance between fundamentals and accessories which was threatened by an authority vested in the infallibility whether of Tradition of or Scripture.[9]

A chapter on Bishop Butler's *Analogy of Religion* at this point would give classic expression to this rationalist movement in Anglicanism.

The Liberal Appeal to Experience

Jeremy Taylor touched the three bases that have been thus far described when he wrote: "I affirm nothing but upon grounds of Scripture, or universal tradition, or right reason discernible by every disinterested person."[10] Bishop Hensley Henson, a modern defender of the claims of reason, emphasized its critical function when he criticized the stock phrase so often quoted by Anglicans that this third reality could be described as "sound learning." "The principle of the English Reformation was, not so much sound learning as such — for every Christian apologist claimed for his own Church the support of sound learning — but a frank acceptance of sound learning as competent to revise the current tradition, both by interpreting afresh the sacred text, and by certifying through independent research the true verdict of Christian antiquity."[11]

This perception of Bishop Henson's about the critical function of reason is beginning to take us well beyond the scholastic uses of the word *reason*. "Experience," whether illustrated by the development of critical methods for testing historical evidence or by the emergence of the natural sciences with their appeal to the scientific method, began to interrupt the older dialogue with painful consequences to the simplicity of the conventional three-term analysis. Many Anglicans have been reluctant to admit a fourth member to the dialogue. It has seemed to them and it does still seem to them that an expansion of the meaning attached to reason would be adequate. The problem, however, is that the umbrella raised over reason cannot be stretched enough to provide the required coverage. Imagine the indignation of a would-be historian of modern philosophy when told that he must use reason to describe both the philosophical rationalism on the continent in the seventeenth century, as typified by Descartes, Spinoza and Leibnitz, and the reaction to this movement in late seventeenth- and eighteenth-century England in the new empiricism of John Locke, Bishop Berkeley and David Hume. He would be asked to call reason and its opposite, "sensory experience," by the same name. The problem is not different for an analysis of Anglicanism as it works its way into the nineteenth and especially into our century. The fact that the advocates of "experience" have not built up a special movement with placards and demonstrations should not blind us to the fact of their emergence out of the earlier criterion of reason. The advocates of experience usually are concerned primarily with their own special interpretation of experience, not with the fact that five or six very different appeals to experience may actually share a common platform. Tillich is sometimes invoked to deny experience a place save as the "medium" for the sources of theology. Actually Tillich lists many examples of the appeal to experience from the Augustinian-Franciscan tradition to Whiteheadian process thought, but because of his decision to deny a place to experience he is forced to describe reason with such various phrases as "critical," "ecstatic," "existential," "objective," "ontological" and "technical." It would be the charge of the linguistic analysts in their radical and positivistic appeal to experience that Tillich's term, reason, is forced to bear a load it can not possibly carry. Tillich's reluctance is probably related to his affinity for the idealistic strand in philosophy; the opposition of many Anglicans to admit experience as different from and coordinate with reason probably results from the Anglican predilection for the Platonic strand in its philosophical alliances.

The issue of whether the fourth term, experience, is justified or needed can probably be solved by observation today. A teacher of theology quickly discovers that many of his or her students identify their version of reality with some psychological theory except that it does not appear as "theory" to them, but naively as "the truth." If, for example, material from the Bible or tradition seems to these students not to be in conflict with, say, the developmental psychology of Erikson, then it is admissible. To another group, drawn by the desperate quest for authenticity and seeking through mystical experiences in many religious cultures some experience of their own, only those elements of the Bible or Christian tradition consonant with such "experiences" are admissible. From this perspective reason often appears as an enemy, as a rationalist denial of the fullness of human feeling. Still others come shaped by the tools of linguistic analysis ready to admit only that from the Bible and tradition which can meet strict verificational analysis or, in more liberal versions of the discipline, are capable of development along the lines of word games and model analysis. The three examples chosen, and they are prevalent among theological students today, are all appeals to experience, but an experience so differently understood that their advocates do not recognize each other as allies in terms at least of classification, but as rivals for the claim of truth. For many of these people experience has begun to take on revelational qualities of its own; but this development leads us beyond the purpose of the analysis, which was simply to establish the need and validity for a four-term description of the components in Anglican identity today.

Because of the growing complexity in understanding Anglicanism in terms of its changing cultural background, it would be impossible to freeze the *via media* into a static formula such as Bishop Paget did when he wrote in his *Introduction to the Fifth Book of Hooker's Ecclesiastical Polity:* "For on equal loyalty to the unconflicting rights of reason, of Scripture, and of tradition rest the distinctive strength and hope of the English Church."[12] The problem with Bishop Paget's rhetorical formula is that one could not determine what "equal" loyalty would mean in real experience. The assumption, moreover, that the rights of reason, of Scripture and of tradition will be "unconflicting" is simply not warranted in reality. Here the *via media* has become a static point at the intersection of vectors, vectors that can even be resolved into such quantitative terms as *equal* and *unconflicting* — a situation perhaps imaginable as a geometric exercise but bearing no relationship to how reason, Scripture and tradition struggle with each other in real life. "No doctrine," writes D. L. Edwards in a description of this fourth group, "can be 'experienced' as true in worship, or conduct, if it contradicts knowledge given by God in answer to historical research, or scientific or sociological investigation, or if it is meaningless or against reason."[13] This fourth pole, with its emphasis upon what "can be experienced," has sometimes been identified as "modernism" in the movement in Great Britain typified by W. R. Inge, Hastings Rashdall, H. D. A. Major and given expression in the Modern Churchmen's Union. It appeared as liberalism in the phrase "liberal evangelical" for another related group within the American Episcopal Church. This group is needed to keep revelation related to the ever changing configurations of culture. Nearly all members of the first three groups now admit experience as a criterion in the exposition of their positions. The fourth group has thereby won a major victory. The emphasis upon experience, however, can become problematic when it goes well beyond the pioneering role that has been described and tends to settle upon some particular method or insight from psychology, or group dynamics, or pedagogy, and to exalt this virtually as a replacement for the Gospel. Of course, the fourth group would not admit the word *replacement* for it tends to see common ground between the Gospel and its special insight. An illustration might be the initial popularity of the Episcopal Church's Seabury Series in religious education and the hard times upon which this useful curriculum has subsequently fallen. There is nothing so odd or cold as yesterday's scientific certainties served up as today's meal. Paul van Buren's *Secular Meaning of the Gospel* rejects everything that cannot stand the test of verificational analysis, but its dogmatic view of experience is so narrowed to a knife-edge that the author soon wisely abandoned the position for a richer view of what constitutes experience. Nevertheless, the book ought to become a classic of the fourth type both in its strengths, for there is much insight in it, and in its subsequently perceived weaknesses.

The freezing upon some one insight or method is of course contrary to the very essence of this fourth position, with its constant appeal to experience. There seems to be a demand, however, of the human mind for certainties, even at the cost of embalming the ever changing results of experience in a given era. Archbishop Ramsey, in his account of Anglican theology from Gore to Temple, argues that the modernists — Hastings Rashdall and Bethune-Baker — were a temporary phenomenon in Anglicanism without staying power because, he says, they had a defective view of the relations between humanity and God. Their liberalism was soon outdated.

Far better than the word *liberalism*, as Alec Vidler has argued, is the term *liberality*, for liberal is not properly the opposite of conservative, as usually assumed, but of bigoted and intransigent. Liberal is larger than any "ism" or set of philosophical assumptions because it refers not so much to the position advocated as to the open way in which the position is held. In a statement that sounds very Maurician, updated for our times, Vidler has grasped and articulated the hope that these dominant notes of Anglicanism are not cacophonous, but really in harmony within the Anglican symphony. "Anglican theology is true to its genius when it is seeking to reconcile opposed systems, rejecting them as exclusive systems, but showing that the principle for which each stands has its place within the total orbit of Christian truth, and in the long run is secure only within that orbit or (in the idiom of today) when it is held in tension with other apparently opposed, but really complementary principles."[14]

The Anglican Dialogue and Its Norms

Enough has now been developed, together with representative quotations, to establish that within Anglicanism there is a four-way dialogue between the catholic, the evangelical and the advocates of reason and of experience. The four basic forms of authority behind the variant positions are obviously Bible, tradition, reason and experience. These authorities are not mutually exclusive, but there is a type of relationship between Bible and tradition which may readily be compared and again a coordinate relationship between reason and experience. The second pair tends to modify the first pair in varying combinations. In preparation for the 1952 World Conference on Faith and Order at Lund, Sweden, representative scholars of the cooperating churches were asked to prepare a study volume on the nature of the church as understood by reference to the official formularies of each communion. Leonard Hodgson, Regius Professor of Divinity at Oxford, who was to contribute an essay called "The Doctrine of the Church as Held and Taught in the Church of England," submitted it first to various parties and scholars within the Church of England, incorporating their comments in footnotes with his own responses. This transcribed dialogue is therefore a tour de force and deserves a wider knowledge than it has received within Anglicanism. The essay has become one of the best representative semiofficial statements about the Anglican understanding of the church. It really summarizes the development thus far in this chapter with a birds-eye perspective on the ongoing process. It unfortunately oversimplifies the third group with the phrase "reasonable scholarship," which may have been adequate at the time of the Anglican reformation but which now, in the interests of clarity to account for subsequent historical developments, requires subdivision into a group centering upon reason and another upon experience. The dialogue today is really four-way and not simply tripartite as in Professor Hodgson's otherwise solid analysis.

> Thus the official formularies of the Church of England can only be rightly understood if they are read in their historical context as reflecting the century-long process in which the Church, while conscious of its unbroken continuity with the Church of the ages, was seeking to purge itself of corruptions and abuses. The continuity with the Church of the past was witnessed to not only in what was said but in what was done, in the maintenance of the inherited church structure with its threefold ministry, episcopal ordination, cathedrals, deans, chapters, archdeacons and universities. The reformation was carried forward by a dialectical process due to the continuance within the Church of catholic-minded conservatives, protestant-minded radicals and those whose first care was for reasonable scholarship. The one thing which has been characteristic of the Church of England as a whole has been and still is the fact that it contains these three elements, maintains them in tension with one another, and is the *locus* of their tripartite dialectic. Because the Church's formularies are the written deposit of that dialectic during the formative century of its separate existence, the successors of the three contributory elements, the Anglo-Catholics, the Evangelicals, and the Modernists, each tend to see in them the expression of that for which they stand and feel themselves to be loyal members of the Church to which all belong. They are united in the conviction that they belong to the Church which can trace its continuous history back to the days of St. Augustine of Canterbury, and that the principle of its reformation, to which it must be true, is conformity to the scriptural revelation of what the Church should be.[15]

The creative maintenance of this four-way dialogue is not an easy matter; it can at times of stress degenerate into a brawl. Conventional Anglicans deprecate the extremists and the extremists deprecate each other. The dialogue cannot be creatively composed by a policy of "peace at any price" or of "never rocking the boat." It fails if it becomes a search for some innocuous least common denominator and for a compromise in principles in the interests of institutional unity. It can sometimes be taken hostage by extremists in any one of the four camps who become absolute about their perspectives and motivated either to convert all others or to exclude them from the communion. The dialectical process implied here is no mere juxtaposition of different views. The talk about the *via media* is really only a description of the dialogue as though it had come to rest in some invisible equatorial point. But the reality behind the dialectical process demands continued discussion, never a premature resolution of the tension as imagined in most concepts of the *via media*. From the very nature of multilateral dialogue there must be vigor, imagination, persistence, determination, respect for differences and a spirit of reconciliation.

Too often people shy away from conflict in an attempt to reach religious truth, whereas the truer view is that conflict, if managed maturely and according to rules of fair play and respect for the opponent, can be very creative. One note of unreality that runs through many of the documents of Vatican II is the absence of any expectation of conflict, as though the bishops in verbally achieving agreement had supposedly eliminated conflict. Whenever, as in Anglicanism, authority is dispersed in many areas the probability of conflict is increased. Bishop John Coburn, who has supported the ordination of women, was asked in 1977 to address an area convention of the Evangelical and Catholic Mission that has strongly opposed the ordination of women, but has not seceded from the Episcopal Church. He frankly embraced controversy as part of "a deeper understanding of the unique spirit of Anglicanism." "We should not apologize," he said to the group, "for tensions within our Church; we should not be frightened of them; and we certainly should not try to pretend they are not there. . . . As you and those who disagree with you remain loyal and discuss, debate, argue, in the unity of spirit and the bond of peace, then we may glory in the goodly heritage God has given us."[16]

No one of the four groups should be missing from the dialogue, nor should any be excluded by the others. What is required is not an exhausted and hostile state of noncommunication, but the enduring of the tension in the confidence that truth will emerge from the dialogue. As Barth said at the Amsterdam meeting of the World Council of Churches,

there must be attention to the disagreements in our agreements and to the agreements in our disagreements. It would
be helpful to apply the Anglican group principle to the production of new symposia, not just by a homogenous group,
but by a mixed group from the four camps in which each
writer commented on the contribution of the others with
reply in a second round. This type of cross-fertilization
springing from rigorous and consistent thinking would render moot any worry that comprehensiveness might be synonymous with lack of thought. It would make a significant
ecumenical advance for all the churches and make outdated
Robert Page's accurate observation that "one cannot escape
the impression that Anglican theology has been too much
content to live off its own fat. What constructive work there
has been is for the most part a continuation of traditions established in an earlier era."[17] Our own study of the "Spirit of
Anglicanism" would have been enriched if there could have
been included a chapter for each of the four groups about
some typical representative; but it would have made the
book unbearably long.

What is required by the very nature of the dialogue is not
compromise for the sake of peace, but comprehension for the
sake of truth. Some Anglicans doubt that "the man in the
street," to use their expression, is capable of such judicial
procedure or nuanced conviction. Bishop Wand does not
avoid smugness and ecclesiastical elitism in the following
statement, which may actually be more ironic than he intended. "On the evidence of friend and critic alike the three
most obvious features of Anglicanism are tolerance, restraint, and learning. None of them is characteristic of mankind in the mass. Taken all together they may well prove a
strange and unattractive climate for the man in the
street."[18] The difficulty with the kind of analysis that Bishop Wand makes in the above statement, apart from its unin-
tended smugness, is that the three "most obvious features
of Anglicanism" are not so much qualities in their own right
as the fruits of the dialogic process when it is working well.
It is far better to rest our analysis of Anglicanism on the
participants in the dialogue and their respective positions
and contributions. These would then appear to an observer
as the "most obvious features in Anglicanism," for when

the dialogue goes poorly or does not even get started there is really intolerance rather than tolerance, ideological blindness about one's one position rather than restraint and the prostitution of scholarship to justify one's tribal affinity rather than learning. It has been observed by many that Charles Gore had "a fanatic streak" in him, but his vision of the vocation of the Church of England was more astute than Bishop Wand's simply because Gore rested his analysis on the dynamic contributions of the Anglican groups rather than on the hoped-for fruits of the process. No one can challenge Gore's catholic credentials, but they were defined by Gore in intimate association with the contributions of evangelicals and liberals for whom he had much less sympathy. If Gore is loyal to his vocation as he sees it in the following quotation, there may well be tolerance, restraint and learning, but they would be the products of successful practice not themselves the generating norms. "I believe," he wrote, "with a conviction the strength of which I could hardly express, that it is the vocation of the English Church to realize and to offer to mankind a Catholicism which is scriptural, and represents the whole of Scripture; which is historical, and can know itself free in the face of historical and critical science; which is rational and constitutional in its claims of authority, free at once from lawlessness and imperialism."[19]

Emergence of the Broad Church Position

The four positions in real life involve some overlapping with others and seldom occur in pure form. There is even a large group that defies any label. Especially critical of any "extreme positions," they seem to gravitate toward the center. They say they despise "party politics," but seem unaware that their own position is probably even more political for not having been thought out theologically with much clarity. Many clergy of this caliber are being elected bishops partly because one senses that they and their electors want to avoid commitment as a quality of episcopal leadership. "Churchmen of the Center," as they have been called, are not to be confused with "broad churchmen." The former group is interested in the inter-Anglican situation often for political reasons; the broad church person sees beyond this situation to the ecumenical implications and responsibilities of Anglicanism. Broad church persons have historically developed out of liberalism. They have such respect for both catholicism and protestantism that they achieve a very real exposure to all four positions in a positive affirmation of the value of the dialogue, of the integrity of the opposed camps and of the expectation that truth will prevail by its own weight and without the nervous shoring up of the edifice by people convinced of their own indispensability to the process. The broad church person is not a latitudinarian indifferent to truth, although the position can degenerate into this. The broad church person is committed to the dialogue of the four partners, convinced that no one partner should wish to swallow up the others. Maurice, in this sense of the word, was a broad churchman, as was Temple, although because the word had become unpopular by Temple's time he was often called a central churchman without, however, the political implications and indifference to theological understanding that have characterized recent uses of the term. It is worth trying to recover the term broad church person for the sake of clarity and completeness in analysis. The broad church person is not an eclectic choosing what suits his taste from the Anglican smorgasbord. It is not the situation of the mullah after a reconciliation of religions who will cry from the minaret: "The early bird catches the worm." He tends to feel that his own position is the only theologically sound way to be a catholic Christian, affirming the catholic tradition under the judgment of Scripture by means of liberal openness to critical inquiry. He justifies his position by the observation from history that it is impossible to be catholic, protestant or liberal alone for very long without losing this single commitment unless there is also simultaneous commitment to the others. The broad church person ought to be aware that his or her position can develop a peculiar blindness by making the imperialistic claim to "true Anglicanism" and thus belying its own insights and presuppositions.

Our description of the four basic Anglican positions has been made primarily with respect to the internal affairs of the Anglican Communion. What is unique within Anglicanism is not the assertion that these four occur only here, for nearly all churches show one or more of these basic positions. They have not, however, generally been admitted officially up to this time by other communions as legitimate ways of interpreting the historic stance of the church involved. What is unique in Anglicanism is not the presence of these positions, but the official comprehension of the positions with their varying permutations and combinations. "The most spacious home" and "the most elastic church in Christendom," commented Einar Molland, a Norwegian Lutheran. Father Van de Pol has asserted that in no other Christian church has the integration and reconciliation of the catholic and reformation positions made such headway. However, the documents of Vatican II show a high level of such integration and the reception of Vatican II within the Roman Catholic Church has made it much more comprehensive than it was. We find liberals like Hans Kung who support the documents and want to press beyond them; we find conservatives like Cardinal Siri who regard the whole council as a mistake; and we find "churchmen of the center" who pay lip service to the council, but are almost totally concerned with "not rocking the boat." On the other end of the spectrum, many of the Protestant Churches through the liturgical movement and the revival of the monastic life have made great strides in a "catholic" direction, illustrating a new comprehensiveness for them.

H. Richard Niebuhr's Typology

All of this suggests a wider dimension to our analysis. Is there possibly something much larger than simply a denominational phenomenon behind the four Anglican positions? Is there perhaps a universal situation about the forces present within all Christian churches not recognized at least officially elsewhere with the explicitness it has developed within Anglicanism? Help for further diagnosis of the problem is available from H. Richard Niebuhr's classic *Christ and Culture.* The five possibilities of relationship between Christ and culture, as Niebuhr saw them, can be applied, as he did not, to alternative stances within a Christian church. His five options were: Christ against culture; the Christ of culture; Christ above culture; Christ and culture in paradoxical, eschatological relationship; and Christ the transformer of culture. While it is probably true that Niebuhr's five relationships have at some time appeared within each of the four Anglican positions, there is a certain sense in which some one of Niebuhr's relationships, by becoming dominant over the other four, can be especially and appropriately identified and correlated with one of the Anglican groupings.

The initial option at first sight would not seem very applicable. The position of a Tertullian hostile to culture is not likely to win many Anglican converts. At times Anglican evangelicals have seemed to want to oppose the world. Recently, they have been criticized for this covert Manichaeanism by James Packer, one of their English leaders. Newman's Anglo-Catholicism had a sharp edge of opposition to the world. Despite these illustrations, the Christ-against-culture option is really the stance of the sect that regards the world as evil and the mission of the faithful community to sever ties with it. Anglicanism, coming from an establishment position as a national church concerned with all types and conditions of people, has always been deeply rooted in a cultural context. The Plymouth Brethren, on the other hand, are the typical sectarian renunciation of the Anglican premise. Although the internal Anglican scene shows few affinities with the Christ-against-culture theme, it is significant that sectarian versions of Anglicanism begin to develop these characteristics. The Reformed Episcopal Church in the United States seceded from the American Episcopal Church largely because it felt an inadequate commitment there to evangelism. It became in a sense anti-catholic and anti-liberal in orientation as the dispute over baptismal regeneration gained momentum. The more recent secession of the Anglican Catholic Church over the ordination of women and over the new Prayer Book is a fracture at the other end of the spectrum. This breakaway group is strongly anti-modern culture. It represents a schism exhibiting the dynamics of the Christ-against-culture theme. Specifically, Christ is seen as against modern "sexology" and could not possibly be represented by a woman priest. The grounds for this opposition are found in tradition and in hostility to cultural changes in the position of women.

Niebuhr's second option is the opposite of his first. Here Christ is identified with cultural movements of the contemporary age. In Germany it could be a Schleiermacher eager to commend the faith to its "cultured despisers." In America it could become a form of the social gospel that felt the Kingdom of God could be voted in by increasing democracy and education. Clearly the applicable Anglican illustration of primary reference here is the liberal movement with the two positions of those who advocate reason and those who favor experience. The danger is that Christ may be swallowed up by the culture. Niebuhr's third option is Christ-above-culture. It is synthesis by the juxtaposition in Western catholicism of an Aristotelian base in natural theology and natural law ethics with a superstructure in the church's teaching about revelation from Bible and tradition (a synthesis which has been given classic expression by Thomas Aquinas). This position is obviously that of the catholic group within Anglicanism. Hooker, Maurice and Temple build their theologies often upon the cultural inheritance of Aristotelian, Platonic and classical Roman insights. The scholastic Anglo-Catholic could be distinguished from the more liberal catholic who switched the cultural base from ancient philosophies to new ones like idealism, or dialectical realism, or Whiteheadian process thought. Christ is seen as the fulfillment of the human cultural drive, the revealed answer to the question of meaning. Niebuhr's fourth option of Christ-and-culture in a paradoxical relationship is represented by the Reformation and more especially by Luther himself. Modern insights of biblical scholarship into eschatology are brought in by Niebuhr to give a contemporary orientation to the position. The Anglican counterpart is obvious in the reformation group which could sometimes stress the paradox of Christ in-yet-above-and-against-culture partly because the Anglo-Catholics had largely preempted the third Niebuhrian position. In the abolition of the slave trade and then of slavery itself the Anglican evangelicals succeeded in bringing a reformist orientation concretely into the historical and political process of Britain.

We have now exhausted the four Anglican options and there is still a fifth Niebuhrian position: Christ as the transformer of culture. Does this mean that the analysis does not fit very well and we are left with an unused side of the Procrustean bed? The question is especially interesting because Niebuhr praises Maurice as the classic exponent of this position. It is the one to which Niebuhr himself most resonates. His enthusiasm has largely been responsible for the American Maurician renaissance. While Niebuhr's fifth point is not one of our basic four, in the analysis thus far made it does correspond to the way in which we have said the four-way dialogue ought to be conducted. It corresponds fully with the stance that we have called that of the broad church person who deeply values the insights of the four Anglican positions, but knows that it is Christ alone who can transform these positions into realistic, fruitful and carefully thought-out dialogue. It is this fifth option of Niebuhr's that provides the living, transforming center of Anglican "comprehensiveness" and makes it an ecumenical prototype of the coming great church.

Pastoral Orientation of the Dialogue

Another characteristic feature of Anglicanism is that the dialogue between the four partners is pastorally oriented. It is possible that this orientation is the legacy of an established church with a sense of pastoral responsibility for all members of the national community and not just for churchgoers. Dogmatics in Anglicanism have been valued chiefly as a guide to leading the Christian life. A study of the moral theology of the Caroline divines amply confirms this thesis.[20] Jeremy Taylor in his magisterial *Ductor Dubitantium* aimed to make the individual Christian responsible for solving his own problems with supportive counseling. John Donne captured the pastoral bent deliberately at the expense of the speculative or merely dogmatic: "Moral divinity becomes us all, but natural divinity and metaphysic divinity, almost all may spare." The often quoted Anglican statement about sacramental confession that "none must, all may, and some should" illustrates again the pastoral direction of the communion. Until about thirty years ago, the

Episcopal Church in the United States regarded pastoral calling in the homes of parishioners as the expected work of a rector and curate to such an extent that it was widely commented upon by clergy and laity in other churches. Professor John T. McNeill from the United Church of Canada and the Presbyterian tradition pays tribute to this pastoral orientation which is more true of the past than of the present. "While the cure of souls is a field of controversy in Anglicanism, this has led rather to its cultivation than to its neglect . . . it is probably safe to say that no other great communion has given more attention to the cure of souls, either in theory or in practice."[21]

Liturgical Orientation

In addition to the pastoral direction of Anglicanism, there is the overwhelming and dominant liturgical orientation. The major controversies in the communion have not been directly on theological topics, but primarily on liturgical ones in which the theological issue, although present, is ancillary. One exasperated non-Anglican exclaimed: "All these people do is fight about the furniture of religion." Prayer Book revision can become a painful process partly because the Prayer Book is conceived not as a book primarily for clergy, but as the equipment for every lay person in leading the spiritual life. Just as the pastoral concern expressed itself in a type of moral theology addressed to the individual to increase his or her responsibility, so the same concern expressed here has stressed the word *common* in the Book of Common Prayer. Confessions, whether Reformation or Counter-reformation, have never played the role in Anglicanism that they have elsewhere. Even the historic catholic creeds have been used chiefly in the liturgy. The Apostles' Creed has invariably been used in baptism and until recently the Nicene Creed invariably in the eucharist. The context of the creeds in worship has emphasized that they are not collections of dogmatic sentences or of conciliar decrees valued primarily as theological doctrines, but that they are acts of personal allegiance and communal commitment to God. They are affirmations "in" God with emphasis upon God's acts as Father, as Son and as Holy Spirit, not statements "that" God exists or "that" God has certain attributes. Even the writing of Anglican theology has usually been done not by organizing the discipline from first principles, but by using these liturgically employed creeds as the basis. Two examples that have had wide impact on Anglicanism in recent years have been *Doctrines of the Creed* by Oliver Quick and *The Creed of Christendom* by John Burnaby. Michael Ramsey, retired Archbishop of Canterbury, in his study of the development of Anglican theology, chose to preface his summary of its characteristics by this revealing observation: "Theological history resembles an iceberg in that there is a part of it which is below the surface, and it is the part which gives ballast and continuity. Among the half-conscious influences there is the influence which a Prayer Book inevitably has in a liturgical Church. The *lex orandi* (law of praying) has its quiet and unobtrusive effect upon the *lex credendi* (law of believing)."[22]

A number of observers have seen in the liturgical orientation of Anglicanism its closest approach to Eastern Orthodoxy in which theological discussion often arises from the liturgical context. It is significant that when Parliament suppressed the Church of England by outlawing the use of the Prayer Book and bishops in the Cromwellian period, it enforced uniformity by use of the Westminster Confession. When Anglicanism had reestablished itself under Charles II it sought to enforce conformity not by a different confession, but by the required use of the Prayer Book of 1662 in the Act of Uniformity. Many non-Episcopalians would testify that the liturgical ethos is what they chiefly associate with Anglicanism. Dean Sperry, a Congregationalist, in his *Religion in America*, wrote such a description. It is far too generous, especially in his comment on the lack of class distinctions, but it does express a characteristic.

> The Episcopal Church knows better than many other Protestant Churches how to greet and to meet the crowds in the city streets, at a mid-day service in Lent. . . . Simple liturgical services, an open door, when far too many other church doors are closed and locked, the encouragement of private devotions at any and all hours of the day, useful manuals for devotions, the patent lack of all class distinctions and the

presence of a sincerely intended catholicity in the services of cathedrals and pro-cathedrals — all these are marks of vitality, sincerity and imagination.[23]

Anglicanism as a Christian Archetype

If the question is raised as to how the three Anglican thinkers of the previous chapters fit into the four positions that have been described as part of the Anglican landscape, it must be said that no one of them represents a "pure" type, but some combination of them, the mix occasionally shifting in emphasis at different times within their lives. Indeed, they have been some of the chief geological forces responsible for carving the Anglican landscape into its present configurations. Hooker has obvious affinities with the catholic group through the great patristic and medieval traditions upon which he drew; but surely he is based more firmly in the Reformation camp with his dependence on his evangelical forbearers and his use of much of Calvin's theology. Yet his very difference from the Puritans is revealed in his relationship to the group which valued reason, he himself contributing much impetus to the development of this third Anglican option. Maurice had a considerable initial affinity with the Oxford group that would place him in the catholic camp, but his dispute with Pusey over baptism separated him from them as he criticized the Tractarians for a sectarian version of catholicism. His affinity with Luther was deep and personal. Maurice expressly lived by the experience of being justified by faith through grace. He disliked, however, the system of protestantism which he felt betrayed the true principles of the Reformation. John Calvin was not one of his heroes. He urged the Church of England to learn what the Reformation was all about. He felt the advocates of reason in the contemporary liberal system came very close to the denial of revelation. What he sought then was none of the groups insofar as they had made themselves into systems or some eclectic system that would comprehend them all, but a genuinely catholic church that would through its six signs incorporate the positive principles that had unfortunately congealed into the rival systems. His position was self-consciously that which has been described here as broad church.

Temple's early theology as reflected in *Foundations* was very close to liberalism, but he soon emphasized with increasing conviction the catholic heritage, particularly in his shift on Virgin Birth and the theology of episcopacy in negotiations for church union. At the same time, toward the end of his life, he sought to give more centrality to sin and the Atonement than to the Incarnation he had earlier made so central. This development brought him closer to the evangelical group. In trying to shift his philosophical base from Hegelian idealism to what he called in his Gifford Lectures a "dialectical realism," with its limited use of Whiteheadean process thought, he was moving toward our fourth position as an advocate of experience. Temple, however, was not a party man, partly due to the influence of Maurice and partly to his own evolution as an ecumenical and social reformer. For all three the liturgical ethos of Anglicanism was a recognized characteristic of their communion and one they contributed to through their activities and writings. In slightly different ways, yet with a central allegiance very much in common in the varying cultural conditions of their times, they illustrate H. Richard Niebuhr's fifth and favorite theme of Christ the transformer of culture. Our interest here, however, is not to show with which of the four positions each of the three had a primary or secondary allegiance, but to demonstrate that each made contributions that would enrich and make the Anglican scene more complex until a fourfold rather than a twofold analysis would be required. The four categories are not eternal norms, but simply the historical developments of evolving Anglicanism responsive to much of their influence and intellectual leadership. The positions should be understood primarily as descriptive of what exists, not normative for what necessarily should exist.

Chapters on Charles Gore, Charles Simeon and Joseph Butler would illustrate the first three "pure types" more adequately than our triumvirate ever could because of their mixture of types. Yet the balance, comprehensiveness and commitment of Anglicanism as a whole shows through the thought and lives of Hooker, Maurice and Temple more arrestingly than in representatives of what might be called "more typical" types. Part of the paradox involved in this situation is that Hooker, Maurice and Temple have enriched the phenomenon of Anglicanism to the point where they no longer fit easily into the usual categories of analysis that are appropriate for most Anglicans.

It now becomes possible to draw together the lines of the discussion up to this point and to state in compressed form a description of Anglican identity in terms of a distinctive Christian archetype. Anglicanism may be defined as a way of being Christian that involves *a pastorally and liturgically oriented dialogue between four partners: catholics, evangelicals and advocates of reason and of experience.* The word *partner* has been deliberately chosen to emphasize the need of the groups to remain in cooperative relations with each other. As we have seen in the development of this definition, many, if not all, of its constituent phrases can be found in non-Anglican writers. Professor Van de Pol, a Roman Catholic, goes well beyond his chosen discipline of phenomenology to prophesy about the future role of Anglicanism. "All Anglican Churches, however, are one in their conscious endeavor to preserve the apostolic faith and character of the Church's worship of the first centuries, though trying to incorporate in it the contributions of the Reformation and those of their own time so far as they have positive and permanent value. This typical Anglican attitude in respect to tradition and enrichment is at the basis of the moderation and comprehensiveness of Anglicanism. It marks world-Anglicanism as being, as it were, a provisional prototype of the reunited *Ecumene*, the world-Christianity of the future. That Anglicanism comprises only a small number of Christians does not detract from that fact."[24]

Whatever may be said of the insight of this analyst and of his prediction in the face of the sorry realities which often characterize Anglicanism when it breaks down under the pressures of its mission, it suggests the need for Anglicans to take themselves more seriously than they often do and to look up from their internal squabbling to a deepened sense of their vocation. What that vocation may actually be needs greater precision than we have yet achieved in this analysis.

The Lambeth Conferences
and Anglican Identity

In order to insulate the situation somewhat from the subjective evaluations of the writer it will be well to turn to the Lambeth Conferences for a view of the episcopate's attempt to define Anglican identity and to see to what degree the insights of Hooker, Maurice and Temple have become digested within the communion itself. At the very least such a survey should reveal some of the problems and pitfalls of the communion today.

The Lambeth Conferences of the bishops of the Anglican Communion began hesitantly and with many reservations in 1867 and have continued since at approximately ten-year intervals. They have been called by the Archbishop of Canterbury, who has kept a tight hand on their planning. Their deliberations and resolutions are only advisory until they have been enacted into legislation within the some twenty-five autonomous Anglican jurisdictions, but their authority has grown over the years largely because of the intrinsic worth of much of their proceedings. Many times the world structure of Anglicanism, which is not a church but a federation of churches, has been compared to the development of the British Commonwealth of Nations. Some American clergy, frustrated by the heavy hand of British dominance in Anglican affairs, have fretted that only in the actions of the Church of England does eighteenth-century colonialism still perpetuate itself. Many have tried to define the Anglican Communion as a fellowship of national churches in communion with the Archbishop of Canterbury, but he has no canonical power outside the Church of England. He is not the Anglican pope, not even officially a supranational patriarch, for his position is purely honorary and ceremonial. Yet the need for a representative leader to act and speak at times on behalf of the twenty-five autonomous Anglican churches that are in communion with each other is an evolving fact of history. That the office has been held in recent years by men of considerable ability and vision has given it a kind of moral authority. When he visits the pope he is understood as somehow to be "representing" the Anglican Communion.

The Lambeth Conference of 1888 produced an important document for the future of Anglicanism in its ecumenical relations especially with the non-episcopal churches. This document is often referred to as the Chicago-Lambeth Quadrilateral from the circumstance of its promulgation by the House of Bishops of the American Church in 1886. It is noteworthy that the American version was not given the approval at that time of the General Convention, which alone would have been the competent constitutional authority. Both the American and the Lambeth versions of the Quadrilateral have been printed in the new Book of Common Prayer (1976).[25] The American document, like so many committee productions, is a mixed bag with pioneering expressions of ecumenism side by side with conservative ultimata against weakening the heritage of the Episcopal Church. It seeks to fulfill the Savior's prayer "that we all may be one"; it "does not seek to absorb other Communions," but is ready "in the spirit of love and humility to forgo all preferences of her own." On the other hand, it is asserted that Christian unity "can be restored only by the return of all Christians to the principles of unity exemplified by the undivided Catholic Church during the first ages of its existence." Fundamentalist reference is made to "this sacred deposit" that has been "committed by Christ and his Apostles to the Church unto the end of the world, and therefore incapable of compromise or surrender by those who have been ordained to be its stewards and trustees." It is instructive to compare the differences between the way the four points are listed in the two docsuments. The long American preface has been jettisoned by Lambeth and replaced by the statement of Resolution 11 that "the following Articles supply a basis on which approach may be by God's blessing made towards Home Reunion." The differences in context are suggestive of subsequent confusion about the Lambeth Quadrilateral. Was it to be interpreted as a maximal or minimal statement of the "essentials" for "organic unity"?

•The simple flat-footed fundamentalism of the American statement: "the Holy Scriptures of the Old and New Testament as the revealed Word of God" has been altered by describing somewhat more carefully the authority of Scripture by a phrase from the Thirty-nine Articles. "The Holy Scriptures of the Old and New Testaments, as 'containing all things necessary to salvation,' and as being the rule and ultimate standard of faith."

•The American statement about "the Nicene Creed as the sufficient statement of the Christian Faith" is expanded by Lambeth to include also "the Apostles' Creed, as the Baptismal Symbol."

•Lambeth added "ordained by Christ himself" to the American description of the sacraments which was otherwise accepted without verbal change. "The two Sacraments ordained by Christ Himself — Baptism and the Supper of the Lord — ministered with unfailing use of Christ's words of Institution, and of the elements ordained by Him."

•It is ironic that the fourth point which has been the most difficult for members of the non-episcopal churches and the most problematic for Anglicans themselves in subsequent negotiations for church union was simply retained by Lambeth in its American phraseology. "The Historic Episcopate, locally adapted in the methods of its administration to the varying needs of the nations and peoples called of God into the Unity of His Church." It would be significant for future controversy that the phrase "apostolic succession" was not used and that the conception of episcopacy suggested by the formula seemed to be chiefly administrative.

Problems of Episcopacy and Liturgy

Meeting after World War I in the full tide of postwar idealism and internationalism, the bishops at the Lambeth Conference of 1920 issued their famous *Appeal to All Christian People,* the highwater mark of Anglican ecumenism. Leaving behind any idea of an ultimatum associated with the original Chicago Quadrilateral, the bishops reworked the fourth point and put their claims into the form of a question.

A ministry acknowledged by every part of the Church as possessing not only the inward call of the Spirit, but also the commission of Christ and the authority of the whole body. May we not reasonably claim that the Episcopate is the one means of providing such a ministry? It is not that we call in question for a moment the spiritual reality of the ministries of those Communions which do not possess the Episcopate. On the contrary we thankfully acknowledge that these ministries have been manifestly blessed and owned by the Holy Spirit as effective means of grace.[26]

That more flexible attempt to restate the fourth and admittedly most difficult point in the Quadrilateral was set in the wider context of an ecumenical vision that saw all churches uniting in a rich and continuing diversity that would introduce each communion to the riches of all the others. "The vision which rises before us is that of a Church genuinely Catholic, loyal to all Truth, and gathering into its fellowship all 'who profess and call themselves Christians,' within whose visible unity all the treasures of faith and order, bequeathed as a heritage by the past to the present, shall be possessed in common, and made serviceable to the whole Body of Christ."[27]

Inspired by this vision, Bishop Azariah of Dornakal returned to India. Twenty-seven years of difficult negotiations followed until finally the Church of South India — reconciling Anglicans, Presbyterians, Congregationalists and Methodists — was inaugurated. It would take another twenty years before Lambeth 1968 would recommend that the members of the Anglican Communion should enter into full communion with it.

The Lambeth Conference of 1930 carried further the corporate discussion of the nature of episcopacy for the united church of the future. It is clear that the "bare bones" statements about episcopacy in the Quadrilateral and in the 1920 restatement were proving insufficient as the wider debate within Anglicanism and the ecumenical discussions with non-episcopal churches demonstrated. An extensive literature about episcopacy appeared. Anglo-catholics under Bishop Kirk produced *The Apostolic Ministry* in 1946 with emphasis upon the *esse* theory of episcopacy. Evangelicals replied in *The Ministry of the Church*, edited by Bishop Stephen Neill with counter emphasis upon the classic theory of *bene esse* that had been so clearly stated by Richard

Hooker. Then in 1954, from a university group of critical scholars under Kenneth Carey, came *The Historic Episcopate in the Fullness of the Church*, a symposium that may be described as initiating the *plene esse* theory. This view involved a more eschatological attitude toward church unity and built on the affirmations of previous Lambeth Conferences. Two excellent studies were produced by individual scholars: Norman Sykes' *Old Priest and New Presbyter: The Anglican Attitude to Episcopacy, Presbyterianism, and Papacy Since the Reformation* and the biblically and mission-oriented *The Pioneeer Ministry: The Relation of Church and Ministry* by Anthony T. Hanson of the Anglican Church of Ireland. Bishop Newbigin has pointed out how Victorian the Quadrilateral really is by asking where in it one can find the church as the people of God or the imperative of mission.

The danger of a too myopic concentration on episcopacy must have been sensed by Temple as he drafted the 1930 Lambeth statement because he struck the note of sharing the varied spiritual treasure of the communions "now separated from one another." Then he reflected on the Anglican contribution to that process by an articulate statement of Anglican identity. "Our special character and, as we believe, our peculiar contribution to the Universal Church, arises from the fact that, owing to historic circumstances, we have been enabled to combine in our one fellowship the traditional Faith and Order of the Catholic Church with that immediacy of approach to God through Christ to which the Evangelical Churches especially bear witness, and freedom of intellectual inquiry, whereby the correlation of the Christian revelation and advancing knowledge is constantly effected."[28] It is doubtful whether Anglican identity has ever been more succinctly defined.

The Lambeth Conference of 1948 achieved a tour de force in drawing the various Anglican views of episcopacy together in a responsible statement that could serve as a guide for those involved in unity discussions with other churches and as a warning to Anglicans themselves not to become polarized over doctrines of episcopacy, but to keep the dialogue creative and continuing under the canon of "comprehensiveness." After asserting that the Lambeth Appeal of 1920 was

fully in accord with the provision of the Ordinal that requires episcopal ordination for the exercise of ministry within the church, the statement made the point that this unity
of practice had not ruled out widespread diversity of interpretation. The *esse* theory and what amounts to the *bene
esse* theory of episcopacy were described.

> Some, holding episcopacy to be of the *esse* of the Church,
> are bound by their convictions to hold that non-episcopal
> ministries are not ministries of the Church, and lack that au-
> thoritative commission without which there can be no guar-
> anteed priestly ministrations. Others, while holding firmly
> that episcopacy is the normal method for the transmission
> of ministerial authority, yet feel themselves bound, in view
> of the manifest blessing of God on non-episcopal ministries,
> to recognize those ministries as true ministries and their sac-
> raments as true sacraments. Yet others hold shades of opin-
> ion intermediate between these views. It is clear that in any
> scheme for reunion or intercommunion all these views must
> be recognized and allowed for.[29]

The statement repeats the necessity for the acceptance of
episcopacy, of episcopal ordination and of the maintenance
of the historic succession in any united church with Anglican participation. It adds that the functions of the episcopate must be "such as have been traditionally assigned to
it" without, however, further defining those functions.
These directives were later largely incorporated in the
united churches of North India and of Pakistan. Then the
statement of 1948, partly anticipating the special description of comprehensiveness in Lambeth 1968, attempts to
mitigate the tensions caused by holding divergent views.
These differences are seen as a prerequisite for the Anglican
vocation to be an instrument of ecumenical reconciliation.

> The co-existence of these divergent views within the An-
> glican Communion sets up certain tensions; but these are
> tensions within a wide range of agreement in faith and prac-
> tice. We recognize the inconveniences caused by the ten-
> sions, but we acknowledge them to be part of the will of God
> for us, since we believe that it is only through a comprehen-
> siveness which makes it possible to hold together in the An-
> glican Communion understandings of truth which are held in
> separation in other Churches, that the Anglican Communion

is able to reach out in different directions, and so to fulfill its special vocation as one of God's instruments for the restoration of the visible unity of His whole Church.[30]

The Lambeth Conference of 1958 went to the heart of the problem of Anglican identity by studying the place of the Bible as authority and of the Book of Common Prayer as a bond of unity. New directions were initiated in this second area of concern. Whereas Lambeth 1948 had spoken of "those features in the Book of Common Prayer which are essential to the safeguarding of the unity of the Anglican Communion," the bishops now denied that "the Anglican Communion owes its unity to the Prayer Book. ... Our unity exists because we are a federation of Provinces and Dioceses of the One, Holy, Catholic, and Apostolic Church, each being served and governed by a Catholic and Apostolic Ministry, and each believing the Catholic faith. These are the fundamental reasons for our unity."[31] This statement has stood the test of time for defining the Anglican Communion. There ought, however, to have been a more precise word chosen than *governed* because, in most Anglican jurisdictions, laity and priests share with bishops in government. The anomaly of the definite article before church and of the indefinite article *a* before Catholic and Apostolic Ministry needed further explanation.

The bishops at Lambeth realized that the old picture of Anglican unity supposedly centered around what many called its "incomparable liturgy" in the Prayer Book of 1662 and in its lineal descendents was outdated. Liturgical scholarship now saw Cranmer's protest against medieval corruptions as largely determined by that context and not as the supposed return to how things were in the early church. Practical advice was given about Prayer Book revision that speeded up the process of revision. The General Convention would in 1976 validate by the first of two needed approvals the Proposed Book of Common Prayer. This very extensive revision, profiting also by liturgical reform in Roman Catholicism since Vatican II, broke in Rite Two with the noble but archaic language of the sixteenth and seventeenth centuries, thereby causing shockwaves that are still reverberating through the American Episcopal Church despite the fact that Rite One retained the old language.

Authority in Anglicanism

During the period in which the Lambeth Conferences were establishing a solid reputation as an articulate expression for things Anglican, there was growing concern about the lack of clergy and lay participation in the shaping of these statements. Partly to meet the need for a more broadly based representation, an Anglican Congress met in Toronto in 1963 with an emphasis upon the mission to the world and the slogan of "mutual responsibility and interdependence in the Body of Christ." Lambeth 1968 dedicated itself to renewal of the church in faith, in ministry and in unity. Drawing upon past statements on authority but focusing on the difficulties presented in ecumenical discussions by the Thirty-nine Articles, it was asserted that authority for Anglicans involved different levels and inheritances.

The first level was understood as shared with other churches throughout the world: "This inheritance of faith is uniquely shown forth in the holy Scriptures and proclaimed in the Catholic Creeds set in their context of baptismal profession, patristic reasoning, and conciliar decision."[32] The second level was the special formularies of the Anglican reformation. "In the sixteenth century the Church of England was led to bear a witness of its own to Christian truth, particularly in its historic formularies — the Thirty-nine Articles of Religion, the Book of Common Prayer, and the Ordinal, as well as in its Homilies." The third level was seen as continuing and broadening this witness through "its preaching and worship, the writings of its scholars and teachers, the lives of its saints and confessors, and the utterances of its councils." This third level illustrated the significant role assigned to reason, whether in historical or philosophical inquiry, or in the claims of pastoral care. Then a summary conclusion is drawn about the concept of authority in Anglicanism which is described as not insulating itself against the testing of history and of reason and as seeking therefore to be a credible authority.

The chief contribution, however, of Lambeth 1968 was a series of recommendations that would result in the setting up by what has now become the twenty-five autonomous churches of the Anglican Communion of the Anglican Consultative Council as an expression by a representative membership including lay persons, priests and bishops of the mind of the Communion. At its third meeting in Trinidad in 1976, the Anglican Consultative Council, in cooperation with the Archbishop of Canterbury, announced an agenda for the Lambeth Conference of 1978. The decentralization that inevitably accompanied the emergence of twenty-five churches in the Anglican Communion produced, when the bishops met in Lambeth in 1978, a countermovement: the creation of a Primates' Committee working with the Archbishop of Canterbury to provide more coordination between the churches on such disputed issues, for example, as the ordination of women.[33]

Anglican Spirituality

If it has proved difficult to reach satisfactory descriptions of the partners in the Anglican dialogue, in their interrelationships and characterizations of Anglican identity, that avoid idolatry and smugness as well as depreciation and caricature, it is clear that it will be even more of a problem to describe briefly Anglican spirituality. The spirit of Anglicanism and Anglican spirituality are intimately related. There is a rich literature that cannot be described here except in telegraph form — the Book of Common Prayer itself, Ken, Cosin, Andrewes, Walton, Taylor, Reynolds, Ferrar, Donne, Herbert, Traherne, Law, Wilberforce, Keble and the anonymous author of the *Whole Duty of Man,* Eliot, Dorothy Sayre, Evelyn Underhill and many others. Two books are available in this area: C. J. Stranks' *Anglican Devotion* provides a description of a recognizable core of Anglican writers.[34] Martin Thornton's *English Spirituality* enlarges the focus to include the full sweep of English spirituality and sets it in the still wider context of Western devotion from St. Augustine of Hippo to Aquinas.[35] The latter includes a useful bibliography. Thornton catches much that we can call the spirit of Anglicanism in his charge at the end of his book to Anglican spiritual advisors: "Empirical guidance, not dogmatic direction; affectiveness curbed by doctrine; recollection, continuous and gentle, not set periods of stiff devotion; domesticity not militarism; optimism not rigour; all leads naturally into a balance, a sanity into what Julian called 'full and homely' and what Taylor meant by 'an amiable captivity of the Spirit.' ''[36]

The most pervasive quality in the literature of Anglican spirituality has been the shaping force of the Bible and the Book of Common Prayer. It has often been pointed out that past calendars for the public reading of Scripture have resulted in Anglicans hearing more of the Word of God in their services than members of any other major branch of Christendom. Hooker counterattacked on the Puritan charge that Anglicans did not preach enough by claiming that the Puritan pastor read only a little of Scripture as a prelude to his preaching whereas the reading in the Anglican services of lengthy lessons in sequence from the Bible was itself a kind of preaching that freed the congregation from the personal idiosyncrasies of the preacher. In all probability, however, the track record of Puritans reading the Bible in private devotions far outdistanced Anglicans in this area. Much later, Maurice would make the same point as Hooker: "The Protestant dissenter says that we set aside the Bible, though we read more of it in any one month in one of our churches than he reads in two years in any of his meetings; and though our reading of it is continuous, his casual and arbitrary."[37]

The impact of the Book of Common Prayer has been immense, for, as has been said before, it has been commended to every member as his or her book. The liturgical ethos of Anglicanism has already been described. What must be added here is the effect of this ethos upon the faithful worshiper in building him or her up in a sacramental mentality through frequent reception of the Holy Communion. While devotional manuals have been much used in Anglicanism, just as in Roman Catholicism, what emerges as distinctive for Anglicans is that the Book of Common Prayer has been itself *the* devotional manual.

There is one point at which Bible and Prayer Book come together in a most interesting way that shows their mutual fortification in Anglican spirituality. The historic form of the General Confession in Morning and Evening Prayer bor-

rowed its phraseology from Titus 2:12 that "we may hereafter live a godly, righteous, and sober life, to the glory of
thy holy Name." Godliness, righteousness and sobriety together sum up the aim of Anglican spirituality. The first
quality needs no further exposition for it is presumably the
aim of every Christian and every method of devotion. A
"righteous life," however, emerges as a distinctive note in
English spirituality. English people are intensely "moral."
They look to their religion to help them "be good." At times
this trait can strike other Christians as dangerously close to
Pelagianism or as self-righteous and smug. It can produce
such doubtful products as the "Christian gentleman" or
"preparatory school religion." At its best it can be represented by the title of William Law's popular devotional
guide: *A Serious Call to a Devout and Holy Life.* The Caroline divines emphasized conscience not so much to build up
a science of casuistry with dependence upon a skilled confes-
sor, but as simply that human faculty most open to the direct molding influence of God. The Cambridge Platonists
knew conscience as "the candle of the Lord." There was
great confidence that the individual could train his intellect
and will, and therefore his conscience, to bring forth good
works through the grace of God. The Anglican was urged to
accept responsibility for "working out his own salvation in
fear and trembling"; sometimes he did this in a too simply
moralistic way, forgetting the scriptural reason "for it is
God that works in you." Bishop Wand has described this
quality as the distinctive note of the Communion.

Finally there is the mark of a deep-seated moralism, which
to those who know it best, is perhaps the most distinctive
feature of Anglicanism. . . . Of the three supreme qualities,
goodness, truth, and beauty, the Anglican has no doubt that
the first is the most important. . . . "By their fruits ye shall
know them" is a favorite text, and an accepted aphorism is:
"It is character and character alone that can truly save us."
The hardest doctrine to bring home to an Anglican is the priority of faith over works. Even his religious revivals are
strongly moralistic. The Evangelical Revival soon found its
most popular expression in works of charity, and the supreme object of the Catholic Revival was not churchliness,
but holiness. Above everything the Anglican wants to be

good, and his strongest temptation is to regard his religion as a mere means to that end.[38]

The third quality described in the New Testament passage appears in the General Confession as a "sober life." It is a quality particularly Anglican, sometimes to a fault. Bishop Angus Dun has called Episcopalians God's frozen people. The trait may be related to a combination of the characteristic understatement of the English people and of the norms of classical severity, but its presence is demonstrated by a simple dignity in the conduct of worship and by restraint in theological controversy. It can degenerate into a weak-kneed acceptance of "anything goes" or it can be a deliberate waiting before premature decision in the confidence that truth is great and will prevail without nervous help from those who consider themselves indispensable to its protection. It has often meant a willingness to tolerate for a time what seemed to be error in an individual or group by an uncomfortable majority reluctant to discipline lest in the process new truth be crushed. The placing of books on an index or the official silencing of a speaker are not methods congenial to Anglicans. Another way of describing this trait is to call it the absence of fanaticism. When any of the four partners in the dialogue break away and adopt extremist positions most Anglicans fault them for lacking what Matthew Arnold called "sweet reasonableness." A communion which places so high an evaluation on sobriety and reasonableness will at times obviously have problems with zeal and conviction.

It almost seems that Anglican writers on spirituality have consciously ordered their presentations around the three norms of "a godly, righteous, and sober life." This expression has led to a generally cheerful, world-accepting and joyous piety. *Surprised by Joy,* the title of a book by C. S. Lewis, could be used to characterize Anglican spirituality. Puritan spirituality nurtured on a profound experience of grace that has found forgiveness of sin through Christ's Atonement retains a sin-drenched ethos illustrated by such a typical work as Bunyan's *Pilgrim's Progress.* Thomas Traherne's *Centuries of Meditations,* on the other hand, expresses an Anglican cheerfulness, hopefulness and felicity, to use his own favorite word, that derives from confidence in God's power in creation and his grace in the Incarnation. Concrete elements of nature fairly shine for him with divine translucence, giving an ecological orientation to his meditation. Einer Molland has attempted to describe Christian communions in terms of one special liturgical day. He associates Eastern Orthodoxy with Easter, Lutheranism with Good Friday and Anglicanism with Christmas. The doctrine of the Incarnation has dominated Anglicanism to a remarkable degree. The Puritans of New England were extraordinarily perceptive of how to be most "un-Anglican" by outlawing the celebration of Christmas. The centrality of the Incarnation can be felt in Bishop Andrewes' sermons on the nativity, studied as a central theme in Hooker, Maurice and Temple, and sung in the carol "O Little Town of Bethlehem" by Phillips Brooks. Temple's title for his chief theological work, *Christus Veritas*, confirms this continuing trend as does the much more recent book, *The Human Face of God*, by Bishop Robinson.

An incarnational piety, however, needs to pass beyond the happy event of Christ's birth to conformity with him in his life of obedience to the will of God, at whatever cost, in opposition and persecution. It must seek to incarnate something of the deeper joy of Christ's sacrifice and the willingness to die to self for the glory of God. Just as Christ is looked upon not only as the agent and expression of the living God but also as a representative human person, so the church must take seriously its task of representing the fullness of humanity.

Anglican Comprehensiveness

The Anglican Communion is pledged to represent in a pastorally- and liturgically-oriented dialogue the four partners — catholics, evangelicals and liberal advocates of reason and of experience. The only way this can be done is to become, through the leading of the Holy Spirit, in Bishop Whipple's phrase, the "church of the reconciliation." It means to be open and attentive to all the partners and not just to the favorite one. Reconciliation at home and within Anglicanism is the presupposition to becoming a reconciling agent abroad and within Christendom and humanity-at-large. This spirit can best be defined as a spirit of comprehensiveness. Lambeth has many times attempted a definition of this quality as, for example, in 1948, but its effort in 1968 is particularly useful for it arose in the context of ecumenical discussions with the Eastern Orthodox churches. They found "comprehensiveness" simply incredible and said so despite its obvious affinities to their own undefinable orthodox concept of "sobornost" ("conciliarity" or "catholicity"). It is interesting that Roman Catholicism since Vatican II has also begun to show more and more the spirit of comprehensiveness without giving official recognition to it as yet. The following description and defense of Anglican comprehensiveness is likely to become a classic statement well beyond its special focus in the dialogue with Orthodoxy.

> *Comprehensiveness* is an attitude of mind which Anglicans have learned from the thought-provoking controversies of their history. We are grateful to the Orthodox for making us think once more what we mean by comprehensiveness, and shall be glad to study the matter afresh with their help; for we realize that we have been too ready to take it for granted. We offer the following reflections to aid discussion. Comprehensiveness demands agreement on fundamentals, while tolerating disagreement on matters in which Christians may differ without feeling the necessity of breaking communion. In the mind of an Anglican, comprehensiveness is not compromise. Nor is it to bargain one truth for another. It is not a sophisticated word for syncretism. Rather it implies that the apprehension of truth is a growing thing: we only gradually succeed in "knowing the truth." It has been the tradition of Anglicanism to contain within one body both Protestant and Catholic elements. But there is a continuing search for the whole truth in which these elements will find complete reconciliation. Comprehensiveness implies a willingness to allow liberty of interpretation, with a certain slowness in arresting or restraining exploratory thinking. We tend to applaud the wisdom of the rabbi Gamaliel's dictum that if a thing is not of God it will not last very long (Acts 5:38-9). Moreover we are alarmed by the sad experience of too hasty condemnation in the past (as in the case of Galileo). For we believe that in leading us into the truth the Holy Spirit may have some surprises in store for us in the future as he has had in the past.[39]

Comprehensiveness can, however, become a snare and delusion when it is assumed that everything can be subjected to it. There are issues and sides to an issue that are not bound together by authentic complementarity. Such an issue is the ordination of women. It is either right or wrong and must be decided by careful theology and a determination to win through to decision. It cannot simply be postponed under a flourish of episcopal trumpets blaring the notes of comprehensiveness and diversity as it was by the Lambeth Conference in 1978. "We recognize that our accepting this variety of doctrine and practice in the Anglican Communion may disappoint the Roman Catholic, Orthodox and Old Catholic Churches, but we wish to make it clear (1) that the holding together of diversity within a unity of faith and worship is part of the Anglican heritage. . . ."[40] The issue, however, is precisely about "the *unity* of faith and worship" for the Anglican priesthood cannot be divided into a male branch acceptable everywhere within the Anglican Communion and a female branch, a local priesthood as it were, accepted within the ordaining Anglican churches, but subject to grievous discrimination elsewhere in Anglicanism. Our lack of self-confidence and our nervous concern for what Roman Catholics, Orthodox and Old Catholics will think of us is a one-sided "ecumenism." If we really believe in the apostolicity and catholicity of our orders and that we are not any more defective without them than they are without us, we should act with confidence in the expectation that they will respect our action even if they differ from it. The tone of the resolutions suggests a weak plea to them to continue dialogue even if some of us have been a little naughty. The resolutions offer no theological interpretation for the ordination of women. One would think these other churches would want to hear such theology and that they would be more likely to continue dialogue if they felt we were not mindless compromisers, but actuated by faith and capable of an articulate theology. The resolution on "women in the episcopate" in effect seems to imply that only male bishops can serve as "a focus of unity." Even on the pragmatic level the overwhelming support for these motions (316 for, 37 against, 17 abstentions) suggests that the conference could have asked for and received a much firmer endorsement of the ordination of women. Such an endorsement might conceivably have been just enough to stimulate a favorable vote on the issue some months later in the Church of England instead of the defeat of the issue in the priestly order. Sometimes the abandonment of the responsibility for leadership simply makes the continuing tasks of leadership and pastoral care more difficult.

It is important here to establish clearly the difference between the way Lambeth '78 handled the ordination of women by an improper resort to the concept of comprehensiveness and the proper use of this great principle in the decision of Anglicans to live together with varying conceptions of episcopacy and divergent views on the Virgin Birth. In the latter cases there has been a thorough theological wrestling with the issues and a resolution to-live-and-let-live in which no person is discriminated against in the exercise of that person's ministry in the church. Lambeth 1978 failed to set its resolutions in a theological context and adopted motions that seriously discriminate against women priests and the possibility of women bishops in their ministries within the Anglican Communion. Much of the vitality and authenticity of the Lambeth 1968 statement on comprehensiveness has been compromised by this misuse of the principle as an expedient dodge for resolving this really difficult issue.

There is another aspect of comprehensiveness in which the finger of accusation should now be removed from the bishops at Lambeth and pointed to many theologians of the liberal or of the broad church category. They may be too ready, in their zeal to protect freedom of inquiry, not to challenge presentations by writers who really have given up the historic faith of the church on such central issues for Anglicanism as the Incarnation and yet who seem to want to maintain their standing as Anglican Christians. The issue here is not the suppression of truth, heresy trials or the denial of the imaginative attempt, say, to understand the divine dimension of Christ through the Jewish categories of Jesus or of the early Jewish Christian communities as against the very different later "incarnational" categories

of Graeco-Roman culture. There is an entirely appropriate
inquiry into the place of the ambiguous word *myth* with respect to the Incarnation. There is also a possible conclusion
from such an inquiry that would deny the truth of Christ's
mission. John Knox has argued in *Theological Freedom and
Social Responsibility* that a denial of the truth presented in
the redemption by Christ, human and divine, should perhaps not be treated "as heresy" but "as unacknowledged
apostasy." He affirms that "such teaching is going on, even
within the Church, and that it is taking a destructive toll.
. . ."[41] One can understand Knox's concern and admit that
any broad church "unitarianism" embraced under the supposed rubric of comprehensiveness would be an irrespon-
sible position. The therapy, however, for this situation is
continuing theological debate and confrontation with the issues in the conviction that truth is great and that it will prevail without too nervous action by "defenders of the faith"
who may simply have mistaken some culturally conditioned
expression of Christian truth for that very truth itself. The
past history of theological conflict warns us against undue
haste in condemning innovative teaching. If comprehensiveness can be wrongly used by ecclesiastics to dodge responsible action and by theologians to avoid responsible theological activity that witnesses to the historic faith in Christ,
there is still another challenge in the appeal to comprehensiveness that touches every member of the Anglican Communion in his or her ecumenical responsibility for other
Christians and for all humankind.

In order to follow its Lord who became a servant to
humanity, the church must be willing to let go its hold upon
its self-serving institutionalism. This is not easy, for
churches, like all institutions, are notoriously conservative
and self-protective. The inability of the church to give credible evidence of following Christ in this fundamental area is
probably the greatest source of people's contempt for and
disillusionment with organized religion. Anglicanism, in
committing itself to follow the way of comprehensiveness,
has dared to face up to the need to die to what is specifically
Anglican in order to be raised up by the power of God in an
ecumenically resurrected church comprehensively Christian
and human. The Anglican vision to be not Anglican cath-

olics in a denominational way, but "mere" catholics in a future church, both catholic and evangelical, was aptly described by Michael Ramsey in an early book of his: "While the Anglican Church is vindicated by its place in history, with a strikingly balanced witness to Gospel and Church and sound learning, its greater vindication lies in its pointing through its own history to something of which it is a fragment. Its credentials are its incompleteness, with the tension and travail in its soul. It is clumsy and untidy, it baffles neatness and logic. For it is sent not to commend itself as 'the best type of Christianity,' but by its very brokenness to point to the universal Church wherein all have died."[42]

Some Anglicans have vociferously repudiated this ecumenical vocation by ridiculing it as "a Freudian deathwish" or "Anglican hari-kiri." Even Lambeth 1948, after commending "the vision" of Anglican churches joining with others in their areas in a reconciled church "no longer simply Anglican, but something more comprehensive," felt it necessary to warn against premature severance from the Anglican Communion. Bishop Bayne, the first executive officer of the Anglican Communion, spoke and wrote tirelessly about the mission of Anglicanism not to believe in itself, but only in the catholic Church of Christ. Paraphrasing Augustine, he described Anglicans as restless until they find their place in that one ecumenical body.

Not only must Anglicanism be prepared to die to its own denominational structure; it must be prepared to die to its "Englishness." The second death may actually be harder than the first because it reaches into subconscious aspects of the psyche. The days of the British Empire and American imperialism are over. Actually, Anglicanism has made encouraging progress in authentic indigenization, especially in Africa where the Anglican churches express local customs and culture. Now at Lambeth there is a mixture of languages and colors as the older Anglicanism, with its too heavy burden of "Anglo-Saxonism," tries to die in order that its really catholic heritage may be born anew in the emerging Anglicanism of the future — which may someday even have to abandon the name "Anglican" as an embarassment.

The shape of the coming great church is turning out to be far more complex than the simple goal of "organic union" envisaged by Lambeth 1920 and expressed impressively in such achieved Third-World unions as the Church of South India, the Church of North India and the Church of Pakistan. The failure of the Anglican-Methodist Union in England and the lack of real commitment to the Consultation for Church Union in the United States has caused serious re-evaluation of ecumenical strategy. The emergence of the Roman Catholic Church as a leader in the ecumenical movement and the greater contributions of Eastern Orthodoxy through the World Council of Churches have enlarged the horizon and shifted the focus from organic union to visible unity. It was therefore appropriate for the report of the Anglican Consultative Council in its meeting in Trinidad in 1976 to assess its own understanding of the Anglican heritage and its relevance for the ecumenical problem of promoting visible unity.

> We believe that Anglican tradition and experience have much to offer in defining more closely the goal of visible unity. In the Anglican Communion we have stressed:
> — a common faith based on the scriptures, creeds, and the teachings of the early Fathers
> — a comprehensiveness which embraces traditions in their fullness rather than seeking compromise
> — common prayer
> — the dominical sacraments
> — the three-fold ministry in the historic succession
> — synodical and conciliar decision-making.
> . . . It has been hitherto assumed that organic union is to be sought for the sake of mission. Our experience seems to be showing that joint action for mission leads to the deepening of commitment to visible unity.[43]

Careful Thinking Needed

Any communion which emphasizes the spirit of comprehensiveness, both as an internal process and externally for the wider reconciliation of Christendom and of humankind, needs to do some very concrete theological thinking about the nature of Christian truth and the responsibility to be more loyal to it than to institutional claims or needs. The

Doctrinal Commission of the Church of England in its report, *Christian Believing* (1976), was properly critical of an automatic, unquestioned acceptance of the principle of complementarity.

> The issues here — on the one hand loyalty to the formularies of the church and obedience to received truth, on the other adventurous exploration and the church's engagement with the contemporary world — appear to point in very different directions and to reflect different conceptions of the nature of religious truth. It is, to say the least, very difficult to explain divergences of this fundamental kind merely as complementary aspects of the many-sided wisdom of God.[44]

The principle of comprehensiveness, however, need not mean that "anything goes" or that Anglicans are too muddled about their hierarchies of authority to present a clear and responsible picture of Anglicanism and to further a spirit based upon this reality. It is the responsibility of any church from time to time to make statements about its own understanding of its ecclesial identity and its conception of the weighting of authorities for belief. It is unfortunate that the American Episcopal Church dodged this responsibility in its latest revision of its ordinal. Instead of making a fresh statement about the nature of Anglican belief, it evaded the issue by repeating the old by-pass: "Will you be loyal to the doctrine, discipline, and worship of Christ as this Church has received them?" This statement presupposes that "the doctrine" is well known whereas this is precisely the question that cries aloud for a contemporary answer. The Episcopal Church has begun the restatement of doctrine in its new "Outline of the Faith," a thorough revision of the catechism, but unfortunately the process did not carry through into the Ordinal. In 1975 the Church of England was driven to make a contemporary statement. This English willingness was partly occasioned by a desire further to relax the 1865 form of assent to the Thirty-nine Articles. It discovered it could not do this without a new and comprehensive statement. Their formulation shows they have presupposed historical methodology for the study of Scripture and the chief contributions of the partners to the Anglican dialogue.

The statement is worthy of adaptation for other branches of the Anglican Communion. It considerably simplifies the task of commentators on the spirit of Anglicanism by presenting a contemporary statement.

> *Preface:* The Church of England is part of the One, Holy, Catholic and Apostolic Church worshipping the one true God, Father, Son, and Holy Spirit. It professes the faith uniquely revealed in the Holy Scriptures and set forth in the catholic creeds, which faith the Church is called upon to proclaim afresh in each generation. Led by the Holy Spirit, it has born witness to Christian truth in its historic formularies, the Thirty-nine Articles of Religion, the Book of Common Prayer and the Ordering of Bishops, Priests and Deacons. In the declaration you are about to make will you affirm your loyalty to this inheritance of faith as your inspiration and guidance under God in bringing the grace and truth of Christ to this generation and making Him known to those in your care?
> *Declaration of Assent:* I, A.B., do so affirm and accordingly declare my belief in the faith which is revealed in the Holy Scriptures and set forth in the catholic creeds and to which the historic formularies of the Church of England bear witness; and in public prayer and administration of the sacraments, I will use only the forms of service which are authorized or allowed by canon.

The Anglican Spirit in Summary

The spirit of Anglicanism is biblical, liturgical and pastoral. At its best it is the spirit of liberality, of comprehensiveness, of reasonableness and of restraint. It stresses the historically given rather than the theoretical, the moral rather than the highly speculative. The spirit of Anglicanism appeals to the conscience and to the individual as responsible for working out his or her own salvation. It perceives the presence and purpose of God in the natural order of things and is therefore open to ecological awareness. In its debate it returns again and again to the ordinary experience of ordinary people. It is pragmatic in temper and greatly values common sense. The spirit of Anglicanism finds its center in the Incarnation of Christ. It is therefore deeply sacramental. It is the spirit of a dialogic process up to this time more the happenstance of a special history, but now demanding acceptance as a special mission that will look upon the groups involved as genuine partners rather than barely tolerated as opposition groups.

When it is most alive to its mission and its insights the Anglican spirit is aware that the only unchanging reality is "Jesus Christ the same yesterday, today and forever" (Hebrews 13:8) and that fidelity to the act of God in Christ to which its favorite doctrine of the Incarnation points is what provides the ultimate orientation of spirit and the strength for pressing on in adventurous pilgrimage toward new spiritual discovery and toward combat with the forces of evil and oppression. Knowing that the center is firm in Christ and his liberating power, the Communion will courageously face change understanding that its time-honored sanctities are carried in earthen vessels. "But we have this treasure in earthen vessels to show that the transcendent power belongs to God and not to us" (II Corinthians 4:7). The spirit of Anglicanism combines tentativeness of statement about itself with finality of commitment to Christ. It is a prophetic spirit daring to act and witness for the liberation of the oppressed. The spirit of Anglicanism ought in its rich resources to find the wisdom to retain its identity and yet to develop through constructive change to meet the demands of the fast-approaching world of the twenty-first century. Unless one changes one cannot even remain the same; yet the change must remain continuous with what went before. The spirit of Anglicanism is the spirit of one way of being Christian in today's world. It needs all the other ways too that the Holy Spirit has revealed and will reveal.

Chapter Notes

Preface

1. Karl Adam, *The Spirit of Catholicism* (Garden City: Doubleday, 1954); and Robert McAfee Brown, *The Spirit of Protestantism* (New York: Oxford University Press, 1961).

2. Ibid., p. 26.

3. Henry R. McAdoo, *The Spirit of Anglicanism: A Survey of Anglican Theological Method in the Seventeenth Century* (New York: Charles Scribners' Sons, 1965).

4. Stephen Neill, *Anglicanism* (New York: Oxford University Press, 1978).

5. W. N. Pittenger, *The Episcopalian Way of Life* (Englewood Cliffs: Prentice-Hall, 1957), p. 186.

6. Stephen Sykes, *The Integrity of Anglicanism* (London and Oxford: Mowbrays, 1978).

7. *Anglican Consultative Council (3) Trinidad 1976* (Canley: Coventry Printers, 1976), p. 23.

Chapter I

1. The bibliography provides an indication of the variety of denominations and professions represented in modern Hooker studies. Olivier Loyer is the French Roman Catholic, Gunnar Hillerdal is the Swedish Lutheran, George Edelen, W. Speed Hill and Paul Stanwood are professors of English literature, Arthur S. McGrade and John Marshall are philosophers and Arthur B. Ferguson is a historian, while C. F. Allison, C. W. Dugmore and H. F. Woodhouse are among the church historians represented.

2. This is *The Folger Library Edition of the Works of Richard Hooker,* W. Speed Hill, general editor, 6 vols. Two have been published. Vol. 1: *Of the Laws of Ecclesiastical Polity: Preface, Books*

I to IV, Georges Edelen, editor. Vol. 2: *Of the Laws of Ecclesiastical Polity: Book V*, W. Speed Hill, editor (Cambridge, Mass.: The Belknap Press of Harvard University Press, 1977).

3. "The Good and Great Works of Richard Hooker," *New York Review of Books*, 24(19), Nov. 24, 1977, p. 55. This is a copy of the address given at the National Cathedral in Washington, D.C., when the first two volumes of the new edition were published.

4. Cited by W. Speed Hill, "The Evolution of Hooker's Laws of Ecclesiastical Polity," *Studies in Richard Hooker: Essays Preliminary to an Edition of His Works*, edited by Hill (Cleveland and London: The Press of Case Western Reserve University, 1972), p. 136.

5. See, for instance, the way in which Hooker begins a discussion of Puritan objections to the celebration of feast days with a profound dissertation on time, in the *Laws*, Book V, Chapter 69, Sections 1–3. Subsequent citations incorporated in the text are by book (Roman), chapter (arabic) and section (arabic) numbers, as these are found in the new edition of Hooker's *Works* (Folger Library Edition) for Preface and Books I–V. For Books VI–VIII see *The Works of... Mr. Richard Hooker*, ed. John Keble, 7th ed., revised by R. W. Church and F. Paget (Oxford: At the Clarendon Press, 1888), Vol. 3.

6. See *Laws*, III.8.14 and J. E. Booty, "Hooker and Anglicanism," *Studies in Richard Hooker*, ed. Hill, pp. 215–30.

7. See Hooker's *Answer to the Supplication* cited below, note 14, for a definition of Reason.

8. See, for instance, *Laws*, III.11.21, citing Rom. 11:33–34.

9. Izaak Walton, *The Lives of John Donne, Sir Henry Wotton, Richard Hooker, George Herbert, and Robert Sanderson*, with an intro. by George Saintsbury (London: Oxford University Press, 1973), p. 177.

10. Cited by H. C. Porter, *Reformation and Reaction in Tudor Cambridge* (Cambridge: At the University Press, 1958), pp. 387–88.

11. *A Christian Letter of certaine English Protestants* ([Middleburg: R. Schilders], 1599), p. 16.

12. See C. J. Sisson's corrections of Walton's *Life* in *The Judicious Marriage of Mr. Hooker and the Birth of "The Laws of Ecclesiastical Polity"* (Cambridge: Cambridge University Press, 1940).

13. See Inner Temple, Petyt MS. 538 (52), ff. 11–12, 22.

14. See Travers' *Supplication*, in Hooker's *Works* (1888), 3:559–560, and Hooker's *Answer*, 3:576–577.

15. See L. Thomson's description of the debate between Hooker and Travers, Dr. Williams' Library, MS Morris A., f. 35.

16. A colorful report is given of Travers' dismissal by Thomas Fuller, *The Church History of Great Britain*, ed. J. S. Brewer (Oxford: At the University Press, 1845), 5:186.

17. See Salisbury Cathedral, Chapter Act Book, Penruddock, pp. 22, 29. For an account of a session of the Sub-Dean's Court presided over by Hooker, see the Act Book of the Sub-Dean of Sarum, Jan. 1589–Sept. 1596, fol. 6 of the Court Records of December 1591. And see the letter to the editor from Elsie Smith, *Times Literary Supplement*, 135(3), Friday, March 30, 1962, p. 223.

18. *A Defence of the Government Established in the Church of Englande* (London, 1587), STC 3734. See Martin Marprelate's *Oh read over D. John Bridges, for it is a worthy worke* (1588), STC 17454.

19. See George Cranmer's letter to Hooker, February 1598, and especially notes made by Cranmer and Sandys on Book VI, in Hooker's *Works* (1888), 2:598–610, 3:108–139.

20. W. H. Frere and C. E. Douglas, *Puritan Manifestoes* (London: S.P.C.K., 1954), p. 20.

21. See W. Speed Hill, "The Evolution of Hooker's *Laws,*" pp. 145–47.

22. The so-called Conventicle Act. See John Strype, *The Life and Acts of John Whitgift* (Oxford, 1822), 3:299–300.

23. For a discussion of the *Letter*, together with a critical edition and commentary, see Vol. 4 of the Folger Library Edition of Hooker's *Works*, forthcoming.

24. This is Corpus Christi College, Oxford, MS 215b; most of the notes are contained in footnotes in the Keble (1888) edition of Hooker, but they are reproduced in their entirety in Vol. 4 of the Folger edition.

25. See Sisson, *The Judicious Marriage of Mr. Hooker*, and especially the documents, pp. 127–56.

26. Concerning the authenticity of Book VI, see W. Speed Hill, "Hooker's *Polity*, The Problem of the 'Three Last Books,' " *Huntington Library Quarterly*, 34(4), August 1971, pp. 317–36. But see also A. S. McGrade, "Repentance and Spiritual Power: Book VI of Richard Hooker's *Of the Laws of Ecclesiastical Polity,*" *Journal of Ecclesiastical History*, 29 (2), April 1978, pp. 163–76, where a strong case is made for its authenticity.

27. Fuller, *Church History*, 5:183.

28. Hooker defines a law as "That which doth assigne unto each thing the kinde, that which doth moderate the force and power,

that which doth appoint the forme and measure of working"
(I.2.1).

29. But see McGrade, "Repentance and Spiritual Power,"
noted above. That which is identified as Book VI in Hooker's work
is of importance as an essay on the Anglican understanding of con-
trition, repentance, absolution and satisfaction or penance.

30. Book V occupies the center of attention in the discussion of
Hooker's theology of participation, the main part of this chapter.
See F. Paget, *An Introduction to the Fifth Book of Hooker's Trea-
tise of the Laws of Ecclesiastical Polity* (Oxford: At the Clarendon
Press, 1907).

31. W. D. J. Cargill Thompson, "The Philosopher of the 'Politic
Society,' " in *Studies in Richard Hooker,* pp. 56–57.

32. That Hooker's views would not have pleased those espous-
ing the divine right of kings has been further proven by newly discovered autograph notes: Trinity College, Dublin, MS 364, ff.
73–84. Of particular interest is Hooker's use of Aeneas Sylvius;
see f. 73. The notes are printed in Vol. 3 of the Folger edition of
Hooker's *Works.*

33. See note 14.

34. Hooker, *Works* (1888), 3:558. See Michael T. Malone, "The
Doctrine of Predestination in the Thought of William Perkins and
Richard Hooker," *Anglican Theological Review,* 52 (1970), pp.
103–17.

35. Ibid., 3:560.

36. Ibid., 3:470.

37. Ibid., 3:471.

38. Ibid., 3:531–2.

39. Ibid., 3:532.

40. See C. F. Allison, *The Rise of Moralism: The Proclamation
of the Gospel from Hooker to Baxter* (London: S.P.C.K., 1966), pp.
1–5.

41. Hooker, *Works* (1888), 3:606.

42. Ibid., 3:594–5.

43. See note 24, above.

44. Trinity College, Dublin, MS 364, f. 80^{r-v}; see P. G. Stanwood, "The Richard Hooker Manuscripts," *Long Room* 11,
spring-summer 1975, pp. 7–10.

45. Trinity College, Dublin, MS 121 (old B.1.13).

46. Fragments, 13; Hooker, *Works* (1888), 2:550; and in Vol. 4 of
the Folger edition.

47. Hooker, *Works* (1888), 3:652.

48. Ibid., 3:670f., sections 10–11.

49. Ibid., 3:696.

50. Ibid., 3:708.

51. Trinity College, Dublin, MS 774, 57ʳ; see P. G. Standwood and Laetitia Yeandle, "The Manuscript Sermon Fragments by Richard Hooker," *Manuscripta* 21 (1977), pp. 33–37.

52. Trinity College, Dublin, MS 774, 58ʳ.

53. Rudolph Almasy, "The Purpose of Richard Hooker's Polemic," *Journal of the History of Ideas,* 39(2), April–June 1978, p. 251.

54. C. H. Dodd, *Interpretation of the Fourth Gospel* (Cambridge: At the University Press, 1954), pp. 195–96.

55. See the 1552 Prayer Book, the third exhortation to communion and the Prayer of Humble Access, where the language of John 6 is used. The language is also found in the 1549 prayer of consecration.

56. Hooker, *Works* (1888), 3:612-3, citing a passage from Gregory of Nazianzus.

57. *Doctrine in the Church of England* (New York: Macmillan, 1938), p. 81.

58. Paul Tillich, *Systematic Theology* (Chicago: University of Chicago Press, 1951), 1:176. See also G. F. Woods, *Theological Explanation* (Welwyn: James Nisbet, 1958). This is a neglected work by a theologian convinced that the personal provides the most viable basis for doing theology today.

59. Cited by David Balas, *Metousia Theou,* Studia Anselmiana 4 (Rome: I. B. C. Liberia Herder, 1966), p. 56.

60. Hooker, *Works* (1888), 3:624.

61. C. W. Emmet, "The Psychology of Grace," in *The Spirit*, B. H. Streeter, ed. (New York: Macmillan, 1921), pp. 157ff.

62. See H. R. McAdoo, *The Structure of Caroline Moral Theology* (London: Longmans, Green, and Co., 1949), pp. 21–23.

63. Hooker, *Works* (1888), 2:542 (Append. I.5).

64. Ibid., 3:471 (Serm. 1).

65. See A. C. Sculpholme, "Anniversary Study of John Donne. Pt. 2: Fraited with Salvation," *Theology* 75 (1972), pp. 75–76.

66. The structure of the sentence here is mine.

67. Hooker here acknowledges his reliance on Cyril of Alexandria, *Commentary on the Gospel according to St. John,* Book 10, ch. 13. His debt to this source is considerable.

68. Hooker, *Works* (1888), 2:549 (Append. I.13).

69. See the Act against Revilers, and for Receiving in Both Kinds (1 Edw. 6, c.1) and Jewel's *Challenge Sermon* and *Apology*, for instance, and S. L. Greenslade, *The English Reformers and the Fathers of the Church* (Oxford: At the Clarendon Press, 1960).

70. Martin Chemnitz, *Secunda Pars Examinis Decretorum Concilii Tridentini* (Frankfurt: Iohannem Feyrebendi, 1596), p. 65: "Non difinimus certum modum illius praesentiae, sed eum humiliter commandamus sapientiae et omnipotentiae Dei."

71. *Christ in our Place* (Edinburgh: Oliver and Boyd, 1957), pp. 98–99.

72. Hooker, *Works* (1888), 2:550 (Append. I.13).

73. Ibid., 2:573 (Append. I.32). Drawing on 2 Cor. 3:5.

74. Malone, "The Doctrine of Predestination," p. 112.

75. See Charles Hardwick, *A History of the Articles of Religion* (London: George Bell and Sons, 1895), pp. 303 (Art. 10), 311–13 (Art. 17), 363–67 (Lambeth Articles of 1595). Hooker ends his fragment on predestination with a version of the Lambeth Articles; *Works* (1888), 2:596–7 (Append. I.46).

76. Compare this with the Post-Communion Thanksgiving of the Prayer Book.

77. See the preface to the Prayer Book which stresses the importance of Scripture, the lectionary, propers and various rubrics which provide for the reading of copious amounts of Scripture, and the Holy Communion which directs that a sermon shall be preached; if that is not possible then it was expected that a portion of the *Book of Homilies* (1547, 63) would be read.

78. *The Sermons of John Donne*, E. M. Simpson and G. R. Potter, eds., (Berkeley, Calif.: University of California Press, 1953–1962), 5:250.

79. See Hooker's emphasis on baptism as the sacrament of divine mercy (V.61.4–5) and as the sacrament of "life and remission of sins" (V.62.15).

80. See John Booty, "The Bishop Confronts the Queen: John Jewel and the Failure of the English Reformation," in the forthcoming *festschrift* for Professor George Williams.

81. In Calvin's *Theological Treatises*, LCC 22 (Philadelphia: Westminster, [1954]), pp. 267–8; *Opera*, Corpus Reformatorum, 9:470–1.

82. Details are given in John E. Booty, "Church and Commonwealth in the Reign of Edward VI," *Anglican Theological Review*, Supplementary Series 7, November 1976, pp. 67–79.

83. Concerning Hooker's use of Machievelli, the prime atheist, see Felix Raab, *The English Face of Machievelli* (London: Routledge and Kegan Paul, 1965), pp. 62-65.

84. See the discussion of Book VIII, note 5.

85. Hooker, *Works* (1888), 3:617.

86. This is the argument of Richard Cosin in *Conspiracie for Pretended Reformation: viz. Presbyteriall Discipline* (London: Christopher Barker, 1592) STC 5823.

87. Eric Voegelin, *The New Science of Politics* (Chicago and London: University of Chicago Press, 1952); see espec. pp. 49-51, 56-59, 75-77, 106-13, 124-52.

88. The problem of civil disobedience was one which deeply troubled apologists for the Church of England and Royal Supremacy; see John E. Booty, *John Jewel as Apologist of the Church of England* (London: S.P.C.K., 1963), pp. 191-97.

89. Hooker seized upon Cartwright's statement that, in Hooker's words, citing the Puritan, "the scripture, must be the rule to direct in all thinges, even so farre as to the *taking up of a rush or strawe*" (II.1.2), and drove it beyond Cartwright's meaning.

90. See Philip Grierson, "The European Heritage," *Ancient Cosmologies*, ed. Carmen Blacker and Michael Loewe (London: George Allen and Unwin, 1975), pp. 249-52.

91. "The First Anniversary," 11.205-8.

92. See John McIntyre, *The Shape of Christology* (Philadelphia: Westminster Press, 1966), Ch. 4.

93. *Moral and Metaphysical Philosophy* (London: Macmillan, 1872), 2:196.

Chapter II

1. *Frederick Denison Maurice 1805-1872: A Commemoration of his Centenary* (London: The Workingmen's College, 1974). The October 1972 (vol. LIV) of the *Anglican Theological Review* is given over to articles on Maurice delivered at the American Maurice Centenary held at Seabury-Western Theological Seminary.

2. Schubert Ogden, *Christ Without Myth* (New York: Harper & Row, 1961), p. 182.

3. See John Francis Porter, *The Place of Christ in the Thought of F. D. Maurice* (Doctoral thesis, Columbia University, 1959).

4. W. E. Collins, *Typical English Churchmen from Parker to Maurice* (New York: E. and J. B. Young and Co., 1902), p. 328. Quoted by Alec Vidler, *Witness to the Light* (New York: Charles

Scribner's Sons, 1948), p. 17. Vidler's many quotations from almost the full range of Maurice's books and his commentary provide a useful introduction to his thought.

5. Frederick Maurice, *The Life of Frederick Denison Maurice* (New York: Charles Scribner's Sons, 1884), I, 41. Referred to hereafter as *Life*. This remains the indispensable biographical source. There is also a very short biography, *Frederick Denison Maurice*, by Florence Higham (London: SCM Press, 1947).

6. Olive J. Brose, in her useful *Frederick Denison Maurice: Rebellious Conformist 1805-72* (Athens: Ohio University Press, 1971), has emphasized the theme of Maurice's conversion at this time. Later her evaluation (p. 279) is that "far from being the Luther or even herald of a new Reformation as he had hoped from the days of his conversion, Maurice had become the Burke of the Church of England." A more nuanced view of Maurice's attitude toward institutions and culture is found in H. Richard Neibuhr's statement that: "It is thoroughly conversionist and never accommodating because he is most sensitive to the perversion of human culture, as well in its religious as in its political and economic aspects." H. Richard Niebuhr, *Christ and Culture* (New York: Harper and Row, 1956), p. 229.

7. Elmer Cleveland Want, Jr., *Frederick Denison Maurice's Eustace Conway, or the Brother and Sister: A Critical Edition with Introduction and Notes* (Doctoral thesis, Vanderbilt University, 1968).

8. *Life*, I, p. 357.

9. *Ibid.*, I, p. 174.

10. John F. Porter and William J. Wolf, *Toward the Recovery of Unity: The Thought of Frederick Denison Maurice* (edited from his letters with an introduction) (New York: Seabury Press, 1964). Some material from the introduction has been incorporated in this chapter by permission of Seabury Press and Professor Porter. Some additional unpublished letters of Maurice are quoted by Frank McClain in his useful *Maurice: Man and Moralist* (London: S.P.C.K., 1972), McClain includes an exhaustive list of the published works of Maurice and of manuscript sources.

11. *Life*, I, p. 167.

12. *Ibid.*, I, p. 237.

13. It is to be hoped that some day the first edition of *The Kingdom of Christ* will be republished because his views are often expressed more clearly there than in the ecumenically richer second and revised edition. Meanwhile it is possible to acquire some feeling for the first edition from the extensive quotations from it made by W. Merlin Davies in *An Introduction to F. D. Maurice's Theology: Based on the First Edition of The Kingdom of Christ*

(1838) and The Faith of the Liturgy and the Doctrine of the Thirty-Nine Articles (1860) (London: S.P.C.K., 1964).

14. *The Kingdom of Christ, or Hints to a Quaker respecting the Principles Constitution, and Ordinances of the Catholic Church.* The second edition, revised and altered. Two volumes, J. G. F. and J. Rivington, 1842.

It is this second edition which was reprinted in England in 1883 with a detailed table of contents (Macmillan), 1891 (Macmillan) and 1906 (Everyman's Library) and which Alec Vidler edited for publication by the SCM Press in 1958 (O.U.P.). All page references in the chapter are to the SCM edition except for a few from the 1838 edition which have been identified by date.

15. *Life,* I, p. 309.

16. MS. letter; September 8, 1852 quoted by McClain, *op. cit.,* p. 128.

17. *Kingdom of Christ* (1838), III, p. 76.

18. F. D. Maurice *Theological Essays* (New York: Harper, 1957), pp. 276–77.

19. *The Kingdom of Christ,* II, p. 314.

20. *The Kingdom of Christ,* II, pp. 346–47.

21. Herbert G. Wood, *Frederick Denison Maurice* (Cambridge: Cambridge University Press, 1950), pp. 77–78.

22. *Life,* II, p. 35.

23. *Ibid.,* II, p. 32.

24. F. D. Maurice, *Tracts on Christian Socialism* (London: Christian Social Union, Oxford University Branch, 1849), p. 2.

25. Torben Christensen, *The Origin and History of Christian Socialism 1848–1854* (Universitetforlaget Aarhus, 1962). Christensen has recently revised his Danish doctoral thesis, *Logos og Inkarnation,* and translated the revision into English as *The Divine Order: A Study in F. D. Maurice's Theology* (London: Brill, 1973). It is the most comprehensive study of Maurice's theology that we have.

26. *Life,* I, p. 484.

27. Maurice B. Reckitt, *Maurice to Temple: A Century of the Social Movement in the Church of England* (London: Faber and Faber, 1947).

28. C. W. Stubbs, *Charles Kingsley* (Chicago: Stone, 1899), p. 16.

29. C. R. Sanders, *Coleridge and the Broad Church Movement* (Durham: Duke University Press, 1942), p. 238.

30. Reprinted by Harper and Row (New York, 1957).

31. *Life,* II, p. 15–23.

32. Two recent doctoral theses: Nancy Sokolof, *Revelation as Education in the Thought of F. D. Maurice* (Columbia University, 1971) and Robert Ketchum, *F. D. Maurice An Assessment of His Contributions to Nineteenth Century English Education* (Syracuse University, 1969).

33. G. L. Phillips in *Theology*, April 1957, p. 167.

34. See the analysis of the Maurice-Mansel debate in Part I of Robert Tom Hall's doctoral thesis (Drew University, 1967) entitled *The Unity of Philosophy, Theology and Ethics in the Thought of F. D. Maurice*.

35. A. V. G. Allen, *The Continuity of Christian Thought* (Boston, New York: Houghton Mifflin and Co., 1893), p. 422.

36. Two doctoral theses: Howard Barth, *Rooted and Grounded in Love; F. D. Maurice's Relational Ethic of Reconciliation and Transformation* (Princeton University, 1965) and Harry Fehr Booth, *The Knowledge of God and the Practice of Society in F. D. Maurice* (Boston University, 1963).

37. *The Prayer Book* by F. D. Maurice (London: James Clarke and Co., 1966) with a foreword by Archbishop Michael Ramsey and *Worship and Theology in England from Watts and Wesley to Maurice 1690–1850* by Horton Davies (Princeton: Princeton University Press, 1961).

38. Claude Jenkins, *F. D. Maurice and the New Reformation* (London: S.P.C.K., 1938), p. 23.

39. R. H. Hutton, *Modern Guides of English Thought in Matters of Faith* (London, New York: Macmillan and Co., 1887), p. 312.

40. *Life,* I, p. 230.

41. *The Kingdom of Christ*, I, p. 236.

42. *Life,* II, p. 16.

43. *Ecclesiastical History,* p. 222.

44. *Life,* II, p. 136.

45. *Ibid.,* I, p. 239–40.

46. *Doctrine of Sacrifice,* p. xli.

47. *Conflict of Good and Evil,* p. 170.

48. H. Richard Niebuhr, *Christ and Culture* (New York: Harper and Row, 1956, p. 229).

49. *Life,* II, p. 317.

50. See Arthur Michael Ramsey, *F. D. Maurice and the Conflicts of Modern Theology* (Cambridge: Cambridge University Press, 1951).

51. *The Kingdom of Christ*, I, p. 177.

52. *Sequel to What is Revelation*, p. 97.

53. *Life*, I, p. 369.

54. Torben Christensen, *The Divine Order: A Study in F. D. Maurice's Theology*, (Leiden: Brill, 1973), p. 297.

55. Op. cit., pp. 227-29.

56. See footnote 60.

57. *Epistles of St. John*, p. 14.

58. *The Kingdom of Christ* (edition 1838), II., p. 87ff.

59. *Patriarchs and Law Givers*, p. 66.

60. *Doctrine of Sacrifice*, p. 194.

61. *Life*, II, p. 615.

62. *The Kingdom of Christ*, II, p. 363.

63. *Acts of the Apostles*, p. 188 ff.

64. *The Kingdom of Christ*, (edition of 1838), I, p. 88ff.

65. *The Kingdom of Christ*, II, p. 45.

66. *The Kingdom of Christ* (edition of 1838), I, p. 287.

67. *Three Letters to the Rev. William Palmer* (London: Rivington, 1842), p. 8.

68. *Epistle to the Hebrews*, p. cxxxiv.

69. For a more detailed discussion see William Wolf, "Maurice and Our Understanding of 'Ecumenical' " in *Anglican Theological Review* (No. 4, October 1972, Vol. LIV), pp. 273-90. Some material from this article has been incorporated in this chapter with permission.

70. L. Bouyer, *The Spirit and Forms of Protestantism* (Westminster, Md.: Newman Press, 1956), pp. 189-90. See also more recent doctoral theses by Roman Catholics: John Haughey, *The Ecclesiology of F. D. Maurice* (Catholic University of America, 1967) and David Murphy, *The Ecumenical Theology of F. D. Maurice* (Ottawa University, 1971).

71. F. D. Maurice, *A Few Words on Secular and Denominational Education*, p. 12. Quoted from Vidler, op. cit., p. 80.

72. *The Kingdom of Christ*, II, p. 340.

73. *Ibid.*, p. 343.

74. "Do not let the Church stand, Narcissus-like, contemplating the comeliness of her proportions and the greatness of her powers. That comeliness will appear most when she moves, these powers will be felt when she is acting." F. D. Maurice, *The Kingdom of Christ* (1838), III, pp. 131-32.

75. See David Murphy, "Maurice and Contemporary Theology," chapter 6 in *The Ecumenical Theology of F. D. Maurice* (unpublished doctoral thesis).

76. *Lincoln's Inn Sermons,* II, p. 86.

77. *Kingdom of Christ*, II, p. 331.

78. *Ibid.,* p. 347.

79. *Life,* I, pp. 258–59.

80. F. D. Maurice, *The Ground and Object of Hope for Mankind* (London: Macmillan and Co., 1868), p. 74.

81. F. D. Maurice, *Three Letters to the Reverend William Palmer* (London: Rivington, 1842), p. 25.

82. *The Kingdom of Christ* (1838), I, p. 315.

83. *Three Letters,* pp. 27–28.

84. *Ibid.,* pp. 26–27.

85. *Life,* I, p. 512.

86. *Three Letters,* pp. 36–38. The preceding quotation is also from this section.

87. *Ibid.,* p. 73.

88. *Essays,* p. 279.

89. *Life,* I, p. 414.

Chapter III

1. John D. Carmichael and Harold S. Goodwin, *William Temple's Political Legacy: A Critical Assessment* (A. R. Mowbray & Co., 1963), p. v.

2. Quoted by A. E. Baker in W. R. Matthews et al., *William Temple: An Estimate and Appreciation* (London: James Clarke & Co., 1946), p. 110; see also p. 99.

3. Ibid., p. 97.

4. F. A. Iremonger, *William Temple Archbishop of Canterbury: His Life and Letters* (London: Oxford University Press, 1948), p. 379.

5. Matthews, *William Temple*, p. 20.

6. Ibid., p. 7.

7. Joseph Fletcher, *William Temple: Twentieth Century Christian* (New York: Seabury Press, 1963), p. viii. I am indebted to my former teacher and colleague for much of the inspiration and information of this chapter.

8. Iremonger, *William Temple*, p. 452.

9. *Christus Veritas: An Essay* (London: Macmillan & Co., 1924), p. vii.

10. *Nature, Man and God* (London: Macmillan and Co., 1934), p. ix.

11. For a thorough analysis of the Gifford Lectures see my book, *William Temple's Philosophy of Religion* (London: S.P.C.K.; Greenwich, Conn.: Seabury Press, 1961).

12. *Doctrine in the Church of England: The Report of the Commission on Christian Doctrine Appointed by the Archbishops of Canterbury and York in 1922* (London: S.P.C.K., 1938), pp. 16–17.

13. *Thoughts in War-Time* (London: Macmillan & Co., 1940), pp. 101–107.

14. Fletcher, *William Temple*, p. 274.

15. *The Church Looks Forward* (New York: Macmillan Co., 1944), pp. v–vi.

16. *Religious Experience and Other Essays and Addresses,* ed. A. E. Baker (London: James Clarke & Co., 1958), p. 21.

17. Page references in this and the following section are to this volume.

18. *Thoughts in War-Time*, p. 104.

19. *Christus Veritas,* p. 164.

20. *Social Concern in the Thought of William Temple* (London: Victor Gollancz, 1963), p. 16.

21. *Nature, Man and God*, p. 478.

22. Quoted in Craig, *Social Concern,* p. 60.

23. *Nature, Man and God*, p. 478.

24. Ibid., p. 486.

25. *Christianity and Social Order* (New York: Penguin Books, 1942), p. 10. Page references in this section are to this volume.

26. *Thoughts on Some Problems of the Day: A Charge Delivered at His Primary Visitation* (London: Macmillan Co., 1931), pp. 88–89.

27. *Religious Experience*, p. 155.

28. Ibid., pp. 155–156.

29. *Readings in St. John's Gospel (First and Second Series)* (London: Macmillan & Co., 1961, pp. 304–305); quoted in *Religious Experience*, p. 18. I am indebted to A. E. Baker, the editor of this volume, for many of the points in the following paragraphs.

30. *Religious Experience*, pp. 153, 157, 158.

31. *The Church Looks Forward*, p. 13.

32. *Thoughts on Some Problems of the Day*, p. 129.

33. *Essays in Christian Politics and Kindred Subjects* (London: Longmans, Green and Co., 1933), pp. 202–203.

34. *The Church Looks Forward*, pp. 30–31.

35. Ibid., pp. 24–25.

36. *Thoughts on Some Problems of the Day*, p. 90. Further page references in this section are to this volume.

37. "The Vocation and Destiny of the Church of England," (1925) in *Essays in Christian Politics*; "The Genius of the Church of England," (1928) in *Religious Experience*; and "Our Heritage in the Anglican Communion," (1930) in *Thoughts on Some Problems of the Day*.

38. *The Lambeth Conference 1930: Encyclical Letter from the Bishops with Resolutions and Reports* (London: S.P.C.K., n.d.), pp. 113–14.

39. *Doctrine in the Church of England*, p. 25.

40. *The Integrity of Anglicanism* (London: Mowbrays, 1978), pp. 28–35.

41. Quoted in Iremonger, *William Temple*, p. 162.

42. *Religious Experience*, p. 90.

43. *Nature, Man and God*, p. 101.

44. *Readings in St. John's Gospel*, pp. xiv–xxiii.

45. *The Church Looks Forward*, p. 5; quoted in Fletcher, *William Temple*, p. 284.

Chapter IV

1. Most of these symposia are identified further in the bibliographies to the chapters.

2. *Catholicity* (London: S.P.C.K., 1947) and *The Fulness of Christ* (London: S.P.C.K., 1950).

3. W. Temple, *Nature, Man and God* (London: Macmillan, 1940), p. 344.

4. F. D. Maurice, *The Kingdom of Christ* (London: Student Christian Movement, 1958), II p. 304.

5. W. R. F. Browning (ed.), *The Anglican Synthesis: Essays by Catholics and Evangelicals* (Derby: Peter Smith, 1964), p. 11.

6. Quoted in H. H. Henson, *The Church of England* (Cambridge: Cambridge University Press, 1939), p. 39.

7. E. R. Fairweather (ed.), *Anglican Congress 1963* (New York: Seabury Press, 1963), p. 232.

8. W. Temple (ed.), *Doctrine in the Church of England* (London: S.P.C.K., 1938).

9. P. E. More and F. L. Cross (eds.), *Anglicanism: The Thought and Practice of the Church of England, Illustrated from the Religious Literature of the Seventeenth Century* (New York: Macmillan Co., 1935), p. xxxii.

10. Heber (ed.), *Works of Jeremy Taylor* (1828), Vol. XI, p. 356.

11. H. H. Henson, *The Church of England* (Cambridge: Cambridge University Press, 1939), p. 59.

12. F. Paget, *An Introduction to the Fifth Book of Hooker's Treatise of the Laws of Ecclesiastical Polity* (Oxford: Clarendon Press, 1899), p. 226.

13. D. L. Edwards, *Not Angels But Anglicans* (Naperville, Illinois: SCM Book Club, 1958), p. 111.

14. A. R. Vidler, *Essays in Liberality* (London, SCM Press, 1951), p. 166.

15. R. N. Flew (ed.), *The Nature of the Church* (London, 1952), pp. 122-23.

16. J. B. Coburn, "Address to the Evangelical and Catholic Mission at All Saints Church, Ashmont, October 16, 1977," p. 3. Used by permission of Bishop Coburn.

17. R. Page, *New Directions in Anglican Theology: A Survey from Temple to Robinson* (New York: Seabury Press, 1965), p. 21.

18. J. W. C. Wand, *Anglicanism in History and Today* (New York: Nelson, 1962), p. 241.

19. C. Gore, *Roman Catholic Claims* (London: Murray, 1892), p. xii.

20. H. R. McAdoo, *The Structure of Caroline Moral Theology* (London: Longmans, Green and Co., 1949).

21. J. T. McNeill, *A History of the Cure of Souls* (New York: Harper, 1951), pp. 245-46.

22. A. M. Ramsey, *An Era in Anglican Theology: From Gore to Temple* (New York: Charles Scribners, 1960), p. 164.

23. W. L. Sperry, *Religion in America* (New York: Macmillan, 1945), pp. 111, 113.

24. W. H. Van de Pol, *Anglicanism in Ecumenical Perspective* (Pittsburgh: Dequesne University Press, 1965), p. 34.

25. *The (Proposed) Book of Common Prayer (1976)*, pp. 876-78.

26. *The Lambeth Conferences (1867-1930)* (London: S.P.C.K., 1948), pp. 120-21.

27. Ibid., p. 111.

28. Ibid., pp. 113-14.

29. *The Lambeth Conference 1948* (London: S.P.C.K., 1948), Part II, p. 50.

30. Ibid., pp. 50-51.

31. *The Lambeth Conference 1958* (London and New York: S.P.C.K. and Seabury Press, 1958), Part II, p. 79.

32. *The Lambeth Conference 1968* (London and New York: S.P.C.K. and Seabury Press, 1968), pp. 82-83. The next two quotations in the paragraph are from the same source.

33. *The Lambeth Conference 1978* (London: S.P.C.K., 1978).

34. C. J. Stranks, *Anglican Devotion: Studies in the Spiritual Life of the Church of England between the Reformation and the Oxford Movement* (New York: Seabury Press, 1961).

35. M. Thornton, *English Spirituality: An Outline of Ascetical Theology according to the English Pastoral Tradition* (London: S.P.C.K., 1963).

36. Ibid., p. 302.

37. F. D. Maurice, *The Kingdom of Christ* (London: SCM, 1958), II, p. 300.

38. J. W. C. Wand (ed.), *The Anglican Communion: A Survey* (London: Oxford University Press, 1948), p. 335.

39. *The Lambeth Conference 1968* (London and New York: S.P.C.K. and Seabury Press, 1968), pp. 140-41.

40. Resolution 206 Women in the Priesthood. *The Lambeth Conference 1978*.

41. S. Bayne (ed.), *Theological Freedom and Social Responsibility* (New York: Seabury Press, 1967), p. 77.

42. A. M. Ramsey, *The Gospel and the Catholic Church* (London: Longmans, Green, 1936), p. 220.

43. *Anglican Consultative Council (3) 1976: Trinidad* (Canley: Coventry Printers), pp. 16-17.

44. Doctrine Commission of the Church of England, *Christian Believing: The Nature of the Christian Faith and Its Expression in Holy Scripture and Creeds* (London: S.P.C.K., 1976), p. 38.

Further Reading
and
Bibliographies

Chapter I

Editions Of Hooker's Works:

The most recent critical edition is that of the Folger Shakespeare Library, volumes 1 (*Of the Lawes,* Bks. 1–4) and 2 (Bk. 5), published by the Balknap Press of Harvard University Press in 1977; four more volumes are scheduled to be published by about 1984. This edition is meant to replace Keble's 7th edition published by the Oxford University Press in 1888, as revised by Church and Paget. One of the most accessible editions of Bks. 1–5 of the *Lawes* is found in the two volumes published in the Everyman's Library, printed from the 7th Keble edition. There is also a recent volume of selections, edited by A. S. McGrade and Brian Vickers, from the *Lawes,* published in 1975 by Sidgwick and Jackson in London.

Useful Works Published in Relation to the Folger Library Edition:

Egil Grislis and W. Speed Hill, *Richard Hooker: A Selected Bibliography* (Pittsburgh: The Clifford E. Barbour Library, Pittsburg Theological Seminary, 1971).

W. Speed Hill, *Richard Hooker: A Descriptive Bibliography of the Early Editions: 1593–1724* (Cleveland and London: The Press of Case Western Reserve University, 1970).

W. Speed Hill (ed.), *Studies in Richard Hooker: Essays Preliminary to an Edition of His Works* (Cleveland and London: The Press of Case Western Reserve University, 1972). This contains numerous important essays, making it a good one-volume companion to an edition of his works.

**Selected Secondary Works
Concentrating on Theology:**

C. F. Allison, *The Rise of Moralism: The Proclamation of the Gospel from Hooker to Baxter* (New York: Seabury; London: S.P.C.K., 1966). Ch. 1.

Richard Bauckham, "Hooker, Travers and the Church of Rome in the 1580s," in *Journal of Ecclesiastical History,* 29(1), Jan. 1978, pp. 37–50.

Leslie Croxford, "The Originality of Hooker's Work," in *Proceedings of the Leeds Philosophical and Literary Society,* Lit. and Hist. Section, 15(2), Feb. 1973, pp. 15–57.

C. W. Dugmore, *Eucharistic Doctrine in England from Hooker to Waterland* (London: S.P.C.K.; New York: Macmillan, 1942). Ch. 1.

Arthur B. Ferguson, "The historical perspective of Richard Hooker: A Renaissance Paradox," in *The Journal of Medieval and Renaissance Studies,* 3(1), Spring 1973, pp. 17–49.

Egil Grislis, "Richard Hooker's Method of Theological Inquiry," in *Anglican Theological Review,* 45 (1963), pp. 190–203.

_____ , "Richard Hooker's Image of Man," in *Renaissance Papers* (The Southeastern Renaissance Conference, 1963), pp. 73–84.

_____ , "The Role of *Consensus* in Richard Hooker's Method of Theological Inquiry," in *The Heritage of Christian Thought,* R. E. Cushman and E. Grislis, eds. (New York: Harper and Row, 1965), pp. 64–88.

W. Speed Hill, "The Doctrinal Background of Richard Hooker's *Laws of Ecclesiastical Polity,*" Ph.D. dissertation, Harvard University, 1964.

_____ , "Doctrine and Polity in Hooker's *Laws,*" in *English Literary Renaissance,* 2(2), Spring 1972, pp. 173–91.

Gunnar Hillerdal, *Reason and Revelation in Richard Hooker,* Lunds Universitets Årsskrift, N.S., 1, 54(7), (Lund: G. W. K. Gleerup, 1962). See Grislis for rebuttal.

Robert Hoopes, *Right Reason in the English Renaissance* (Cambridge: Harvard University Press, 1962).

Olivier Loyer, *L'Anglicanisme de Richard Hooker,* doctoral thesis, University of Paris, 1977. Useful in relating scholastic to Hookerian doctrine. 3 vols.

Arthur S. McGrade, "Public Religion: A Study of Hooker's *Polity* in View of Current Problems," Ph.D. Dissertation, Yale University, 1961.

_____ , "The Coherence of Hooker's Polity: The Books of Power," in *Journal of the History of Ideas,* 24 (1963), pp. 163–82.

_____ , "The Public and the Religious in Hooker's *Polity*," in *Church History,* 37 (1968), pp. 404-22.

Michael T. Malone, "The Doctrine of Predestination in the Thought of William Perkins and Richard Hooker," in *Anglican Theological Review,* 52 (1970), pp. 103-17.

John S. Marshall, *Hooker and Anglican Tradition: An Historical and Theological Study of Hooker's Ecclesiastical Polity* (Sewanee, Tenn.: The University at the University of the South; London: A. and C. Black, 1963).

Peter Munz, *The Place of Hooker in the History of Thought* (London: Routledge and Kegan Paul, 1952).

Francis Paget, *An Introduction to the Fifth Book of Hooker's Treatise of the Laws of Ecclesiastical Polity* (Oxford: The Clarendon Press, 1899; 2d. ed., 1907).

F. J. Shirley, *Richard Hooker and Contemporary Political Ideas* (London: S.P.C.K., 1949).

C. J. Sisson, *The Judicious Marriage of Mr. Hooker and the Birth of* The Laws of Ecclesiastical Polity (Cambridge: Cambridge University Press, 1940). Dated, but still useful.

Lionel S. Thornton, *Richard Hooker: A Study of His Theology* (London: S.P.C.K.; New York: Macmillan, 1924). Dated, but there's nothing else quite like it, except for Hillerdal, perhaps, and he's so negative that his opinions are always suspect.

Basil Willey, "Humanism and Hooker," in *The English Moralists* (London: Chatto and Windus; New York: W. W. Norton, 1964; rpt. Garden City, N.Y.: Doubleday, Anchor Books, 1967), pp. 100-23.

H. F. Woodhouse, *The Doctrine of the Church in Anglican Theology 1547-1603* (London: S.P.C.K.; New York: Macmillan, 1954).

_____ , "Permanent Features of Hooker's Polity," in *Anglican Theological Review,* 42 (1960). pp. 104-08.

Chapter II

The beginner in Maurice does well to take the plunge and first read his classic *The Kingdom of Christ* (2 vols. edited by Alec Vidler: London, SCM Press, 1958) and then the *Theological Essays* (New York: Harper and Brothers, 1957). Both books are, unfortunately, out of print. An abridgement of *The Kingdom of Christ* into one volume entitled *The Keys to Maurice's Kingdom of Christ*, with introduction by William Wolf, is being prepared for publication by Greeno, Hadden and Company. From this point on the reader can follow his own line of interest aided by the descriptions of the books in Chapter II. For the Maurice afficionado his letters are required reading, whether in the two volumes edited by his son Frederick Maurice in 1884 as *The Life of Frederick Denison Maurice Chiefly Told in His Own Letters* (London: Macmillan), or in a one-volume collection, *Toward The Recovery of Unity*, edited by John F. Porter and William J. Wolf (New York: Seabury Press, 1964). An extensive bibliography of Maurice can be found in Frank McClain (see below).

Subscription No Bondage, by Rusticus (London: J. H. Parker, 1835).

Three Letters to the Rev. W. Palmer (London: John W. Parker, 1842).

The Kingdom of Christ: or, Hints to a Quaker Respecting the Principles, Constitution, and Ordinances of the Catholic Church, two volumes (London: J. G. F. and J. Rivington, 1842). Second Edition.

The Epistle to the Hebrews. With a Preface containing a Review of Mr. Newman's Theory of Development (London: J. W. Parker, 1846).

The Religions of the World (Boyle Lectures) (London: J. W. Parker, 1847).

Moral and Metaphysical Philosophy: Originally published in the Encyclopedia Metropolitana. It grew into four parts (1850, 1854, 1857, 1862) and was collected in two volumes with a new preface, 1873 (London: J. J. Griffin and Co.).

The Prayer-Book. Nineteen Sermons preached in the Chapel of Lincoln's Inn. (London: J. W. Parker, 1849. Third edition with the *Lord's Prayer*, 1880).

Tracts on Christian Socialism (London: George Bell, 1850). Tracts 1, 2, 3, 7 and 8 are by Maurice, the others by Charles Kingsley and J. M. Ludlow.

The Church a Family: Twelve Sermons on the Occasional Services of the Prayer-Book. (London: J. W. Parker, 1850).

The Prophets and Kings of the Old Testament: A Series of Sermons preached in the Chapel of Lincoln's Inn. (London: Macmillan, 1853).

Theological Essays (London: Macmillan, 1853).

The Unity of the New Testament (London: J. W. Parker, 1854).

The Doctrine of Sacrifice (London: Macmillan, 1854).

Learning and Working (Six lectures of Workingmen's College) (London: Macmillan, 1855).

The Gospel of St. John (London: Macmillan, 1857).

What is Revelation? (Cambridge: Macmillan, 1859).

The Conscience: Lectures on Casuistry delivered in the University of Cambridge (London: Macmillan, 1872).

Olive Brose, *Frederick Denison Maurice: Rebellious Conformist 1805-1872* (Columbus, Ohio: University Press, 1971).

Torben Christensen, *Origins and History of Christian Socialism 1848-1854* (Aarhus: Universitetsforlaget, 1962).

_____ , *The Divine Order A Study in F. D. Maurice's Theology* (London: Brill, 1973).

Merlin W. Davies, *An Introduction to F. D. Maurice's Theology* (London: S.P.C.K., 1964).

Florence Higham, *Frederick Denison Maurice* (London: SCM, 1947).

Frank McClain, *Maurice: Man and Moralist* (London: S.P.C.K., 1972).

Arthur Michael Ramsey, *F. D. Maurice and the Conflicts of Modern Theology* (Cambridge: University Press, 1951).

Alec Vidler, *Witness to the Light: F. D. Maurice's Message for Today* (New York: Scribners, 1948).

Chapter III

One of the best places to begin reading Temple is his Oxford Mission addresses, *Christian Faith and Life* (New York: Macmillan Co., 1936). Perhaps the most direct way to grasp the spirit of his approach to faith and life is his *Readings in St. John's Gospel* (London: Macmillan and Co., 1961). One of his most important books for the life and work of the church today is *Christianity and Social Order* (New York: Penguin Books, 1942). The heart of his theology is found in *Christus Veritas* (London: Macmillan & Co., 1924) and his main philosophical work is *Nature, Man and God* (London: Macmillan and Co., 1934).

The definitive biography is F. A. Iremonger's *William Temple, Archbishop of Canterbury: His Life and Letters* (London: Oxford University Press, 1948) which also contains a chapter by Dorothy Emmet on Temple as a philosopher. There is an abridged edition of this volume by D. C. Somervell. The best single treatment of his life, work and thought is Joseph Fletcher's *William Temple: Twentieth Century Christian* (New York: Seabury Press, 1963), which contains a complete annotated bibliography.

Chapter IV

Anglican Consultative Council (3) 1976: Trinidad (Canley: Coventry Printers, 1976).

L. Andrewes, *Preces Privatae,* ed. by Brother Kenneth C.G.A. (London: Hodder & Stoughton, 1974).

S. F. Bayne, *An Anglican Turning Point* (Austin, Texas: Church Historical Society, 1964).

G. K. A. Bell, *Christian Unity, the Anglican Position* (London: Hodder and Stoughton, 1948).

E. J. Bicknell, *The Thirty-nine Articles of the Church of England* (London: Longmans, 1961).

J. Booty, *John Jewel As Apologist of the Church of England* (London: S.P.C.K., 1949).

Y. Brilioth, *The Anglican Revival* (London: Longmans, 1925).

W. R. F. Browning (ed.), *The Anglican Synthesis: Essays by Catholics and Evangelicals* (Derby: Peter Smith, 1964).

J. Burnaby, *The Belief of Christendom* (London: S.P.C.K., 1959).

K. Carey (ed.), *The Historic Episcopate in the Fullness of the Church* (London: Dacre Press, 1954).

J. Carpenter, *Gore: A Study in Liberal Catholic Thought* (London: Faith Press, 1960).

Catholicity (London: Dacre Press, 1947).

W. O. Chadwick, *The Reformation* (Grand Rapids: Eerdmans, 1965).

Doctrine Commission of the Church of England, *Christian Believing: The Nature of the Christian Faith and Its Expression in Holy Scripture and Creeds* (London: S.P.C.K., 1976).

P. M. Dawley, *The Episcopal Church and Its Work* (New York: Seabury, 1955).

W. Temple (ed.), *Doctrine in the Church of England* (London: S.P.C.K., 1938).

E. Selwyn (ed.), *Essays Catholic and Critical* (London: S.P.C.K., 1926).

The Fulness of Christ (London: S.P.C.K., 1950).

C. Garbett, *The Claims of the Church of England* (London: Hodder and Stoughton, 1947).

C. Gore (ed.), *Lux Mundi* (New York: E. and J. B. Young, 1890).

A. T. Hanson, *Beyond Anglicanism* (London: Darton, Longman and Todd, 1965).

H. H. Henson, *The Church of England* (London: Cambridge University Press, 1939).

A. G. Hebert, *Liturgy and Society* (London: Faber and Faber, 1935).

G. Herbert, *A Priest to the Temple (Works of George Herbert,* ed. by F. E. Hutchinson (Oxford: Clarendon, 1941).

K. Kirk (ed.), *The Apostolic Ministry* (London: Hodder and Stoughton, 1946).

The Lambeth Conferences (1867–1948) (London: S.P.C.K., 1948).

Lambeth Conference Reports 1948, 1958, 1968, 1978.

W. Law, *A Serious Call to a Devout and Holy Life* (Philadelphia: Westminster Press, 1948).

H. R. McAdoo, *The Structure of Caroline Moral Theology* (London: Longmans, Green, 1949).

H. R. McAdoo, *Being an Anglican* (Dublin and London: S.P.C.K., 1977).

J. R. H. Moorman, *History of the Church in England* (London: Black, 1953).

P. E. More and F. L. Cross, *Anglicanism: the Thought and Practice of the Church of England, Illustrated from the Religious Literature of the Seventeenth Century* (New York: Macmillan, 1957).

S. Neill, *Anglicanism* (New York: Oxford University Press, 1978).

R. Page, *New Directions in Anglican Theology: A Survey from Temple to Robinson* (New York: Seabury, 1965).

D. M. Paton (ed.), *Essays in Anglican Self-Criticism* (London: SCM, 1958).

N. Pittenger, *The Episcopalian Way of Life* (Englewood Cliffs: Prentice-Hall, 1957).

F. J. Powicke, *Cambridge Platonists* (London: Dent, 1926).

O. Quick, *Doctrines of the Creed* (London: Nisbet, 1938).

A. M. Ramsey, *An Era in Anglican Theology: From Gore to Temple* (New York: Scribners, 1960).

A. E. J. Rawlinson, *The Genius of the Church of England* (New York: S.P.C.K., 1947).

A. E. J. Rawlinson, *The Anglican Communion in Christendom* (London: S.P.C.K., 1960).

R. Rouse and S. Neill (eds.), *A History of the Ecumenical Movement 1517–1948* (Philadelphia: Westminster, 1954).

M. Shepherd, *Oxford Prayer Book Commentary* (New York: Oxford University Press, 1950).

C. J. Stranks, *Anglican Devotion: Studies in the Spiritual Life of the Church of England between the Reformation and the Oxford Movement* (New York: Seabury, 1961).

B. H. Streeter (ed.), *Foundations* (London: Macmillan, 1913).

S. Sykes, *The Integrity of Anglicanism* (London and Oxford: Mowbrays, 1978).

N. Sykes, *Old Priest and New Presbyter: The Anglican Attitude to Episcopacy, Presbyterianism, and Papacy Since the Reformation* (Cambridge: Cambridge University Press, 1956).

O. Thomas, *William Temple's Philosophy of Religion* (New York: Seabury, 1961).

M. Thornton, *English Spirituality: An Outline of Ascetical Theology according to the English Pastoral Tradition* (London: S.P.C.K., 1963).

Today's Church and Today's World (Lambeth Conference 1978 Preparatory Articles) (London: CIO Publishing, 1978).

T. Traherne, *Centuries of Meditations* (New York: Harper and Bros., 1960).

W. H. Van de Pol, *Anglicanism in Ecumenical Perspective* (Pittsburgh: Duquesne University Press, 1965).

A. R. Vidler (ed.), *Soundings* (Cambridge: Cambridge University Press, 1962).

J. W. C. Wand (ed.), *The Anglican Communion: A Survey* (London: Oxford University Press, 1948).

J. W. C. Wand, *Anglicanism in History and Today* (New York, Toronto: Thomas Nelson and Sons, 1962).

A. T. P. Williams, *The Anglican Tradition in the Life of England* (London: Macmillan, 1947).

W. J. Wolf (ed.), *Protestant Churches and Reform Today* (New York: Seabury, 1964).

Official Yearbook of the Church of England, latest edition.